“This book isn’t just for Anglicans or those used to high church liturgy. It’s for any church leader, regardless of tradition. When you read this, you’ll better understand that the historic practices of the Church were deeply missional and are what we need today to start missionally effective churches. I highly recommend this book for all church planters and leaders.”

Daniel Yang, Director of the Church Multiplication Institute, Wheaton College Billy Graham Center

“This book is a must-read to see the importance of Anglican missiology in our North American twenty-first century context. It is also timely because the church needs not a new vision but a renewed vision for sacramental, liturgical, and biblical mission. I highly commend it to you.”

The Rt. Rev. Alan J. Hawkins, Chief Operating Officer, The Anglican Church in North America; Bishop Coadjutor, The Diocese of Christ Our Hope

“Writing from within the Anglican tradition but in a manner accessible to others, Alger beautifully articulates what it means to cultivate new Christian communities that are grounded in both the Word and the Table. This is an essential read for all who care about not only church planting but what it means to be the church.”

Gordon T. Smith, PhD, President, Professor of Systematic and Spiritual Theology, Ambrose University

“Dan Alger’s new book, *Word and Sacrament*, meets a critical need in the literature on this topic. This page-turning, well-written work on ecclesiology and missiology should be required reading for Anglican as well as non-Anglican church planters.”

The Most Rev. Dr. Ray R. Sutton, Presiding Bishop of the Reformed Episcopal Church; Dean of the Province and Ecumenical Dean of the Anglican Church in North America

"While believers are questioning the essence of the church and her mission, *Word and Sacrament* will enliven our hearts and minds to confidently plant churches in the fertile soil of the historic church."

Scott Thomas, Lead Servant of Church Planting Partners; former President of Acts 29 Network; author of *The Gospel Shaped Leader*

"*Word and Sacrament* is an excellent resource for anyone wanting to better understand the intersection of church planting and Anglicanism."

The Rev. Dr. Bradley P. Roderick, Associate Professor of Missions, Director of the Stanway Institute, Trinity School for Ministry

"What a well-researched and resourceful work for every church leader! This book brings out clearly the two aspects of discipleship that matter most—Word and Sacrament."

The Rt. Rev. Dr. Manasseh Gahima, Bishop Ordinary, Diocese of Gahini, Rwanda

"In *Word and Sacrament* you will find a guidebook full of ancient wisdom and present-day practicalities. These pages will certainly energize, empower, and equip you along the church-planting journey, but most importantly, they will draw you into a deeper love and dependence on Jesus."

The Rev. Drew Hill, Anglican priest; head of school at The Covenant School in Greensboro, NC; author of *Alongside: Loving Teenagers with the Gospel*

Word and Sacrament

....

Ancient Traditions for Modern Church Planting

....

DAN ALGER

New Growth Press, Greensboro, NC 27401
newgrowthpress.com

Cover Design: Studio Gearbox, studiogearbox.com
Interior Typesetting and eBook: Lisa Parnell, lparnellbookservices.com

ISBN 978-1-64507-303-1 (Print)
ISBN 978-1-64507-304-8 (eBook)

Library of Congress Cataloging-in-Publication Data on file

Printed in the United States of America

30 29 28 27 26 25 24 23   1 2 3 4 5

Dedication

To my wife, Karen.
You are my partner in planting and my crown.

To my sons, Eli and Silas,
may you continue to grow in wisdom and stature,
and in favor with God and man.

I love you deeply.

Almighty God, to you all hearts are open,
all desires known, and from you no secrets are hid:
Cleanse the thoughts of our hearts by the inspiration
of your Holy Spirit, that we may perfectly love you,
and worthily magnify your holy Name;
through Christ our Lord. Amen.

— *2019 Book of Common Prayer, Prayer for Purity*

Contents

....

Foreword

My spiritual journey started in the Anglican tradition—I first heard the gospel through a charismatic Episcopal church near Orlando, Florida. I remain ever grateful for the gospel witness at that retreat center long ago. Through the years, I've had the opportunity to interact with Anglicans in a variety of settings and have developed friendships with many leaders, including Canon Dan Alger.

In the pages that follow, you will find a book that rises above others interested in church planting for two important reasons, one indirectly and one directly related to the field of church planting. The first reason to read this book is seen in the book's title, *Word and Sacrament.* This is a book written by an Anglican about Anglicanism and church planting.

I remember asking Dan, "Why is there no book on church planting from and for Anglicans?" You see, the stream of Anglicanism that Dan serves has been focused on church planting—and they have made good progress. Yet there is more to do.

So the reasons an Anglican should read this are obvious, but why should others read it?

Books like this matter, regardless of your own doctrinal persuasion or tradition, because the world is getting both bigger and smaller today. This means being engaged with the global church is both possible and essential for church leaders. The Anglican tradition is one of the more influential and important global traditions and is worthy of being understood in its own right. Increasingly we need to be aware of traditions outside our own who love Jesus and his Word and are on the same mission.

Today Anglicans number over 85 million adherents globally, making it as Dan notes, the third largest communion globally. And it's important for all of us who name the name of Jesus to remember that God's global church is bigger than our own tradition, no matter how important that tradition may be to us personally. We are far better as the people of God when we take the humble posture of seeking to learn from one another first over starting with those things that divide us. As Dan reminds us, we are all members of the "one, holy, catholic, apostolic church."

Dan writes with humility; his words show his deep conviction about the good news in Jesus, the urgent need for new churches, and his own walk with Jesus. You will read here his unambiguous devotion to the Anglican way while he demonstrates a winsome and irenic posture toward those of other traditions. Surely his example is needed in our time.

All of our traditions have strengths and weaknesses. We can learn from one another. Alger is quick to note not only the strengths of the Anglican tradition, but its flaws as well.

Second, this book is important because of the wealth of content about church planting found in its pages. The wisdom found here is deep and helpful. While every chapter ends with a word of explanation for those who are not Anglican, the church planting content applies to all. His expertise in the field of church planting will help any reader who desires to understand both the need and the practice of starting new churches.

Though he writes enthusiastically and unapologetically from his Anglican heritage and convictions, Dan has given us a book that will help any church planter or church planting network to serve the Lord more faithfully and effectively for the gospel. He champions ecclesiology as vital to planting, an area too often neglected by planting leaders.

Requisite questions on the topic serve to outline his content, from the *why* we plant, to *what kind* of churches we plant, to the practical *how* of planting. Dan deals with objections to planting, and these are pretty much the same objections I have dealt with for years. His responses are helpful and encouraging. His section on under- and over-contextualizing will be helpful to any church leader—planter or not. He warns potential planters of common mistakes and implores them to seek coaching and assessment.

Whether you are a Christian on the Canterbury Trail or not, you will be encouraged, informed, and inspired to be more engaged in planting new churches because of this book.

Ed Stetzer, PhD

....

Introduction

Let your way be known upon earth,
your saving health among all nations.
Let the peoples praise you, O God;
indeed let all the peoples praise you.

— *Psalm 67, Deus Misereatur*

I feel as though I am introducing you to two of my dearest friends. On one hand, we have the beautiful and rich Anglican heritage that has been my home since infancy. On the other, we have the complicated world of church planting in which I have served for more than half my life. I have lived in this middle space for a long time, having planted two Anglican churches as the lead planter and having trained, guided, and supported dozens more across the world in the last couple of decades. I can assure you that you are standing at an exciting intersection where the voices of the ancient church are brought to bear on the contemporary work of mission. In this space, two things happen: (1) Anglicanism is kept faithful to the missional call of the universal church and (2) innovative church planters are held accountable to plant actual churches rather than whims of fancy. It is an intersection of old and new, order and chaos, frustration and fun. I pray that no matter what perspective you to bring to these pages, you will leave with a greater appreciation for both the beauty of the Anglican tradition and the essential work of church planting.

The ancient church has something to say to modern church planters. Most contemporary church planting is approached as an endeavor that is fundamentally new, entrepreneurial, and innovative. Overly focused on the pragmatic, church planting can be primarily concerned with what "works," seeking an effective methodology for gathering people, resources, and notoriety, even before asking what is "right." This approach leads to extreme pressure on the planter as he is tasked with simultaneously deciding what a church is and how to properly start a new one.

A lens of Word and sacrament helps us begin the work of planting with a different perspective—one of submission to something greater than ourselves, a deep awareness of a carrying on of something of profound value rather than simply creating something new. This perspective affects both what we plant and how we plant it. The definition of the church has been decided for us, we have the example of thousands of years of church planters to guide us, and we can breathe deeply in the truth that we are simply stewards of the present moment of what the faithful church has been participating with God to do for millennia. The church planter is no longer creating *ex nihilio* but rather engaging in a creative fidelity as he "brings out of his storeroom new treasures as well as old" (Matthew 13:52 NIV). What a relief!

Planting in Word and sacrament means that we find our calling and our guide for church planting in the truth of God as revealed in his Word written and echoed in his sacraments, the Word visible. The truth of God has put on flesh in the person of his Son Jesus and continues to be made manifest in the church as the body of Christ. The sacraments call us to experience that mysterious intersection of the divine and the physical—the same place we find ourselves when planting a church. We should view our planting efforts as sacramental in nature as we create this new physical expression of the people of God, ensuring that we are a means of grace, a proper sign of the God we signify, and we remain fully dependent on the power of his Word and Spirit. For the majority of history, the church has lived in this reality. The Anglican tradition carries on this way of life and offers us a way to bring the unchanging truth of the Word of God to bear on our mission through the incarnational lens of the sacraments.

These two realms—Anglicanism and church planting—have been adequately mapped individually in other books. This book is more interested in the space where they overlap: the liturgical and missional world of Anglican church planting, for which there has been a dearth of resources and navigational charts. So far, the brave pioneer who would step into this nebulous world has been left to do so with little guidance, knowing perhaps a good deal about the mountains on either side but less about the fertile valley in between.

As we look at church planting through this particular lens, I hope to show how Anglicanism can be a gift to the work of church planting and how church planting is natural and healthy for the Anglican Church. Whether you are a planter exploring Anglicanism or an Anglican trying to understand church planting, I hope you find instruction, enlightenment, and inspiration here.

My goal is in no way to set up Anglicanism as over and above any other tradition that is faithful to Jesus and his Scripture. I do not wish to portray any sort of Anglican arrogance, and if I get carried away in extolling its virtues, I pray I am balanced to also show its vices. I desire to communicate its value only to the degree of its own faithfulness to Jesus's commands and never in comparison to any other tradition.

This is also not a book only for Anglicans. If you are planting a church through a different tradition, I hope that being introduced to an alternative perspective on church and mission will encourage you to examine your assumptions to either broaden your thinking or strengthen your convictions. To this end, I have included at the end of each chapter a particular note to non-Anglican readers to help you consider the implications of what you are reading for your ecclesiastical tradition. The hope of this book is to strengthen the church universal, which I am sure is our mutual aim. I am so grateful you are here.

With regard to church planting, I do not desire to be only a theoretician, but to remain a practitioner. My goal is not to study the science of ecclesiastical agriculture; I want to get my hands in the dirt with you to actually plant churches, and not just any churches—gospel faithful, missionally effective, sacramentally imagined, communally intimate Anglican churches. I love this work with all of my heart, and I truly love you too for your willingness to even enter into a process of discernment over your role in this important gospel ministry.

This is a "start here" book that I hope will pique your interest in both the historic church and church planting. I pray that this book will be a help to you if you are:

- An Anglican who wishes to understand church planting as a part of your heritage

- A missional non-Anglican searching for something rooted, transcendent, and bigger than your own entrepreneurial vision
- A potential planter looking for discernment and encouragement
- An active planter seeking a teaching tool for you and the people of your plant
- Part of a diocese, structuring the systems and the training of planters
- A bishop further exploring your role in planting
- Part of a diocesan standing committee, wanting to understand your role in supporting planters
- Part of a local church that desires to plant more churches—reading it as a vestry, a staff, or a congregation
- A church planter from a different tradition who seeks to hear another perspective on our work
- Anyone who desires to learn more about the uninterrupted work of the ancient, universal church on mission

If you are going to plant a church, you will need more than this primer for preparation. This book is a starting place to introduce many important themes and truths that will form the foundation of how you approach church planting, but it would be impossible for this small book to explore how these truths are applied in every situation and cultural context. From here you need to engage in assessment, training, and coaching. Before you take tremendous risk to step into this work and before you ask others to do the same, please take the time for thorough preparation by those in the church who can help you.

Most of all, I pray that you will see Jesus in these pages—his love for his church, his majesty and glory, his mission in the world, and his passion for you. May the Spirit guide us as we walk this journey together, and may we see many faithful churches planted for the glory of God the Father, according to the commission of Jesus, and by the power of the Holy Spirit.

Part 1

Why Should We Plant?

CHAPTER 1

. . . .

The Two Topics at Hand

"This must be a simply enormous wardrobe!"
thought Lucy, going still further in . . .

— *C. S. Lewis, The Lion, the Witch, and the Wardrobe*

SUMMARY: The Word and sacrament tradition helps us plant faithful and deep churches, and planting churches helps us ensure our tradition has real life.

It was a door to a whole new world. As a child, I attended St. Andrew's Episcopal Church, a red brick building whose steeple was nestled in among the live oaks and salt spray of a coastal town in North Carolina. I would shuffle up the brick walkways, climb the cement stairs, and grab hold of the twisted, wrought-iron handles of the arched, thick oaken doors. As I pushed open the heavy doors with my shoulder, I remember being flooded by a sense of awe. It came from the kind, wrinkled hands of the smiling greeters handing us bulletins, the colors that washed over the long wooden pews as the sun splayed through the stained-glass windows, and the long, red carpet leading up to the ornate Table that read "Holy, Holy, Holy" on its front. Above the Table was a glowing window depicting Jesus holding a lamb and a crook, gazing down lovingly with a smile. The organ was bold and loud, and the liturgy rang from the vaulted ceiling as the church spoke in unity. From the raised pulpit I heard faithful and challenging preaching about the person and work of Jesus. At the wooden baptismal font, many times I saw both children and adults dressed in white and dripping with the waters of life. I remember the bishop coming to confirm me, laying his hands on my head, and handing me a Book of Common Prayer as he commissioned me to live into my calling as a member of the church. Three steps up to the Communion Table, I ate as my family and friends knelt next to me and our priest smiled as he pressed the bread into my hands. In the years to come, on those same steps, still as a boy I would attend the funeral of my father, and as a young man I would kneel as I took my vows of ordination. In that sacred space I was formed, shaped, and sent out by an ancient faith.

Since my boyhood, I have worshipped in many dozens of Anglican churches. Some of those church buildings and worship services looked similar to what I experienced growing up. Others were aesthetically very different. I have worshipped with Anglicans in living rooms, high school cafeterias, stone cathedrals, and dance studios. Even the church of my youth would have to take a stand for the truth of the Scripture, leave that building, and worship for a time in a storefront. I have worshipped alongside priests in flowing robes and others in designer jeans. I have heard the liturgy recited in formal, aged language and in quick, modern style. The music has been choral, acoustic, folk, and rock. The preaching has ranged from ten-minute homilies to forty-five-minute exegetical teachings. All of this is legitimately Anglican. We may be known for our outward adornments, but Anglicanism is deeper than a particular aesthetic. Since Anglicanism is the particular perspective through which we are exploring church planting in this book, let's look first at what exactly it means to be Anglican.

What Is Anglicanism?

First and Foremost, Anglicans Are Christians

Much of what we share in the Anglican tradition we claim as our own simply because it is sourced in the Great Tradition of the church to which we belong—that is, the authoritative tradition of the universal church. Anglicanism is a part of the greater whole that is the church catholic, which in this usage means "universal." The foundations of our doctrine and practice are rooted firmly, first and foremost, in the Scripture and have been developed over the two-thousand-year history of the church. Primarily, Anglicanism is all about God—Father, Son, and Holy Spirit—his glory, his truth, his people, and his mission.

Secondly, We Are Bearers of a Particular Tradition within the Greater Church

Our way of being has been shaped by how the Lord has worked through the church in the British Isles. Try to move beyond a modern picture of England buzzing with double-decker buses and red phone booths. The tradition we are discussing is much more ancient than that.

It is insufficient to look at a specific point in the history of the English church, like the foibles of Henry VIII, and define Anglicanism by that moment. Anglicanism is the sum total of the experience of the life of the church before there was an

England, through the Reformation, and after the church that developed in England had spread across the globe to take root in other lands.

Although firmly grounded in the ancient undivided church, the Anglican tradition has been profoundly shaped by people and events as diverse as the monastic and Celtic traditions, the Synod of Whitby, the Protestant Reformation (although our experience of the Reformation was a bit different from that of continental Europe), Puritanism, evangelicalism, the Oxford Movement, and revivalism. Missionaries, clergy, and settlers carried the Anglican tradition to places that would become independent nations in Africa, North America, Australia, and throughout the world—lands whose cultures have further shaped the Anglican Way. More recently, thinkers and authors such C. S. Lewis, J. I. Packer, and N. T. Wright have given modern voice to Anglican thought.

These influences, and more, have produced a unique tradition grounded in the Scripture, carrying forward the ancient sacramental practices of the church, and giving rise to many legitimate local expressions of our shared historic faith. Our doctrinal foundations and missional impulse are best expressed in our Book of Common Prayer, which serves as the rule of faith for Anglican life. The Book of Common Prayer is not to be mistaken as a substitute for the Scripture, nor is it in conflict with our firm belief in the sufficiency of Scripture. On the contrary, its use is primarily for the purpose of teaching and celebrating the Scripture. A chief motivation of the Protestant Reformers was to get the Scripture into the hands and ears of the common person in a language they could understand, employ in their worship, and apply to their everyday lives. The intention of Thomas Cranmer, who compiled, curated, or created much of the earliest authoritative edition of the Prayer Book, was to "attain intelligibility, edification, and corporateness, by producing, for regular use, a single, simple liturgy in the vernacular, in which the Scriptures are read and expounded in an orderly way, biblical teaching is incorporated throughout, all that is misleading or meaningless is excluded, words are audible, actions are visible, and congregational participation in speaking, singing, and reception of the sacrament . . . is encouraged."[1]

The English Reformers, unlike many other Protestants, elevated the written and proclaimed Word of God while also emphasizing the importance of the sacraments. Perhaps due to their hearts shaped by both Celtic and Roman roots, they saw the communal and experiential participation in the sacraments as indispensable to scriptural faithfulness and discipleship. The great British Bible translator William Tyndale said, "The sacrament doth much more vehemently print lively the faith, and make it sink down in the heart, than do bare words only: as a man is more sure of that he heareth, seeth, feeleth, smelleth, and tasteth than what he heareth only."[2] Anglicanism views Word and sacrament as one. They are each an encounter with the revealed truth of God—one proclaimed, the other visible.

The experience of Word and sacrament should be a saturation in the gospel of Jesus Christ, with his glorious grace bestowed and his call to action extended. Anglicanism is a living tradition where the wisdom of those who have gone before—who worshipped the same Savior, studied the same Scripture, immersed in the same water, and ate at the same Table—continues to shape our modern experience and our future hope.

Thirdly, Anglicanism Is a Modern Movement of the Gospel

Anglicanism's lens is now much bigger than the British Isles, as it is the third largest communion in the world with more than eighty-five million adherents. Scholarship, thought, and practice is being defined by a global family of Anglicans in Africa, Asia, and the Global South along with revivals of faithful Anglicanism in the West.

We feel the healthy tension of being formed and rooted by our ancient history while engaging in the continued missional impulse of the church today. Our desire is to bring our Anglican perspective—built on the foundation of the Scripture, the Great Tradition, and our global heritage—to bear on the current global missional landscape. Anglicans recognize that the way, the truth, the life, and the wisdom and practice of the church are not ours to invent, but to carry on. And at the same time, our ways of being are not stuck irrelevantly in the past as we recognize that the Holy Spirit is still at work today to bring the unchanging truth of Christ to an ever-changing world. So, our view of mission is one that both protects and proliferates. We guard the good deposit entrusted to us, while also inviting missional innovation that submits to the doctrine, discipline, and worship of the church.

This concept is sometimes referred to as *creative fidelity*. We are faithful to the Christian faith, the Great Tradition, and our Anglican heritage, but that faithfulness is not unnecessarily restraining. Rather, it provides the framework for modern mission. It carries on the essentials, the ethos, and the institutional memory of the church while also speaking winsomely to the current culture.

What Is Church Planting?

Church planting is the starting of new local churches. This book is about starting new churches as approached through the Anglican tradition. The history and influences of the Anglican church have created a unique way of being the church and that should affect our motives and methods when we start new local churches in contemporary society. This book attempts to be a bridge between the particular and often misunderstood work of church planting and the peculiar tradition of Anglican Christianity.

Church planting elicits significant questions of both ecclesiology (what is the church?) and missiology (what is the mission of the church and how do we go about it?). We need to know both what we are planting and how we should plant it. To look at church planting through an Anglican lens is to find answers to these questions in our unique heritage.

Church planting is a complex and risky endeavor. Church planting not only forces us to ask philosophical questions of the church's identity and purpose, but also to find practical solutions to how we start new churches in our own local areas. Church planting is a broad discipline demanding engagement with practical issues ranging from structural processes (how to incorporate, how to open a bank account, how to get insurance, how to form a vestry, how to keep children safe in the nursery, how to choose a name, how to find meeting space) to missional questions (how to reach the community, how to build an initial group of people to start the church, how to serve those in need, how to make disciples). There are also questions of funding, strategy, polity, and worship, just to name a few more. All the while, the planter is striving to remain faithful to Jesus, effective in mission, and personally healthy. Our Anglican heritage frames our philosophy of planting and helps answer these questions.

Anglican Church Planting

The coming together of the historical juggernaut that is Anglicanism with the creative and passionate work of modern church planting is a beautiful convergence. Each benefits the other. Anglicanism provides a prolific amount of direction, focus, accountability, and gifts to church planting. And church planting ensures that Anglicanism is not merely a reflection on past glories, but a continuation of an ongoing work of God.

It is an unfortunate truth that many within Anglican circles do not understand the purpose or the practice of church planting, or why it is essential to continue to plant churches. Our emphasis on the ancient sometimes lulls us into celebrating the depth of our roots while forgetting about the new green leaves that are required for continual life and reproduction. Frankly, although church planting has long flourished in the Anglican church in the Global South, it had until recently become all but lost to Anglicans in the West.

Church planting should not be foreign to Anglicans. This gospel work should not be left up to our faithful brothers and sisters in mission-minded, non-denominational, Presbyterian, Assemblies of God, or Baptist traditions. We have a lot to offer this work. With its high view of the church and its missional roots, church planting should be natural to the Anglican church. When properly engaged, the relationship of Anglicanism and church planting is symbiotic, as Anglicanism brings depth to church planting and church planting brings life to Anglicanism. We should strive to live out what is built into our heritage.

I believe Anglicanism will grow stronger as we continue to wake up to our missional calling to plant churches, and in doing so our unique voice can add a healthy new perspective to the current ecumenical church planting conversation. This should mean more than simply using selected elements of Anglicism as a new set of "tools" to be employed (or not) in planting a church. Anglicanism is not a dead tradition that can be dissected and the parts leveraged for trendy church planting. Lighting candles and reciting a psalm does not make one Anglican. Anglicanism is a living global family with a rich history, a vibrant present, and an exciting trajectory for its future. Anglicanism is not a model to be employed; it is a way of being to be embraced. Anglicanism is not an aesthetic skin laid over the work of church planting until cultural preferences change and a fresh facade is needed; it is the steadying force that shapes the family, history, and ethos of the new church. The Anglican tradition does not submit to our church planting; it calls us to submit our planting to the church.

. . . .

The churches that result from our shared pursuit may, and in many cases should, aesthetically look very different from the Anglican church of my youth. There may or may not be arched doors, stained windows, or white vestments. But there must remain the heart of Anglicanism: the continued life and work of the church ancient and catholic, lived out in Word and sacrament for the glory of Christ, for the care of the found, and for the sake of the lost.

Anglicanism is uniquely positioned to harness the missional fervor that has existed within the church since Jesus's commissioning of the apostles by gathering the wisdom and community of the ancient church, bringing to bear the gifts of Word and sacrament, allowing the fresh movement of the Holy Spirit, entering well into contemporary cultures, and planting churches that are simultaneously faithful and effective in the work of mission. Church planting is a command for the church universal and pursuing this command as Anglicans means that we go about planting churches in a particular way.

A Note to Non-Anglican Readers:

Again—welcome, I am so very glad we are exploring church planting together. As we begin, I would encourage you to ask how your particular church tradition engages the living history of the church. Even if your tradition does not intentionally emphasize the authority or continued presence of those who have gone before, how should the witness and example of the previous millennia inform your present work of mission? Of course, there is the legitimate fear of a dead, legalistic religion, but there is also an equal danger of an unrooted church left to unrestrained change. Immersing in your own heritage, how do you ensure that neither one of these realities are true for your church plant or your process of planting? There may be some translating you have to do as I use the example of the Anglican Church in these pages, but there are principles and perspectives here that I encourage you apply to your own tradition to strengthen what is commendable and rethink what may need reforming. Church planting gives you the opportunity to ask why we do what we do in the way we do it.

CHAPTER 2

• • • •

The Reasons We Plant

Jesus said to them again, "Peace be with you.
As the Father has sent me, even so I am sending you."

—*John 20:21*

SUMMARY: We need to build a common foundation for our motivations for church planting so that church planters can be equipped to give a winsome explanation for why they are doing the work they are doing, and so that all clergy, laity, leaders, and members can be confident in their support of church planting.

"Why should we plant churches?" is a legitimate question. Church planting requires significant energy and resources, so it requires a robust justification. Beyond that, I am making the case that church planting should be a primary focus of every diocese and local church, and that every faithful church member should at the least be aware and supportive of church planting. That's a strong pitch, which deserves an equally strong defense. Church planting is also foreign to many in the West, especially Anglicans, so many people have not ever been a part of a church plant or heard a clear explanation for why we plant churches at all. They deserve answers.

Also, do not be surprised if "Why should we plant churches?" is an emotionally-charged question for many. For church planters, this question can prick a nerve. After all, the planters are risking so much at significant cost to themselves and their families, and here is someone questioning the very validity of the endeavor they have sacrificed so greatly for. There is relational baggage in this question as well, because many times it is asked more as an accusation than an honest inquiry. Often, the planter is frustrated not so much with the individual asking, but with the fact that planting has become so removed from the normal life of the church that this question even comes up.

We need to build a common foundation for our reasons for church planting, so that church planters can be equipped to give a winsome explanation for why they are doing the work they are doing, and so that all clergy, laity, leaders, and members can be confident in their support of church planting.

Fundamental Presuppositions

I want to begin with two presuppositions that rest at the heart of the reason we plant churches. I am convinced that if you are not in agreement with these assumptions, there is little hope that data or empirical evidence can convince you church planting is a proper pursuit—for although church planting is strategic, it is first and foremost a command from God.

First Presupposition: The Centrality of the Gospel

We cannot be faithful Christians and not be on mission, for our work of mission is a part of the gospel. The gospel is more than simply a legal transaction that determines what happens to you when you die. The gospel (which of course means "good news") is the entire story of redemptive history. God created the world. Humankind rebelled, introducing sin into the world. God began the saving process by making a people for himself through Abraham: "I will be their God" (Genesis 17:8). God foreshadowed salvation in Christ by bringing them out of oppression in Egypt and into the promised land, emphasizing not only that he will be their God, but that they will be his people (Exodus 6:7). He showed us our great need for a Savior through the law that we were not able to keep and the prophets who prosecuted us for it. He showed us our need for his sovereignty through the ineptitude of the line of kings of Israel.

The long-awaited Messiah came in the person of Jesus Christ, born of the virgin Mary. Jesus lived a sinless life, fulfilling the law and the prophets, and not deserving of the penalty of death that comes through sin. Yet out of obedience to God and love for us, he died a substitutionary and very real death on the cross to atone for our sins. He defeated death on the third day by rising to life again, opening for us a reconciled relationship with God by grace through faith in his Son. Jesus ascended to heaven and is seated at the right hand of the Father where he now intercedes for his people.

The Holy Spirit was sent to the church on the day of Pentecost to empower her for the work of mission to be his witness "to the end of the earth" (Acts 1:8). Through Christ, God has made a people for himself—the church. And the people of God have been sent, just as Christ was sent: "As the Father has sent me, even so I am sending you" (John 20:21). We are a sent people, commissioned to bring the news of Christ's redemption to the world by making disciples of all nations, baptizing them and teaching them (Matthew 28:19–20). After his resurrection, Jesus made a point to show his disciples that worldwide mission has been promised throughout all of Scripture and is part of what he accomplished in his death and resurrection.

> Then he opened their minds to understand the Scriptures, and said to them, "Thus it is written, that the Christ should suffer and on the third day rise from the dead, and that repentance for the forgiveness of sins should be proclaimed in his name to all nations, beginning from Jerusalem. You are witnesses of these things." (Luke 24:45–48)

The full story, according to Jesus, consists of both salvation achieved in Christ and salvation proclaimed in his name. There is no bifurcation of the two, no separation of these events. If we are to believe in the fullness of the gospel, we must simultaneously be beneficiaries of the gospel and witnesses of the gospel. Until finally, one day our mission will find its fulfillment when Christ returns the same way he ascended to make all things new and "at the name of Jesus every knee should bow, in heaven and on earth and under the earth, and every tongue confess that Jesus Christ is Lord, to the glory of God the Father" (Philippians 2:10–11). The final chapter is the fruition of the message to which we are witnesses, when all things are reconciled unto him.

No one part of this is the gospel—it is *all* the gospel. From creation, to fall, to redemption, to mission, to the consummation, it is all the good news of Jesus Christ, the progress of redemptive history, and the central truth of our identity and work as the church.

It would be easy for us to strip away all but what we would deem as the essential work of Christ on the cross and mistakenly call that the gospel. But if we do so, we will see outward mission as a mere addendum to the truth of the gospel. In other words, we will imagine the gospel is the salvific work of Christ, and mission is telling others about it. The problem is that when mission is seen as an addendum to the gospel and not one of its central events, we often begin to think of mission as optional, or an activity meant only for those who are particularly called. The gospel is both that God is reconciling the world to himself through Jesus Christ and that we are ambassadors through whom God is making his plea (2 Corinthians 5:20) until his final return. These things cannot be separated.

Peter tells us explicitly that we have been saved for the purpose of mission. He says, "But you are a chosen race, a royal priesthood, a holy nation, a people for his own possession, that you may proclaim the excellencies of him who called you out of darkness into his marvelous light" (1 Peter 2:9). Jesus did not simply command us to make disciples, he saved us for this purpose. We proclaim his excellencies through our worship as a royal priesthood and our witness as his holy nation. To fully participate in the gospel, we must be a people on mission.

Our first presupposition is that the gospel of Jesus Christ is at the core of our belief and identity as Christians. Everything else that we say, do, and think should be based on the gospel. And that gospel inextricably includes the work of Christ and the continued work of his church.

Second Presupposition: The Critical Necessity of the Local Church in Gospel Mission

The work of the gospel is by nature incarnational. The concepts of redemption, covenant, community, and mission are meant to be embodied by the people of Christ, which is why the church is called the body of Christ. These things are not just meant to be written about or preached; they are meant to be lived out by the people who are transformed by them. That means fleshy individuals must put their actual hands, feet, heads, and hearts to work in tangible interaction with other people in their local communities. My wife had a roommate in college who used to say, "I know the promises of God and I am thankful for them, but sometimes you just need someone with skin on to make you realize they are true." The local church is the place where the grand story of God's redemptive work comes alive and becomes tangible. We are people with skin on to make the promises of God a reality to our communities.

Our second presupposition is that the local church is an essential part of the redemptive plan of God. The church is not a gathering of like-minded people who all happen to hold the gospel in common and self-select to come together once a week and discuss our shared interest. The gospel is not that individuals are being saved from Satan, sin, and death and can add on the church if it would enhance their personal spirituality. No, the gospel is that God is saving a people—the church—and individuals are saved, through Christ, *into his church* through repentance, belief, and baptism. The church is the recipient of the promises of God and his chosen instrument to proclaim those promises to the world.

The local church, then, is more than a place for Sunday gathering. Although our regular corporate worship is an essential aspect of the life of the church, it is not the entirety of the life of the church. The local church is a place of cosmic and eternal importance where the kingdom of God takes root in a geographic location and the people of God live out the sending commands of God. Just listen to the words we pray each week in our worship services (emphasis mine):

> Heavenly Father,
> We thank you for feeding us with the spiritual food
> of the most precious Body and Blood
> of your Son our Savior Jesus Christ;
> and for assuring us in these holy mysteries
> that *we are living members of the body of your Son*,
> and heirs of your eternal Kingdom.
> And now, Father, *send us out to do the work you have given us to do,*
> to love and serve you as faithful witnesses of Christ our Lord.
> To him, to you, and to the Holy Spirit,
> be honor and glory, now and for ever. Amen.[1]

The church is the saved people of God locally gathered for worship and formation, a people sent to love and serve, and a people who will one day assemble around the throne of Christ together in the new heavens and the new earth. When we are planting churches, we are planting local embodied expressions of this greater gathering. Here is where the action happens. Here the truth of the gospel comes crashing into everyday life, and the Lord adds to our number daily those who are being saved. The local church is essential to God's great work of redemption.

Conclusion: Planting Churches

The implications of these two presuppositions are clear: if the gospel is the hope of the world and is the life and mission of the church, then more local churches means more embodied gospel. It is as simple as that. We plant churches because more local churches means more disciples, more evangelism, more worship, more tangible expression of the kingdom of God.

People have said to me (sometimes laden with snark), "There is no command in the Scripture to plant churches, only to make disciples." The Scripture itself must find this statement ridiculous. There is no making of disciples without the church! Disciples are not free radicals; making disciples requires baptism into the church, catechesis and formation are pursued within community, and sending happens through the church. When Jesus's original disciples heard the Great Commission from Jesus to go and make disciples, what did they do? We see in the book of Acts that they planted churches. Preaching and evangelism led to baptism and starting new churches that led to more disciples who preached, baptized, and started more churches. If we are to be faithful as the people of God, we should see the same natural pattern in our disciples and churches.

In fact, any entity that is not making disciples is not really a church. Call your gathering what you will, if disciples are not being made, then you may have started a civic organization or a fan club, but you have not planted a church. This statement is challenging to some existing churches as it roots our definition of a healthy and faithful church not in the local congregation's age or size, but in its faithfulness in worship, mission, and discipleship. Part of the value of church planting is challenging the status quo. We plant churches to remind the greater church of its missional purpose.

Church planting is a living expression of the gospel that is centered on a sending God—a God who in his essence is in perpetual loving community in the Trinity, and who sends from that loving community the Son and the Spirit into the world to redeem what has been lost. Church plants are the children of the bride of Christ, meant to grow strong and reproduce more disciples, more churches, more worshippers gathered around the throne of God.

The Missional Effectiveness of Church Planting

There also remains the justification for planting that the proof of the pudding is in the tasting. In other words, experience and research reveal that church planting is simply the most effective method of evangelism and discipleship we can pursue. Bear with me as there is no other way to communicate this truth than to quote the research.

For a deeper dive into this subject, read Tim Keller's article, "Why Plant Churches?" Let me give you a taste of the force of his argument:

> The vigorous, continual planting of new congregations is the single most crucial strategy for (1) the numerical growth of the body of Christ in a city and (2) the continual corporate renewal and revival of the existing churches in a city. Nothing else—not crusades, outreach programs, parachurch ministries, growing megachurches, congregational consulting, nor church

> renewal processes—will have the consistent impact of dynamic, extensive church planting. This is an eyebrow-raising statement, but to those who have done any study at all, it is not even controversial.[2]

Keller goes on to say that planting has been statistically proven to be our most effective method of reaching the unchurched, younger people, new people groups, and new residents. There are many sociological and anthropological reasons for this, which Keller will winsomely lead you through.

Another fantastic resource on the significant need for church planting is "The Great Opportunity," a report written by the Pinetops Foundation. This report synthesizes the data from several studies plus original research. The work led to startling findings:

> The bottom line: the next 30 years will represent the largest missions opportunity in the history of America. It is the largest and fastest numerical shift in religious affiliation in the history of this country. Even in the most optimistic scenarios, Christian affiliation in the U.S. shrinks dramatically, and in our base case, over 1 million youth currently at least nominally in the church today will choose to leave each year for the next three decades. 35 million youth raised in families that say they are Christians will say that they are not by 2050.[3]

However, Pinetops did not leave us simply with doom and gloom. They provided solutions to prevent and reverse this trend—six areas which need significant attention from the church, the first of which is planting new churches:

> Church planting in the U.S. will need to double to triple from current rates to address population growth and anticipated church closures of older congregations. The American church needs to plant more than 200,000 churches in the next 30 years, and to meet the needs of the unaffiliated, nearly 270,000 churches. In addition, there is a dramatic need to invest specifically in planting in emerging urban cities with those who have left the church; Gen Z (which follows the Millennials) is the largest generation in American history and will likely increase urban density over the next two decades. The church will need to find new models for lowering the cost of planting while increasing the number of leaders who reflect the increasing diversity of urban populations, all without sacrificing historic orthodoxy.[4]

More than 200,000 churches in the next thirty years simply to meet the needs of population growth, and another 70,000 to make headway with the unaffiliated? That is quite the task. Anglicans need to step up to the plate with our sister traditions to spread the good news of the gospel through the planting of churches.

It Is Part of Our Anglican Heritage

Planting churches is not new to Anglicanism. The reason there are Anglican churches throughout the world is because Anglican missionaries planted them. If you are a part of an Anglican church today, it was at some point a church plant. It is true that the expansion of the Anglican Church is partially due to the spread of the British interests throughout the world, but do not be deceived into thinking that planting Anglican churches was historically just a pragmatic necessity of an expanding empire. Long before there was a British Empire, there were faithful Christians in England who were planting churches.

As we previously mentioned, our Anglican roots are not, as some may falsely understand, limited to, or defined by, the cavorting of Henry VIII. Anglicanism stems from a long history of gospel missionaries that predate Henry.

It is impossible to know exactly when Christianity reached the British Isles, though some have speculated it could have been as early as AD 67. What is known, however, is that separated from the continent of Europe and farther from the influence of Rome, a distinct expression of Christianity developed in the British Isles in what we now call Celtic Christianity. Leaders like Patrick, Columba, Aidan, and Brigid led expanding and multiplying Celtic churches. In AD 595, Pope Gregory sent a missionary named Augustine to visit Britain and give a report on the church. Augustine reported that the Christian faith was vibrant, but the church was distinct from the Roman church in its more organic expression.

The missionary tradition that would become Anglicanism continued within the monastic traditions, the actions of the Reformers, the Wesley brothers, William Wilberforce, the Church Mission Society, and missionaries like William Temple, Lilias Trotter, and Roland Allen. We also cannot forget Joe Church who was an Anglican missionary instrumental in the work of the East African Revival in the early twentieth century that resulted in thousands of new believers and new churches. This list does not even begin to scratch the surface of the missionary work done throughout the world by countless men and women in the Anglican tradition.

Anglicans have a long history in mission and church planting. Sadly, we also have an infamous history of sacrificing missionary work on the altar of order and territory. For example, John Wesley and George Whitfield both found many Anglican churches closed to them based on the nature of their missionary work, so they moved to preaching outside the walls of the church. As a people who highly value tradition, we should celebrate our long heritage of missionary endeavors so we may emulate that success, and we should learn from the mistakes of the moments when we let our structure squelch the work of the missionary, so we are not doomed to repeat them.

Our high ecclesiology, our devotion to the Scripture, and our sensitivity to the work of the Holy Spirit makes Anglicans a church-planting people. May we live into our heritage and our history and continue to fervently plant churches in our time.

Why Isn't It Obvious That We Should Plant Churches?

The longer you are involved with the work of church planting, the more tempting it is to assume that the answer to the question of why we plant churches should be obvious. I assure you, however, that for many reasons it is not obvious to the average person inside or outside of the church.

Genuine Unawareness

Many people have not stopped to consider where new churches come from or why it is important to start them. Many who have been part of a local church for a long period of time have never been discipled in this radical way of living. Planting is an endeavor as foreign to them as splitting atoms is to me. Their unfamiliarity may sometimes be expressed as opposition or contempt, but a little education can make them believers. If you are a planter, be patient and willing to give an answer for the work you do.

Idolatry and Sin

Church planting is about giving away. We give away our lives, our time, our money, our safety, and our security for the glory of Christ and the sake of the lost. We give away our best leaders from our churches and send out key members of our parishes. Jesus said it is better to give than receive (Acts 20:35), but honestly, he said many things that are extremely difficult. It is not in our fleshly nature to turn outward and put Christ and others before ourselves. Instead, we are quite good at worshiping the idols of our own comfort and security. If you are a skeptic or are opposed to church planting, I humbly ask you to prayerfully consider whether your opposition is grounded in the generosity of our sending God or in the idols of predictability and safety.

Idolatry and sin require a good deal of conviction, repentance, and forgiveness to overcome. As supporters of church planting, we must be like the prophets who speak boldly against the complacency of the church, leading by proclamation and action in this aspect of her mission. We must also be full of grace and mercy as we recognize that facing down idols is a difficult task.

Fear and Scarcity

Church planters are missionaries whether our efforts are foreign or domestic. There is inherent uncertainty and unpredictability in what we do. There is a great possibility of rejection, a hugely complex task that can seem very daunting, and a large amount of risk tolerance is required. We tend not to want to discuss the things that scare us.

There is also a fear of scarcity of resources. If we are committing leadership and financial resources to church planting, something previously funded may no longer be. A move away from old programs to a new focus on church planting can be challenging to those who found success in the previously-emphasized ministries. There is fear in something new and a grieving over the perceived loss of what once was.

But true love casts out all fear. God's love for us, our love for the church, and the church's love for the lost must move us beyond fear and into sacrificial action. We must lean not on the sanctity of programs, but rather, as Paul tells us, be compelled by the love of Christ to go and persuade others (2 Corinthians 5:11–15).

The church also often develops an attitude of scarcity where we feel like we will lack the resources to survive, so we act like a body dying of exposure: we pump all our heat and life away from the edges to warm our core and allow the vital organs to live. We decide church planting and mission are extremities—expendable so we can stay alive. But the truth is that when mission and church planting have become dispensable, we are already dead.

Does our God not own the cattle on a thousand hills? "Yes, he does," you say, "but he has not put those cattle in our budget." But have you asked? I mean really asked, even begged the Lord of the harvest? Communally, as a local church and as a diocese, have you fasted and prayed for the funding you need to plant churches? Or have you capitulated to a balanced budget and giving shortfalls, and determined that you cannot afford to plant? James brings us difficult words when he says,

"You do not have, because you do not ask. You ask and do not receive, because you ask wrongly, to spend it on your passions" (James 4:2–3). Why is planting only funded after those things that serve ourselves? Are we prioritizing outward mission? Let us not give up on church planting due to a perspective of scarcity. Let us together beg the Lord for the resources to do the work he is calling us to do. Let us call upon the faithfulness of our people to give to this important work. If you are wealthy and can give large amounts, please do. If you are poor and can give very little, please do. When we truly value the work of church planting as central in our life and ministry as a diocese or local church, we will give what we are able. If planting is a siloed ministry for the radical and strange, our budgets will never be large enough to plant.

Territorialism

Another common fear comes from misunderstanding the local church's claim over a geographic area. I have heard many people say that planting a new church in a particular area will simply shrink the number of people in other Anglican churches in the city. This thinking misunderstands the purpose of church planting. There are not a finite number of Anglicans in an area so that adding another church dilutes their distribution like watered-down wine. Church planting is about reaching those who do not yet know Jesus. I guarantee you there are enough of those to go around.

A church planter once told me about his experience with a pastor of an established Anglican church who conveyed to the planter that he was fine with the planting of a new church nearby as long as it wasn't in his church's sphere of influence. He then took a map and marked his sphere by drawing a circle around an entire city of millions of people! Friends, we must move beyond territorialism and welcome others into our corner of the vineyard.

Of course, there's no excuse for planting churches without communicating this to sister churches in the area. Christian unity and our Anglican ecclesiology require a collaborative approach. But we also must not be limited by clergy or laity who spend more energy fending off effective mission than engaging in it.

One Reason to Rule Them All

Above all else, beyond all other reasons for the work we do as church planters, we must long to participate in the work of Jesus Christ. We must have a heart for the lost that mirrors his. We must have a love for the church that reflects the kind of love Christ has when he calls her his bride.

Church planting is not a growth strategy. In human reproduction, there is a difference between procreating solely for the numerical advancement of a species and bearing children as a mystical cooperation with God. Church planting is church birthing. We cooperate with God as co-creators who usher in new life. Birthing hurts. Parenting is hard. Kids are expensive. But we long for children, and it is painful if we cannot bear them. Church planting is difficult and risky, but we should long for the new life it brings to the souls of the lost, and the affection for Christ it stirs in our own.

Answering Some Common Objections to Church Planting

In my time of leading church planting within dioceses, provinces, and local churches, I have encountered a few objections which are repeated quite regularly and are worthy of being addressed quickly here. Although I am an ardent defender of church planting, I also strive to never come across as defensive. Church planting needn't be an argument. We are like a married couple discussing having children. Although many of our concerns about logistics, money, timing, etc. come from the fear and selfish tendencies of our hearts—I understand, I have them too—we are called to support one another in community as we overcome those fears and break down our idols through Christ. As we work through some possible objections to church planting, picture us sitting together over coffee, logically and respectfully working through our big decision to have more children.

Objection #1: Church Planters Compromise Their Anglican Heritage

I am literally writing hundreds of pages to prove that church planters don't have to compromise their Anglicanism, but I readily admit there are times when it has been true. There are horror stories of how some planters have ignored the Great Tradition, misused Word and sacrament, and planted something that is Anglican in name only. Honestly, that happens with clergy and laity of established churches as well.

There is often a phenomenon where liturgical folks have experienced dead liturgical churches and wish for the vibrancy of what they see in churches from some other traditions. While at the same time, those from other traditions who have been good at gathering larger but shallow crowds look longingly at the ancient roots of the liturgical church. They are like two passing ships on different trajectories, each trying to navigate the narrow channel where deep tradition and cultural engagement meet. The danger is that each will overcorrect and run aground on opposite rocks. The church looking for more tradition will become pseudo-liturgical. They will import some liturgy without truly understanding its purpose. They will light candles, talk about cool ancient stuff, and maybe say the creed (but change some words to better fit their context), all without grasping what it really means to be a historically-rooted church. Meanwhile, the church looking for more cultural engagement will become awkwardly missional. They will try to conjure up some missional wizardry by adding trendy dress and removing parts of the liturgy that don't feel comfortable or entertaining enough. Either way, the result is a half-baked liturgy that is neither pleasing to the eye nor good for food.

Diocesan and local church leaders see the sloppy thing that emerges and presume that church planting leads to unhealthy liturgical expression and questionable ecclesiology. But our response to this quandary should not be to dismiss church planting, but rather to create effective resources (of which I hope this book is one) that can help equip churches who desire to maintain the integrity of both liturgy and mission. Instead of pointing fingers and grumbling where we see it not going well, let's go plant churches that model how the Anglican tradition properly pursued is well-suited for church planting.

Objection #2: Planting Is Only for Low-Church Evangelicals

I have seen beautiful, faithful, and missional churches that run the spectrum of churchmanship. I have sat at the table with high-church Anglo-Catholics who dripped with passion for mission. Pursued properly, their expression of the faith that focuses on beauty and the holiness of God can be startlingly effective in mission. A dear friend of mine planted one such church in Waco, Texas, off the campus of Baylor University, that is ministering to professors and students from the university as well as many Waco natives. He's always genuflecting, lifting, and smoking. And his church is vibrantly reaching the community. Many of our church plants have higher churchmanship and see a significant missional value in bringing a profoundly different offering to a culture in search of something deeply transcendent.

Objection #3: We Need to Focus on Strengthening the Churches We Already Have Before Starting New Ones

This objection is common, but somewhat nebulous. In what specific ways should we first strengthen existing churches? What do existing churches look like when they are finally strong enough? Why should strengthening existing churches keep us from planting churches?

Honestly, I believe this objection is more often a veiled concern over rights to the budget. If a diocese or network is giving significant resources to start new churches, there are fewer resources available to established churches. Like with cell phone companies, the new customers seem to get all the good deals. The answer to this objection is a change in perspective.

I weed my garden every day because if I didn't, the little green parasites would steal the water, nutrients, and sunshine needed by the plants I actually want to grow. If we see church plants as invaders and competitors for resources, we will want to pluck them like weeds in the garden. We instead should view our church plants not as weedy resource thieves, but as children of our diocese.

Healthy adults should not need as many resources as new children. Sometimes it feels like my two young boys are going to consume everything in my house, but I am happy to provide dump trucks full of food to help them grow strong. I would do anything to find that food for them. They are not thieves; I provide for them joyfully. At the same time, that will change if they are thirty years old and hoping to live in my basement. So we provide for our children in their early years and develop a plan for them to become self-sufficient. The same is true for our churches: established churches may need funds for special initiatives or obstacles but should not be dependent upon diocesan funds for survival. If we have churches living in our diocesan basements, we should not fund inactivity. They need to get off the couch and pursue the work of mission.

What about churches that are weak and need assistance? Yes, there are times when an existing church needs help in revitalizing after a difficult season and the diocese should come to her aid. Having said that, let me give three caveats.

First, an existing church needs to have been vital to begin with in order to revitalize. Too often, I see churches that never got any traction at their start asking for money to revitalize after years of being plateaued. Discernment needs to be given to decide whether these churches need help developing and funding a strategy for revitalization or whether it is time for them to close. We should not be ashamed to close local churches as long as it is done with pastoral concern for the few people who remain in the dying church. Too often what is called revitalization is in reality only life support, keeping the church statistically alive but with no signs of life.

Second, it is too simplistic to think that giving money to an unhealthy church will be its saving grace. Much work needs to be done to develop a proper culture, reorganize leadership, and ensure a missional focus. Many churches that ask for help with revitalization are systemically unhealthy and simply want money to replace a clergyperson who left due to the dysfunction. This strategy does not go well for the new clergy or the church. I have heard it said, "It is much harder to raise the dead than to have babies." A diocese cannot simply become a hospice for unhealthy churches; it must keep open its maternity ward as well.

Third, there are good and legitimate times to invest in revitalizing an existing church, so I am happy to report that revitalization and church planting are not antithetical. In fact, church planting helps revitalize existing churches. It is church planting that will develop the courageous and innovative leaders who can turn these churches around. Church planting will create the missional culture and adaptive methods that will assist these churches in reaching their communities. Church planting will ultimately bring more funds into the diocesan budget, and a rising tide lifts all ships. Throwing money at a dying church without leadership and strategy is bad stewardship because the money alone will not save it. Let's revitalize when it is wise, close churches when that is what is needed, and start new churches that can help bring new life to the diocese.

Objection #4: We Have Enough Churches Already

The thought goes that in places like the southern United States there seems to be a church on every corner, so why do we need more? But remember that statistics show we do not have near enough churches to fit even the current generation of people, much less future generations. If we have a missional optimism—if we believe we will actually reach people with the gospel—we need thousands more churches. Plus, if we truly want to reach the lost, we continuously need new churches on the front lines. Tim Keller writes,

> Dozens of denominational studies have confirmed that the average new church gains most of its new members (60–80 percent) from the ranks of people who are not attending any worshiping body, while churches over ten to fifteen years of age gain 80–90 percent of new members by transfer from other congregations. This means the average new congregation will bring six to eight times more new people into the life of the body of Christ than an older congregation of the same size.[5]

There is simply no factual justification to a claim that we have a sufficient number of churches. However, there is significant data to show how continual church planting increases our missional effectiveness.

Objection #5: There Is Already a Church in That Area

This objection is a bit more complicated. There is a tension between respecting the work of an established church and continuing to pursue new mission in a community. I have seen existing churches that have embraced new church planters and have been of immense support to the new work. Other times, I have seen frosty relationships from the beginning. Since we need more churches, not fewer, our churches must learn how to interact with one another in life-giving ways.

A brash young planter entering into a town without as much as a courtesy phone call to the existing church is unwise at best and more probably in violation of our Anglican values, since we are not autonomous local churches. The opposite problem is often true as well, when planters are met with scorn, anger, or suspicion from existing churches.

Let me say this very clearly to local church leaders: planting another church in the same city or town where an established Anglican church already exists is not a judgment upon the effectiveness or worth of the existing church. It does not necessarily mean you are falling short in your mission to your community; you simply have missional reinforcements. If your existing church is flourishing in worship and mission, then you have a new partner in town. If it is not, then you have someone who may encourage you with new missional zeal and creative methods. And if you don't want to flourish in mission, then to oppose the planter may actually mean you are kicking against the goads of conviction as he represents what the Lord is calling you to do.

The existing church should also recognize that the new planter is going to go about things in different ways, and that's perfectly fine. We do not need to roll our eyes in contempt, but rather applaud their efforts for Jesus. We can either pursue contention or cooperation. The first will make everyone's life more difficult, and the second will create a partnership that strengthens both churches.

Don't think in terms of an appropriate distance between churches, I know many churches that have planted churches within ten minutes of their existing congregation with great success. The new churches are reaching different people in different ways. There is no excuse for claiming a geographic area as our own. Jesus did not say, "One of you will be my witness in Jerusalem, one in Judea, another one in Samaria." We need strength in numbers.

One time I received a call from an irate priest who was furious that someone was thinking about starting another church in his town. His was a choral-singing, incense-burning, expensive-vestment-wearing, very beautifully high church, reaching people in a wealthy part of town. Wonderful. The potential new plant was proposed for the other side of town, next to a university, with a more informal approach and lower churchmanship aimed primarily at students. Although geographically close, these two churches were not fishing in the same pond.

When the person who was beginning to pray about starting this church called the rector of the established church, the rector laid into him, furious and offended that this was the first he was hearing about the new plant. His church was already established and doing just fine in reaching the community. Why would this town need another church? etc. etc.

When the rector called me, the diocese's canon for church planting, he read me the riot act as well. I tried to calm him down, explaining that the first call I had the planter make was to the rector of the local church. There was no vast conspiracy happening behind his back. I tried to talk to him about the significant differences in missional approaches between his church and the potential plant. He would have none of it. His people wrote letters to the bishop complaining about the possible new plant. Some of his vestry went so far as to call the planter himself to tell him that he shouldn't plant in their town.

Frankly, this attitude is blasphemous, sinful, and utterly un-Christlike. If you are a planter, do not assume that this will be the response of the rector of an existing church near your potential plant. Seek relationship and have grace. You may find the rector in your area to be one of your biggest fans.

If you are the rector of an existing church, do not respond out of fear and scarcity to a new church plant in your town. It is not there to compete with you, but to join in the work you are doing. Find a way to support one another in mission. Begin by responding well. If you respond with suspicion or anger, of course that planter is not going to pursue a further relationship with you. Instead of seeing the plant as an intruder, be overjoyed that new gospel work is coming to your community. The Lord has seen fit to bring more workers to this corner of the vineyard. Find a way to be a partner. At the very least, pray publicly for the plant in your weekly worship services. Develop a relationship with the planter, offer the use of your copy machine—whatever it takes to stir the affections of your heart for the planter and his work. See the planting of a new church as the beginning of a church family, a network of churches supporting one another in pursuing mission and faithfulness. A new plant in your area is not a threat, it is a gift.

Objection #6: We Should Only Plant When Convenient, Fully Funded, and Risk-Free

If I am correct that church plants are the children of a diocese, then there is never a "right time" to have them. No prospective parent ever said, "We now have more than enough money, a proper level of maturity, a completely free schedule, and assurance that all will go perfectly well—so let's have a baby." There is always risk in birthing new life. There are also always associated costs. If we wait until we can answer every objection, assuage every fear, and raise enough money that all the needs of the diocese are taken care of and we can put the extra funds into something like church planting, we will never plant churches. So why do we have babies if they are so risky and costly? Because they bring life. New parents swoon, grandparents get a new glint in their eyes, and friends rejoice—because the new child is a gift. So are church plants.

A Note to Non-Anglican Readers:

This may be one of the easiest chapters of this book to apply to all denominations and traditions. All of the biblical foundations for planting are equally shared, and most of the statistical data I cite is not from Anglican sources. It is also a universal truth that you will have objectors both within your denomination and without. Take some time to contemplate how you would answer the objections posed in this chapter. Also, ask other planters from your denomination to discuss with you some of the common arguments or questions they have fielded in their planting work. Some of the nuances may be different, but we are all planting for the same reasons and we face very similar pushback from those who do not yet understand why we are engaged in this important ministry. May the Lord give us all wisdom, peace, and patience.

Part 2

What Are We Planting?

CHAPTER 3

Ecclesiology and Missiology

The church's task is defined for it. It is the herald and foretaste of the Kingdom of God. For that it exists, and for the service to that end it must be organized and equipped.

— *Archbishop William Temple*

SUMMARY: Before we jump into the nuts and bolts of *how to plant a church*, we first need to understand *what kind of church* we are planting. This proper starting point significantly affects our methodology.

The Anglican tradition is an expression of the historic Christian church with its own peculiar practices, ethos, and charisms. Anglican churches are different from those in other traditions, and how we plant them is different as well.

This does not mean Anglicanism values distinctiveness in and of itself. We do not desire to be novel, only faithful to who the church has always been. We seek catholicity, not uniqueness. Archbishop Michael Ramsey said it this way:

> For while the Anglican church is vindicated by its place in history, with a strikingly balanced witness to Gospel and Church and sound learning, its greater vindication lies in its pointing through its own

> history to something of which it is a fragment. Its credentials are its incompleteness, with the tension and the travail in its soul. It is clumsy and untidy, it baffles neatness and logic. For it is sent not to commend itself as "the best type of Christianity," but by its very brokenness to point to the universal Church wherein all have died.[1]

Still, the meanderings of church history have given rise to other denominations so that some of our striving to be faithful now makes us different from other traditions. This means someone from a Presbyterian tradition, for example, can value from learning how an episcopal polity system affects planting. Or it means someone coming from a Baptist heritage might not yet have had lengthy discussions about the role of sacraments in church planting. I pray we can approach the uniqueness of Anglicanism without pretense or tribalism, and not disparaging other traditions.

That being said, before we jump into the nuts and bolts of *how to plant a church*, we first need to understand *what kind of church* we are planting. We must not gather people first and then start doing Anglican-y things. Even how you gather the people matters, for how you win them is how you keep them, and if planting an Anglican church, you are winning them through a way of life. So it is important, then, that we explore what the church is supposed to be and do.

Which Comes First?

There is an important philosophical conversation we must have if we are to share a common approach to church planting. In the world of mission and church planting, the first step is much debated. Do we begin with our ecclesiology (our understanding of the church) or our missiology (our understanding of the work of mission)? Which point of this compass you follow will decide much of where you will go and how you will get there.

Here is what is at stake: Does the church have an objective form and function that shapes how we go about the work of mission (our ecclesiology determines our missiology), or does the need to be effective in mission dictate what the church should be (our missiology determines our ecclesiology)? Stick with me for this discussion. Don't skim this for the sake of getting to the pragmatics, because our answer here has a profound effect on how we plant churches.

First of all, and most importantly, our understanding of both the church (ecclesiology) and mission (missiology) must be founded upon our understanding of the person and work of Jesus Christ (Christology). All we are and do as the church is by Jesus, with Jesus, and in Jesus. If your church is not built upon this Rock, your labor is in vain. You cannot plant based on either your ecclesiological or your missiological convictions unless those convictions find their source in the gospel of Jesus Christ. If this truth is not incontrovertible for you, stop reading this book and explore Jesus first. With that truth firmly in place, we now move to the next, more controversial, step.

A Helical Approach

I believe that our approach to church planting should begin with our ecclesiology and lead into our missiology. In other words, I believe we start with what the church is, rather than what the church does. Put another way, I believe we begin with the identity of the church and move to the function of the church rather than first determining our mission and reverse-engineering it in order to determine the form the church should take.

In truth, the interplay of missiology and ecclesiology from an Anglican perspective is less linear (one is determined by the other) than it is helical (shaped like a helix, or spiral). Our understanding of the church shapes our pursuit of mission, which informs our work as the church, which makes us more passionate about our mission, which causes us to examine everything we do in light of our mission, which more clearly defines our understanding of who we are, and so on, ever influencing one another and spiraling upward like a strand of DNA to greater degrees of purity and effective practice. Ecclesiology and missiology serve both as correctives and catalysts to one another: the pursuit of mission constantly keeps the church from becoming lifeless and stagnant, and faithfulness to the church's identity keeps mission from becoming formless and undefined.

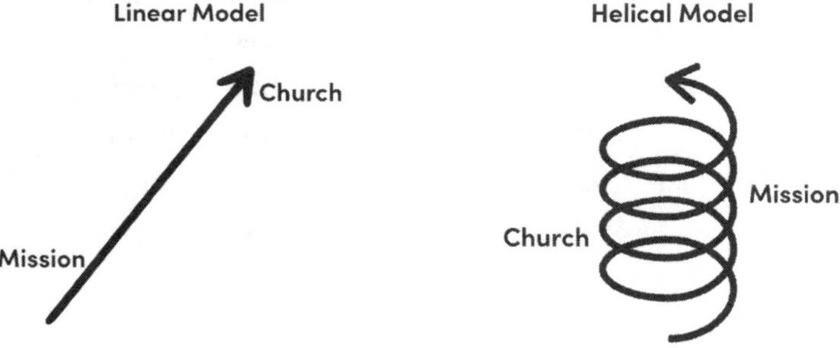

But if one or the other has to be first in our helix, I say we should start with the church. If the church is composed of those who are being saved, and mission is the act of God's people proclaiming the gospel in order to see more people repent, believe, and be baptized into the church, then we must begin with the church as established by Christ. Else we have no people for the work of mission, nor anywhere to bring the lost once they are found.

I see a linear missiology-determines-ecclesiology approach as dangerous. If we begin by asking what we hope to accomplish and then determine what we must make the church into in order to accomplish it, the forms of the church fall victim to pragmatism and lose any intrinsic value. On the other hand, a helical understanding of ecclesiology and missiology sees propriety in the forms of the church as essential to the work of mission.

In their book *The Shaping of Things to Come*, Alan Hirsch and Michael Frost, two influential modern missiologists, claim that if we put our ecclesiology first, we will, "never really engage in mission and so lose touch with Jesus. These churches spend all their time discussing (or arguing) about the forms of worship, the church furniture, and the timing of services and programs."[2] I truly respect the heart of these brothers in their fear of a dead church and their desire to see mission as the central focus of the church, but I disagree quite significantly with their reasoning. In fact, I propose the opposite to be true—that behavior such as they are describing actually comes from a weak ecclesiology; a lack of understanding of who the church is leads to a malpracticed mission.

Most significantly, the Scripture is clear that Jesus had a strong ecclesiology. In the Great Commission he begins his work by gathering a people, he then tells these disciples to make more disciples by first baptizing them into the Father, and the Son, and the Holy Spirit. Mission resulted from this group in Acts 2 when "the Lord added to their number day by day those who were being saved" (v. 47). Jesus gathered the church, who were by nature a missional people, and the Lord added to their number. Once added, these people did much more than move the furniture.

Since the church is inextricable from God's saving mission, and mission from the church, it would be odd for the Lord to set the mission but leave the form and nature of the church undefined, amorphous, and up to the whim of man. And so, he doesn't. The structure, purpose, and function of the church are, in fact, described in Scripture. The Bible clearly outlines subjects such as church leadership, orderly worship, church life, authority, the church's role in protecting doctrine, and many more. A strong ecclesiology sees all of these aspects of the life of the church having meaning in themselves and as essential to what the church is to be about.

A strong ecclesiology sees church as God's people united with Christ in our baptism, the heirs of God's promises, and ambassadors of Christ as God makes his appeal through us. We are the church that the very gates of hell will not prevail against. Gates are not offensive weapons; they are defensive structures—it is we who are advancing! Ambassadors are not silent—it is we who are bringing the message of God to the world. Heirs are not simply workers; they are family. When these descriptors of the church are read, marked, learned, and inwardly digested, when our ecclesiology supplies us with this sort of identity, we do not argue about furniture, we beat on the gates of hell.

Limiting the church to purely a function of mission is to dismiss the great plan of God to redeem more than just our local communities, but the entire cosmos itself. Paul says, "through the church the manifold wisdom of God might now be made known to the rulers and authorities in the heavenly places. This was according to the eternal purpose that he has realized in Christ Jesus our Lord, in whom we have boldness and access with confidence through our faith in him" (Ephesians 3:10–12). Somehow in the mystery of God, the church will preach the good news of the gospel to powers and principalities and will judge the world and the angels. This is a mission whose scope is beyond our human ability to pursue.

Our ecclesiology gives us eyes to see the magnitude of what is truly taking place missionally when we plant a church. In planting, we are doing more than trying to start a new church for the purpose of a solid paycheck and a crowd of people on a Sunday. What is really going on is that the gospel, through the church, is being proclaimed not only in the earthly locations where we live but also to the very heavenly realms. The glory of God is being revealed to all that is visible and invisible. This truth is mysterious and wondrous, and it makes church planting so much bigger than simply entrepreneurial ministry.

If our missiology requires of us the converting of powers, principalities, and angels, but the ecclesiological task of reverse-engineering that mission in order to create the form of church adequate for such a task is left solely up to our human ingenuity, I am afraid we are outmatched. Instead, the church must rest on being faithful to who we are in Christ as we strive to do what we are called to do through his power. Praise Jesus that his Great Commission to go is accompanied by his great promise that he will be with us always until the very end of the age.

Beginning with our ecclesiology and moving to our missiology keeps us from an unhealthy pragmatism where the forms and functions of the church only have value if they achieve outward missional goals. Take the Eucharist, for example. If we believe the celebration of this meal is a command of the church and central to who we are as the church, we celebrate the Sacrament out of our identity not out of its functionality. We cannot then examine the practice of the Eucharist, determine that it may be strange for visitors, and decide not to engage in it because it may hinder our visitor retention rates. Rather, if we begin with an ecclesiology that sees the sacraments as a part of who we are, we celebrate the Lord's Supper as integral to our identity and function as the church and our mission is to invite others into the community of faith so they may share in it as well. The sacraments, therefore, are not optional based on our missiology; they are deemed beneficial and essential *because* of our ecclesiology.

There are no Anglican divines that I can quote to you directly saying, "Anglicans put their ecclesiology before their missiology." This understanding of the church, however, is implied in every fiber of our way of being—from our awareness of the great cloud of witnesses that surround us, to our participation in ancient practices that foreshadow the future consummation, to our submission to authority, and our intentional "otherness" in our worship, to our value of beauty for beauty's sake, to our emphasis on subsidiaries and the importance of the local church. All these thoughts and emphases reveal our conviction that the church is a primary actor in God's work of redemption through Christ and our mission subsequently flows out of who we are. This robust ecclesiological context brings about a different perspective on church planting than if you were to plant without it.

Anglican missiologist Christopher Wright says:

> "Mission belongs to our God." *Mission is not ours; mission is God's.* Certainly, the mission of God is the

> prior reality out of which flows any mission that we get involved in. Or, as has been nicely put, it is not so much the case that God has a mission for his church in the world but that God has a church for his mission in the world. Mission was not made for the church; the church was made for mission—God's mission.[3]

Wright's point supports what I am calling a helical approach. God's redemptive mission is the context for both the church and her mission. God created the church to be the agent of his mission. Therefore, there is no such thing as a mission-less church or else it ceases to be the church. Simultaneously, there is no such thing as disembodied mission, since God's mission in the world is rooted in the church. The church cannot remain isolated and unaffected by our mission work, and there are many aspects of the church that can be appropriately changed according to local context, but neither can our mission work be devoid of the church or left to take the shape of the mold of the culture it is poured into.

We do not start church planting with a blank white board, a marker, and the question, "What do we want our new church to be so we can reach this city?" as if the mission is God's and the church belongs to us. Instead, we acknowledge that *both* the mission *and* the church are his, so we ask, "How do we bring God's church to this city?" The difference may seem subtle, but the change in our approach to church planting is profound.

Implications for Church Planting

Many wise leaders who have gone before us have searched the Scripture to define the church. The Nicene Creed says the church is "one, holy, catholic, and apostolic" a phrase which we will return to again in this book. More specifically, our Thirty-Nine Articles of Religion say, "The visible Church of Christ is a congregation of faithful men [people] in which the pure Word of God is preached and the Sacraments be duly administered according to Christ's ordinance. And all those things that are necessity and requisite to the same" (Article 19).

It is easy to overlook the missional impulse of that statement. This article does not list Word and sacrament and mission, but Word and sacrament only. However, the reason mission is not explicitly stated here is because mission is implicit in every phrase. Word and sacrament are inherently missional practices. Why are we preaching the Word of God if it is not for the work of mission? You cannot read the Scripture and see it any other way. The Word of God is going out to the people who don't know him and building up the people who do know him so they can be sent out and spread his glory and gospel. The sacraments are given to receive the people, build them up, and send them out into the world. It makes no sense to have a church where the pure Word of God is preached and the sacraments are duly administered if there is no mission, or else the preaching is useless and the sacraments are window dressing.

Again, looking at Acts 2, we see that as the church "devoted themselves to the apostles' teaching and fellowship, to the breaking of the bread and the prayers" (v. 42), they grew by the thousands at the initiative of God. The life and essence of being the church is in itself a missional endeavor.

In Acts 13, the Holy Spirit tells the church to set apart Paul and Barnabas for the work God had them to do, so the church came together and "after fasting and praying they laid their hands on them and sent them off" (v. 3). Note that it was the Lord who initiated the mission, it was the Lord who issued the commission, but he did not go directly to Paul and Barnabas with his call. He went to the church and said, "You send them out." Here again, ecclesiology leads to a proper missiology as the church is God's agent for mission.

Church planters must be sent by the church. You are not entrepreneurs. You are not renegades and rebels, you are members of the one, holy, catholic, apostolic church. God has said to the church, "set them apart for the work that I have called them to do," and the church's responsibility is to fast and pray, and if it is good to the Holy Spirit and to them, to lay hands on you and send you out. You are never to do this on your own or by your own strength. A strong ecclesiology relieves the pressure cooker of church planting as it brings the weight and support of the church universal behind your individual work.

Planting with what I would call this proper Anglican perspective on ecclesiology and mission should inspire us to inspect our goals and methods. What do we hope to accomplish with our church planting? What forms of planting best reflect the true nature of both the church and mission? How do we go about planting in such a way that remains faithful to the biblical form and function of the church? Let me name a few implications as I see them.

Implication #1: Anglican Church Planting Begins with Submission

Our church planting work does not begin with our plans and our vision; our planting work starts in submission. If you want a megachurch and a book deal, don't plant an Anglican church. We begin at the cross, in submission to Christ. We submit to the Scripture as God's Word written. We submit to the doctrine, discipline, and worship as this church has received it. We submit to the great cloud of witnesses. We begin in submission to our bishop through both confirmation and, for some, ordination. We submit to one another out of reverence for Christ.

Planters are often bold self-starters, gatherers, and leaders. These can be wonderful traits, but they also lead to pride, ambition, greed, and lack of accountability. So many celebrated pastors and church planters have suffered severe public failing and falling when their strong leadership surpassed their humble submission.

The best jazz improvisors must first learn their scales. It is out of knowing what is universal, unchanging, and standard that appropriate deviation brings beauty. It is by remaining lovingly in check that we stay on the path of righteousness and holiness and run the race with perseverance. Submission is beautiful. In the midst of your dreaming of your church plant and stressing over how it will flourish, reflect first on church planting as an act of submission. Both you and your church will be healthier for it.

Implication #2: Anglicanism Affects Methodology and Timing

Most church-planting resources teach the concept of launching large. While Anglicans also teach the need for a critical mass before moving to public worship, our scale is quite different. One of the most popular books on this topic teaches a process that encourages beginning with preview services that are hopefully attended by 300 people or so—then you will have a good core group with which to start your megachurch. But for North American Anglicans, 300 people *is* a megachurch. If we read this methodology and then pursue Anglican church planting, we might think, *My plant is not growing fast enough, what am I doing wrong?*

I am not speaking against other ways of being church, but I want to convince you that Anglican planting is approached differently and therefore has different values, methods, and timelines. If your plant experiences tremendous growth in a short period of time, praise Jesus! This is not always true, however, at least in the West. My experience is that planting an Anglican church is often a long obedience in the same direction. We are not gathering a crowd and then hoping to disciple them. Ours is often a slower pace that seeks depth, formation, and long-term sustainability. We plant oaks, not bamboo.

The potential of slower growth should be considered as we form our planting strategies—in levels of funding, timing of a public worship launch, structure of curacies, expectations for relationships with a mother church, etc. We should not base our methodologies on our Anglican ecclesiology and missiology only to then gauge our effectiveness based on the results seen in other traditions.

Our methods may not be as quick, but there is extreme value in what we are doing. There is substance, there is beauty, and there is longevity. Faster is not always better. Church fads are going to come and go. The newest megachurches are going to wax and wane. But the liturgy, ethos, polity, and way of life within the Anglican tradition is thousands of years old with no ending in sight.

Implication #3: Anglican Church Planting Is Worship-Centric

Worship is at the center of who we are as the church. We believe that in the worshipping community we share a moment that is intrinsically expressive, transcendent, evangelistic, and formative.

Our worship is *expressive* because we are allowed to publicly and passionately worship the triune God. We ascribe to him blessing, honor, glory, and power.

Our worship is *transcendent* because we participate with activities taking place in the heavenly realms. We join our voices with angels and archangels and all the company of heaven to proclaim the holiness of God.

Our worship is *evangelistic* not because we primarily shape our services around the seeker or unbeliever, but rather because we do the opposite by seeing God as our primary audience. A group of people who are worshipping something other than themselves, in deep community with one another, invites a visitor to explore the worth and value of the object of their worship. When our response to visitors is intentionally not to convince them that we are gathered primarily to appease them, but to worship God, we invite them to turn their gaze outward toward the one who truly can fulfill their needs. This is not an excuse to be standoffish or cold—by no means! Rather, our welcome should reflect the warmth and welcome of the God who welcomes us. Our hospitality in welcoming visitors is immensely important, but secondary to the giving of glory to God, or else we are engaging in a bait and switch.

If our outward message is primarily that our worship is all about the visitor—their experience, their needs, their family, their marriage, their children—then it will be quite shocking when we bid them come and die. In your church planting work, do not begin to worship the number of attendees or else you will use the message of God simply as a means to increase your attendance. In worship you are bringing people to an experience of the holiness of God, to learn how to reject the idols they have been pursuing and turn their praise toward the one true God. Do not appeal to their idols in order to sneak in the glory of God. Our Anglican framework is meant to keep our focus in its proper place, insisting upon the imminence of the transcendent God. We move from glory to invitation, not the reverse.

We will discuss how our worship is formative in upcoming chapters. Suffice it to say here that our worship is a two-way street. The forms that we use in worship not only express what it is in our hearts, but also shape our thoughts and loves as God works through them to transform us.

Implication #4: Anglican Church Planting Is Not Meant to Be Pursued Alone

Church planting is too much for you to pursue alone. The good news is that you do not have to. Church order and governance is a gift from God. You have a bishop, you belong to a diocese, you are a part of something bigger than yourself. In leading up to planting, your diocese can help prepare you through assessment, training, and coaching. And when you are in the work of planting, the diocese provides ongoing care and guidance. The decisions are not all on your shoulders. Your burdens are not yours alone to carry. The isolation of church planting is tempered by your relationships with other churches, clergy, laity, and leaders. You have a pastor in your bishop.

I know you also have your doubts. I know that sometimes you wonder if a diocese just gets in the way, if they are too bureaucratic and institutionalized. You are correct; there will be some struggles as a planter within a group of established churches. This is where you can help your diocese as well. We need to be involved in our dioceses because as church planters we are a vital part of the diocese. Our mission is not just to our local church, but to the church catholic for the spread of the gospel to the ends of the earth. The influence of planters changes culture. You will keep the diocese on task. Because of your presence and your missional work, the diocese with her existing churches and many future church plants will be healthier in the long term, and so will you.

We are planting churches that will raise up a disproportionate number of leaders with a heart for church planting and mission. These men and women will be the next generation of priests, deacons, bishops, and faithful laity. Planting as a part of a diocese means support for you now and a healthy future for your diocese.

Implication #5: Anglican Church Planting Is Pursued Through Word and Sacrament

We must give the people the Word proclaimed in the sermon and invite them to participate in the Word visible in the sacraments. Our understanding of the sacraments—their incarnational nature, their mystery, the eminent presence of God within them, and their function as a means of grace—is of vital importance and extreme influence on everything that we do as church planters, as we will discuss more in further chapters. Our bold preaching of the Word is all the more effective because it is rooted in the liturgy. Our missional message as church planters is, "Repent and believe." And the sacraments let those who hear it respond, expressing their repentance and belief in an outward and visible way. They enter into the church through holy baptism, and they participate in Table fellowship in the Holy Eucharist. In this way, we call people to the worship of our holy God. The invitation of Jesus lingers, the place for washing is ready, the Table is set, won't you come? Our role comes from the Master of the feast: "Go out to the highways and hedges and compel people to come in, that my house may be filled" (Luke 14:23).

Implication #6: Anglican Church Planting Must Be Dependent on the Work of the Holy Spirit

Anglicanism is not a liturgical to-do list that if followed will guarantee the beautiful, deep, and holy church you desire to plant. Our mission, like all true Christian mission, is dependent upon the work of the Holy Spirit. The disciples themselves were instructed by Jesus not to try and be witnesses of the gospel until they were given power from on high. Perfectly executed Anglicanism (as if there is such a thing) will not bring life to a church any more than the swaying of the trees creates the wind. God must breathe into the nostrils of our liturgy, our preaching, our sacramental practice, our reaching out to the world. As a Christian, this concept should be of no surprise to you, but trust me, you will forget this foundational truth in the busyness of church planting. This is precisely why we have prayers like this in our Prayer Book:

> O God the Holy Spirit, Sanctifier of the faithful: Sanctify this Congregation by your abiding presence. Bless those who minister in holy things. Enlighten the minds of your people more and more with the

> light of the everlasting gospel. Bring erring souls to the knowledge of our Savior Jesus Christ; and those who are walking in the way of life, keep steadfast to the end. Give patience to the sick and afflicted and renew them in body and soul. Guard those who are strong and prosperous from forgetting you. Increase in us your many gifts of grace, and make us all fruitful in good works. This we ask, O blessed Spirit, whom with the Father and the Son we worship and glorify, one God, world without end. Amen.[4]

Implication #7: Anglican Church Planting Must Begin with the Pursuit of Personal and Corporate Holiness

I have attended many church planting classes and conferences and read most of the books. Holiness does not come up very often. Strategy does. Methodology does. The mechanics—the nuts and the bolts—they come up a lot. How are we going to attract people, fund the mission, find a place to meet, etc.

Although these details are important, they are not our starting point. Beginning with our ecclesiology means that we are primarily concerned with the gospel and the pursuit of Christ. So, when we talk about church planting, we must first discuss personal and corporate holiness. We must ask, "Would I rather have a large church or a holy church?" If your answer is "large," stop planting churches. We do not need large, unholy churches; we need churches that are hungry and thirsty for righteousness. We need disciples who are longing for the holiness that comes from the gospel of Jesus Christ. Not that such churches can't also be large, but numerical growth must never come at the expense of the pursuit of holiness—starting with our individual lives as planters.

In church planting, there is often a competitive culture in which we are either comparing ourselves to others or we have contempt for the way someone else is planting. We must be above that. We need holiness of heart and life, because what we are creating through the grace of God and the power of the Holy Spirit is a holy people. We must not compare ourselves to megachurches or to other traditions. We must find our markers for success in our pursuit of righteousness.

Church planting has to begin with the pursuit of holiness and from there move to strategy and methodology. You reverse this at your peril. There are many people who planted churches within the last fifteen to twenty years who are now falling very publicly. Their plants grew rapidly for a long time and people celebrated them: "Look at how big this church is and look at how many people they are reaching. This must be great." They were in glossy magazines and Forbes reports. But underneath they were hollow, and sins had to be covered up to keep the momentum going.

Anglicanism is a Prayer-Book tradition because we desire our life together to be based on the person and work of Christ. Through praying the words of Scripture regularly and passionately, we set apart Christ as Lord so that, as the Prayer Book says, "we may delight in his will and walk in his ways, to the glory of his name."[5] When we are planting, we are building a Prayer-Book culture in which all things move to the rhythm of Christ. Our sense of time is Christ-centered as our daily patterns are shaped around prayer and our calendar revolves around Christ's life. Through prayer we see that our very source is found in God, or as Anglican poet George Herbert said, prayer is "God's breath in man returning to his birth."[6] In prayer we remember that we come from God, and we mark each hour as belonging to Christ. That is why Anglican church planting is not simply about successfully starting a well-attended worship service, but rather cultivating a community sharing a life of holiness, worship, and service.

Christ is not calling you to plant at the expense of your soul, nor is he calling you to gather a group of people so you can balance a budget. You are planting a people—and not just any people, a people who share a way of life in which Christ's righteous will, his holy ways, and his profound glory are pursued in all things.

In light of this truth, I encourage you to see the development of your own devotional habits as part of your preparation for church planting. Regularly pray the Daily Office. Build into your weekly schedule sabbath and rest. Adapt your experience of time through following the seasons of the church calendar. Practice hospitality and being a person of peace. Foster faithful tithing and generosity. Pursue the spiritual disciplines of solitude and simplicity. It is from these deep wells you will draw the cool water that will nurture and sustain you through the difficult work of church planting.

. . . .

So you want to plant an Anglican church? Anglicanism is more than an aesthetic or a style of worship. It is more than vestments and setting up candles on a table. Anglicanism is a way of life, a culture, a response to a strong ecclesiology, an expression of a robust missiology, and a tradition with a particular ethos and methodology. Most of all, Anglicanism is a tradition centered on knowing, honoring, and proclaiming the gospel of Jesus Christ. Every aspect of the Anglican life is intentionally focused on the person and work of Christ, so that we can walk in his ways to the glory of his Name.

A Note to Non-Anglican Readers:

Regardless of whether you are Anglican or not, this discussion of ecclesiology and missiology is an important one. I do not believe that the helical approach I have suggested should be uniquely Anglican; it is true for the church as a whole. Does your tradition tend to emphasize one over the other? If so, what are the implications for this singular focus? Also, the seven implications of a helical ecclesiology/missiology are universal as well, although how they are worked out in your tradition may differ. I encourage you to turn each one into a question. For example, "What does it mean for me to begin church planting from a state of submission? What role does worship play in my planting work? How do I ensure I do not go about this process alone?" I also encourage you to read this section with others from your tradition to see what you can learn from communal comparison to what I suggest here.

CHAPTER 4

....

Planting in Godly Tension

What is the manner of our ingrafting into Christ? . . .
The first answer is, briefly, that we are incorporated in Christ
by hearing and believing the gospel. The second is that
we are incorporated by sacramental participation in the life
of the historically continuous Church. The third is that we
are incorporated by receiving and abiding in the Holy Spirit.

— *Lesslie Newbigin*

SUMMARY: Our church planting must take into account the authority of Scripture, the tradition of the church, and the ongoing work of the Holy Spirit.

After the service one Sunday in our first church plant, I was greeting people at the back of the church, hoping to introduce myself to visitors before they left. As I shook hands with one couple, I told them I hoped we would see them again. The husband replied, "We come from a Roman Catholic background and this is a Pentecostal church, so it is not what we are looking for." I just smiled. If they were in the same service I just left, clearly these folks had never actually been in a Pentecostal church. I asked them to tell me more and they said that some people were raising their hands during worship and that is what Pentecostals do. I encouraged them to come a few more times just to see if some of the more familiar aspects of who we are may outweigh the things that are a bit different.

Within five minutes I greeted another visiting couple and repeated the same invitation to return. The wife replied—and I'm not kidding here—"Well, we come from a Pentecostal background and this is a Catholic church." For a moment I thought I was on a hidden camera show. Then I remembered that I'm Anglican. They determined we were Catholic due to our liturgy, our vestments, and our celebration of Communion.

Anglicanism is its own box. To be a part of the Anglican family is to be willing to live in a healthy tension that recognizes there is acceptable diversity within the Anglican tradition that stems from our history and ecclesiology.

Three Streams

In relatively recent years, this diversity of Anglican expression has come to be pictured as three streams flowing into one river. Although he did not use these specific words, this analogy has been attributed to Bishop Lesslie Newbigin and his book *The Household of God*. Newbigin asks, "If the church is the body of Christ, how does one become a member of that body?" He provides three ways this question has historically been answered:

1. **An evangelical approach.** We become part of the body of Christ by hearing and believing the gospel.
2. **A catholic approach.** We become a member of the church through participation in the sacraments, which places a high value on the role of the church in salvation.

3. **A Pentecostal (or charismatic) approach.** Membership in the body of Christ is by receiving and abiding in the Holy Spirit.

Newbigin makes it clear that these are not isolated avenues but that there is, and should be, overlap between these expressions. He says: "It is at once apparent that they are far from being mutually exclusive, that very few Christians would deny the truth of any of them, and that there is an infinite variety of combinations of and approximations to these three positions."[1] According to Newbigin, each of these streams or historic traditions is insufficient in isolation to give a complete picture of the church. When looked upon together as three streams conjoining to form one river, however, a more robust and comprehensive picture of the church emerges.

Stream #1: Evangelical

Sometimes the word *evangelical* is confused with the concept of "doing evangelism," but they are not the same thing. Evangelicalism is a particular approach to theology and practice. This word has also become politically charged in recent years in the American culture, and has grown so broad that it scarcely has any useful meaning. Today the term would include both J. I. Packer and Jerry Falwell—two people with very different approaches to the Christian faith. When used in our three-streams analogy, we will define evangelicalism historically as a stream within the church that emphasizes the authority of the Scripture, pure doctrine, defense of the faith, personal evangelism, and the centrality of the atoning sacrifice of Jesus on the cross. There has also been a strong focus on discipleship, teaching, and global mission. A few historical figures attributed to this stream would be Packer, John Stott, Charles Simeon, William Wilberforce, and J. C. Ryle.

Stream #2: Catholic

There is confusion around the word *catholic* as well, since many think of it as synonymous with *Roman Catholic*, but that is not the case. Roman Catholicism is a different branch of the church. The term *catholic* in this usage does not refer to a particular denomination, but rather means "universal." The Nicene Creed utilizes the word in this way when we pronounce our belief in "one, holy, catholic, and apostolic church." The catholic church is the church that has existed for all time, consisting of both those on earth and those who have died in Christ and now live as part of the great cloud of witnesses. The catholic emphasis is on the Great Tradition, the centrality of the sacraments, the role of the church in salvation, and the authoritative structures of the church. There is a focus on beauty and liturgy in worship as leading to an appreciation of the holiness of God and the call to a righteous life. Discipleship in the catholic tradition has often taken the form of catechesis. Although less so in recent years, historically the Anglo-Catholic branch of Anglicanism was known for its focus on social justice in serving the poor and less fortunate, and there are many contemporary Anglo-Catholics who wish to reclaim that focus. A few historic examples of Anglo-Catholics would include John Keble, John Henry Newman, and Edward Pusey.

Stream #3: Charismatic

The charismatic (or Pentecostal) emphasis is on the continued work of the Holy Spirit. Imbued with passion, the charismatic stream focuses on the closeness and realness of God. It stresses the importance of the work of the Holy Spirit for sanctification and for the work of mission. This stream places high value on bringing action to faith and on bringing feeling to the experience of a life with Christ. The charismatic renewal in the Episcopal and Anglican Church is responsible for the awakening of a significant number of hearts to the gospel, and many influential leaders in the Anglican Church were profoundly influenced through traditions such as the Vineyard. Anglicans in this stream have included Dennis Bennett, Terry Fullam, and Nicky Gumbel (creator of the Alpha Course).

One River

If these are the three streams, Anglicanism is then the one river within which all these traditions comingle. Although a complicated man, John Wesley is a good example of someone who could be referred to as a three-streams Anglican. Wesley was an Anglican clergyman who started the Methodist movement. He described his conversion experience in his journal: "In the evening I went very unwillingly to a society in Aldersgate Street, where one was reading Luther's preface to the Epistle to the Romans. About a quarter before nine, while he was describing the change which God works in the heart through faith in Christ, I felt my heart strangely warmed. I felt I did trust in Christ, Christ alone, for salvation; and an assurance was given me that He had taken away my sins, even mine, and saved me from the law of sin and death."[2]

Wesley's own words describe his embodiment of two of the streams: he comes to repentance through the hearing the reading of Scripture (evangelical), and he has an emotional response recognizing the nearness of Christ (charismatic). Wesley was also a high churchman, valuing greatly the form of the church (catholic). Clearly, Wesley waded deeply in the evangelical stream by leaving the safety of the walls of the church and preaching in the fields. At the same time, R. N. Danker notes, "It would be the amalgamation of high churchmanship and heart religion that would define Wesley's theological outlook and evangelistic impulses throughout the rest of his life."[3] Wesley does not fit neatly into any one particular stream. Many would seek to claim him as exclusively their own, and all would have some quibbles with him as well. That's the point: he was shaped and formed by each as he went about the work of the kingdom inside and outside the church.

Whereas this framework is quite popular, there has also been disagreement over the use of "three streams, one river" language. A portion of the dispute comes from a lack of generosity and humility by individuals in any one particular stream and proves the point of the need for all three, but some of the critique is legitimate. A full treatment of this subject is far beyond our scope here, but I will offer a couple of examples. For instance, are there only three streams? What about Orthodox or Celtic Christianity? Still others prefer the term "Reformed Catholic" to describe the Anglican heritage. Another problem is that these categories can also end up being caricatures painting over the nuances of these traditions with broad brushstrokes. There is also trouble in that each of these categories deals with both belief and practice, and there are some differing theological and methodological claims between the streams that can seem antithetical to one another.

Certainly, there are limitations of the three streams analogy, but I still find it helpful as a starting point for describing a distinct aspect of Anglican identity—its breadth. Modern Anglicanism is distinctive in its emphasis on correct doctrine in the Word proclaimed while also holding to the importance of the sacraments and emphasizing the ongoing work of the Holy Spirit. No analogy can neatly categorize all of the historic and cultural influences that have formed the Anglican tradition, but this general framework is a good place to begin.

Three Notes

An additional analogy may be helpful. Instead of streams, let us discuss notes. In music, a basic chord is made up of three notes. When played together, these three distinctive notes result in something complimentary and so much more beautiful than any single note alone. However, if the string on which one of these notes is played is out of tune—a bit sharp or flat—the other two notes reveal the error and provide a basis for returning that errant note back to true.

Anglicanism is the chord and each tradition a note. Each note compliments the others for the sake of purity and results in something profoundly more beautiful. There's also accountability, because when the theology or practice of one note strays, its error stands out as it is heard as a part of the whole. Each note, then, is at its purest when played as a part of the full chord.

Each of the notes has particular strengths and is more susceptible to certain errors:

- *Evangelicalism* is strong on the supremacy of the Word of God, but evangelicalism can also stray either into either dry intellectualism or rigid fundamentalism. The passion and sentiment of the charismatic tradition can rescue the evangelicals from disconnected knowledge, and the focus of the Anglo-Catholic tradition on the holy otherness of the church can rescue evangelicalism from drifting into shallow legalism.

- *Anglo-Catholics* have historically been champions for social justice and purity in worship, but can stray into ritualism and dead tradition that leads to theological error. The evangelical note keeps the sacraments and liturgy grounded in the Word of God, and the emphasis on the working of the Holy Spirit by the charismatic note makes sure there is life in ritual expression.
- The *charismatic* flow has led to significant revival in many parts of the Anglican church, but this note is susceptible to being guided by emotionalism and unreliable inspiration. If left unchecked by the Anglo-Catholic's grounding in historic ecclesiology and the doctrinal emphasis of the evangelicals, it can lead to strange and unfaithful practice.

Together, these three traditions, notes, or streams collectively make each individual tradition stronger and purer. There will be many different local and regional expressions of Anglicanism as some Anglicans emphasize one note a little more than the other, but there is room for that. We should define ourselves less by which note in the chord we are, but rather by the chord as a whole. We are Anglicans, and some happen to be a bit more evangelical, charismatic, or catholic. I do not know any Anglo-Catholics who deny the work of the Holy Spirit, nor do I know any charismatics who would downplay the importance of Scripture, nor any Anglican evangelicals who do not acknowledge the importance of the sacraments—but I do know all can grow deeper in their understanding of these things if we pursue the wisdom of the other streams. There is much we can learn from each other and much we can do to protect one another.

The Trouble in the Tension

I will call out two particular sources of trouble. First, we all tend to moralize our own preferences. I have had the honor of serving Anglican church planters throughout the world, and the problem I am describing is a global issue. Anglicans in Sydney, Australia, have a particularly Reformed evangelical bent to their theology and practice, and many churches in Africa have been influenced by the charismatic stream, while churches in the United States often have higher churchmanship than even those in England herself. I have had conversations with friends from each of these continents as they question the propriety of the Anglicanism expressed on the other continents. For example, I have heard people say, "That is not Anglican" in reference both to those who wear vestments and those who do not, flippantly excluding millions of people who hold to the opposite practice. I recently overheard someone claim that no church that engages in music other than Anglican chant is legitimately Anglican. Certainly, there are beliefs and practices that truly are not Anglican, but we must be generous in how narrowly we define our tradition's legitimate expression.

The second cause of stress is that every church planter needs accountability, but we often bristle when faced with it. Calling one another back to faithful Christian identity is not pleasant, but an out-of-tune chord remains grating until corrected. On top of this, we have to sort out which actions require correction and which are simply diverging views that all fit together underneath the large orthodox Anglican umbrella.

The need for accountability and for corporate learning is real. Coming out of our echo chambers is healthy. These things can only be done through real and intentional relationships. That is why I believe Anglicanism is poised to be such a healthy and missionally effective tradition—because although we are not perfect, we are a global family. As a family, we have people who love us and are willing to speak difficult truth to us and receive correction from us as we mutually learn together. So, instead of looking with suspicion on one another, let us live into the healthy tension that holds us as Anglicans. Let us see that the Great Tradition holds a place for many different nuanced expressions and that Anglicanism is beautifully broad.

I will reiterate that breadth does not mean a total lack of boundaries. It is not mere relationship or sentiment that defines the Anglican Way. Our historic formularies along with more contemporary statements such as the Jerusalem Declaration give a solid definition of our stance on particular matters of theology, morality, and practice. Anglicanism is by no means universalism—properly founded in the Scripture, Anglicanism should guard against such heresy. It does, however, allow room for a significant amount of mystery and grace that result in what I am calling "breadth." We will explore this further in the next chapter.

Others have used different labels than streams or notes to describe this breadth. Thomas McKenzie calls Anglicans evangelical, catholic, charismatic, orthodox, activist, contemplative, conversational, liberal, and on mission.[4] J. I. Packer describes mainstream Anglicanism as biblical, liturgical, evangelical, pastoral, episcopal, national, and ecumenical.[5] Whichever of these illustrations or lists you prefer to employ, it is clear that Anglicanism is multifaceted.

As much as we appreciate order, Anglicanism is not neat and tidy. It is what my mother used to call "lived in." Our house was never dirty with the threat of tetanus or cholera looming—there was a proper standard of cleanliness to be maintained—but our house was comfortable. It was meant to be lived in. Things were not always in their place, and sometimes we didn't even know where an item actually belonged. There were patterns that temporarily clashed when a striped blanket was laid on a floral couch, or a stray shoe and uncollected toys in our living room. Our house was not merely a house in concept, but a house for the purpose of harboring our life together. This is Anglicanism. It is not always clean and orderly, but it is our home.

What Does This Have to Do with Church Planting?

I believe this is an important conversation for us to have as students of Anglican church planting for numerous reasons.

First, you need to know what you are planting. Anglicanism is more than an aesthetic; there is more to Anglicanism than outward adornment. Anglicanism is a global family and a way of being. With that comes a responsibility for knowing the family you are a part of and for learning how to introduce others into this tradition as well. You must contemplate how this generous Christian tradition will be expressed in your local plant.

Second, it is important for you to recognize that there is a breadth to Anglicanism so that you can collaborate well with others both inside and outside of our tradition. Local churches that see themselves as Anglo-Catholic can, with integrity, work together with Anglicans who are low-church in their expressions. You can both teach something and learn something. The same is true for all the other streams. Be intentional in working with other expressions within the church. This is also true in how we work ecumenically. I have found that with few exceptions, churches from other traditions enjoy relationships with Anglicans. Since we have something in common with nearly every tradition, we can be a significant factor in ecumenical relationships.

Third, breadth is not the hallmark of all Christian traditions. If the area in which you are planting has any memory of the Christian church, many people who enter into the church you are planting will surely find something unexpected. Although many will consider this a breath of fresh air, many will also find it disconcerting as they attempt to categorize the church: "Are you a Catholic church or a Pentecostal church?" Visitors will see our generous but faithful understanding of Scripture, our liturgical practice, and our passionate worship, and although many will find some part familiar, experiencing all three may be new. We must be intentionally hospitable in reassuring them and making this new reality accessible.

Finally, rejoice and give thanks for the family and tradition you are a part of. Anglicanism is uniquely poised to reach a culture that is simultaneously globally aware and searching for roots. Plant with the intention of living into the strength of each of these streams and allowing their influence to guide you to distinctive, faithful, and lively mission.

Whatever analogy you are most comfortable with—streams or notes or something else—rejoice in the fact that we can bring the ancient truths of the Word, the sacrament, and the Spirit to bear on a hurting world, and we can do it together with one another and with all those who have gone before.

A Note to Non-Anglican Readers:

Newbigin's work that is the basis for our discussion here was not centered on the Anglican Church, but on the church as a whole. Various traditions emphasize different aspects of this framework, but all three streams are unavoidably present throughout church history. As you reflect on your tradition, where are there areas of flexibility and freedom and where has your particular tribe intentionally narrowed some of these expressions? It is important that you have integrity to the tradition in which you are planting. You will have to decide where you can flex, but I encourage you to be wisely challenged by those faithful Christians who would emphasize a different stream than you are used to swimming in. I have shown how my particular tradition has to work through the relational issues that come with living in this tension. How is that true for your tradition and how does that affect your church planting work? Finally, how can the concept of breadth within biblical bounds be helpful to you as you explore starting a new local expression of the catholic church through the lens of your chosen tradition? I pray this framework and discussion is beneficial to you and you explore the fullness of what you are planting.

CHAPTER 5

....

Contextualizing Word and Sacrament

It has been the wisdom of the Church of England, ever since the first compiling of her Public Liturgy, to keep the mean between the two extremes, of too much stiffness in refusing, and of too much easiness in admitting any variation from it.

— *Preface to the 1662 Book of Common Prayer*

SUMMARY: We now turn to the practical discussion of how we embody the ancient traditions of the church in a contemporary setting in a way that keeps the integrity of the tradition but speaks with relevance to today's culture.

The Anglican tradition is ancient, and aspects of its communal life are hundreds to thousands of years old. The beauty and benefit of Anglicanism's doctrine, formularies, polity system, and liturgy is that they provide a level of steadiness that transcends the whims of external culture. At the same time, Anglicanism is meant to be nimble enough to adapt what is not essential in order to be effective in communicating the gospel to a changing cultural context.

The preface to the 2019 Book of Common Prayer describes our heritage by saying, "What emerged in Britain, by God's grace, was a Church that saw herself, in each of her local manifestations, as part of the One, Holy, Catholic, and Apostolic Church: culturally attuned and missionally adaptive, but ever committed to and always propagating 'the faith that was once for all delivered to the saints' (Jude 1:3)."[1]

What Is Firm and What Is Flexible?

The English Reformers understood the need to parse and explain the difference between what is firm and what is flexible. Article 34 of the Thirty-Nine Articles of Religion is entitled "Of the Traditions of the Church," and states:

> It is not necessary that Traditions and Ceremonies be in all places one, and utterly like; for at all times they have been diverse, and may be changed according to the diversities of countries, times, and men's manners, so that nothing be ordained against God's Word. Whosoever through his private judgement, willingly and purposely, doth openly break the traditions and ceremonies of the Church, which be not repugnant to the Word of God, and be ordained and approved by common authority, ought to be rebuked openly, (that others may fear to do the like,) as he that offendeth against the common order of the Church, and hurteth the authority of the Magistrate, and woundeth the consciences of the weak brethren.

This article allows local expression to be adapted to "the diversities of countries, times, and [people's] manners." This is what we would now call *contextualization*. The article, however, also importantly outlines two constraints for the work of contextualization.

The first and primary constraint is that nothing we do in an effort to reach the people of our local communities can be contrary to the Word of God.

Second, the article gives authority to a communal approach to the process of contextualization. Our own personal preferences and desires (what the article calls our "private judgement") do not override the authority of our bishop who has charge over the common worship of the church. Neither do they override the authority of the received doctrine, discipline, and worship as expressed in the formularies of the Anglican Church. You cannot simply choose which parts of the tradition you will follow as if Anglicanism were an ecclesiological buffet where you pick and choose according to your preference. At the same time, the margins of Anglicanism are wide. Think of the formularies as fences rather than chains. Fences keep in what should remain safe and keep out what may be a threat. Our fences give us the freedom to have room to run safely.

Liturgy and authoritative structures should not squelch local expression. Your weekly worship service may have incense and genuflecting or it may have guitars and drums—or all of the above. Last year our church set up an interactive service of stations of the cross during Holy Week. It was a self-guided experience of reading Scripture and tangibly participating in aspects of the story like rolling dice at the casting of lots for Christ's clothes and pounding a nail into a cross at the reading of his crucifixion. The most powerful Anglican services I have been a part of have been Easter vigil services that intersperse the prescribed readings and responses with expressions of visual art, musical performance, poetry, and dance.

The Word and sacrament tradition comes alive when engaged through local language, art, and culture. I have worshipped in Anglican churches throughout the world. I have danced in the dust of Rwanda until I was too tired and sweaty to move. I have sat serenely in the stone cathedrals of England. I have wept in Chile, surrounded by the colorful and boisterous South American culture. I have preached barefoot in a church in Hawaii and have shined my shoes before preaching in a more formal church in Texas. The same liturgy was said (in different languages), the same doctrine taught, the same tradition honored—but every experience was different as it was contextualized in the local church.

Think of Anglicanism as the structural engineer that ensures your creative architecture and design are structurally sound. Your house may be contemporary, traditional, modern, or rustic, but in each case the footings must be sunk deep into the moorings of Scripture. Anglicanism, as outlined in its formularies and embodied in your bishop, serves as a check to make sure that whatever you build is safe for those who find shelter within its walls.

Contextualization or Compromise?

If one concern is the possibility that Word and sacrament can be restricting, an opposite knee-jerk reaction to the concept of contextualization is to assume we are discussing compromise. Some fear that in even considering the reaction of external culture to our practice we are on a slippery slope of compromising either our Anglican identity or our biblical foundation. I taught on contextualization in a church one time and a very angry woman stood up in the middle of my presentation and yelled, "Are you saying we have to bring banjos and drums into the church!?" No, that was not what I was saying at all (even though I do happen to like banjos and drums). I was saying, however, that if we live in Kentucky, perhaps we *should* look at banjoes. And we can do so without being disingenuous to our Anglican way of being.

In the same group, another frustrated person asked, "Are you saying we have to take our beliefs from our culture?" No again. Contextualization does not mean that our cultural context decides our identity. Rather, contextualization helps us decide how we will locally adapt the broad options that Anglicanism gives us. We keep the unchanging gospel unchanged, and then learn to communicate it well to our communities.

There are two considerations in contextualization: (1) how to maintain integrity in your church's mission and worship, and (2) how to communicate the gospel in ways your local culture will understand and respond to. Your cultural context does not dictate everything, but to be a missionary you must reflect on how your decisions will be perceived and find ways to make what you are doing accessible and your church hospitable.

A few years ago, I had a Bible that was worn out. The binding was broken and the glue separated to the point that sometimes 2 Timothy would fall out and I had completely lost Titus. We decided it was okay to retire it, but how do you properly dispose of a worn-out Bible? It did not seem appropriate to just throw it in the trash bin. So, after asking around to some of my clergy colleagues, we decided that we would pray to give thanks to God for his Word and then we would burn the Bible, returning it to the dirt from which the trees that made it had come—ashes to ashes, dust to dust.

On our next camping trip, my wife and I gathered our young children around the campfire. We talked about how the Bible is different from any other book. We talked about the nature of the Scripture, the need to spend time in God's Word, and how we wanted to give this special book a splendid send-off as we prayerfully burned it. Just as I put the Bible in the flames, kids from the next campsite over, whom my children had been playing with earlier in the day, called to see if my boys could come have a marshmallow with them. My six-year-old son yelled out, "We'll be there in just a minute, we have to burn some Bibles first!" There we were in central Georgia, smack in middle of the Bible Belt, and he announces that we are burning the Good Book. Lord, have mercy. Most of the people in the surrounding campsites had never really read any of it, but they figured nobody should burn it. Heads turned and looked at us suspiciously. I stood up and, in the moment, said the first thing that came to my mind: "It is okay. I am a pastor." The gasps I received in response proved that my eloquent speech did not help. I could only sit down and quietly watch the embers of God's Holy Writ crumble in the wind of my embarrassment as I prayed we would make it out of the wilderness alive.

What we meant as a solemn and holy moment, those around us assumed was an act of defiance and disrespect. It was all about context. The things we do as Anglicans in our worship and way of being can also be strange and misinterpreted. Although we embrace our peculiarity, we must realize that we are not operating in a vacuum and that our actions evoke response. Contextualization asks how we remain true to our biblical and Anglican identity in a way that creates intrigue and investigation rather than suspicion and standoffishness.

Under-Contextualizing

There are two ditches on either side of the road to contextualization: under-contextualizing and over-contextualizing.

On one side, church planters in our tradition often times fail to make the Anglican way of following Jesus accessible to new people. They may do this out of fear of compromising some important aspect of our faith or, more likely, because they are pursuing their personal preferences. If you are suspicious of what I am writing, concerned that I am advocating we take our cues from the surrounding culture and mimic its way of being in order to better reach it—well, I am and I am not. We make contextualization choices in everything we do. Here in the United States most of our people speak English, so most of our worship services are in English. But if you are planting to reach a specific ethnic group within the United States—a Latino community, for example—you will speak in Spanish. That is basic contextualization. Contextualization does not mean giving culture the authority to change our identity, but rather capitalizing on the broadness of our tradition to make the gospel and the Anglican way accessible to our communities.

Part of our calling as the church is to be something wholly other and transcendent, calling the surrounding culture to something different and true. But we need to remember that we are dealing with people who have certain preconceived notions of truth, God, the church, and life itself. What we mean to be an invitation to something beautifully different can become a wall of impenetrable strangeness. Anglicanism should not be a labyrinth that needs to be solved, but rather a clearly lighted path to Jesus. If you do not explain the what and the why of the peculiar things you are doing, the very things that you hope will serve to engage the people will turn them away. They will fill in the meaning for themselves, and their conclusions may not be what you are hoping for. You do not need to give a complete explanation of what it means to be an Anglican church the first time someone steps through your door, but at least explain that there are well-conceived, historical, biblical, and practical reasons for why we do what we do and give them assurance that there is excitement in the learning.

Let me give an example: I once worked with a small church plant that had started with fewer than ten people and a number of years later still had just ten people. The planter was a warm-hearted man who truly loved Jesus. He reached out to me for help. Over lunch, he described the church plant. For their liturgical expression, they chose to use the 1928 Book of Common Prayer, which contains much more traditional language, utilizing pronouns such as *thy*, *thou*, and *thee*. It is beautiful prose that can be used effectively in some instances, but it is a farther step away from normal for most people in our current society. The church plant was also highly charismatic, with gifts of the Spirit such as speaking in tongues and being slain in the Spirit displayed weekly. The fusion of the 1928 with being highly charismatic is quite unique, so people they might have reached with one expression may be alienated by the other. They also were without a musician when they began their church, and so they sang hymns acapella and decided to keep that style of music as part of their life as the church. For a meeting space, the group gathered in a room above the garage of one of the members.

The person such a church is trying to reach must be willing to enter the side door of a garage, which will feel strange to most people whether they have a church background or not. They will think, *Is this safe? Why is this church hiding in a garage?* The visitor will then need to be willing to endure being very conspicuous in a small group of people they do not know, which is the stuff of nightmares to many. It gets worse: the new visitor is now handed a strange book with unfamiliar language and asked to speak aloud in front of other people—one of the biggest fears in our culture. In this small setting, others will clearly hear any mistake they make. Then, to their terror, they are asked to sing acapella hymns. Their social anxiety is now through the roof as they have essentially engaged in both public speaking and musical performance. After all of this, people around them begin speaking in a different language and some fall onto the ground. If the visitor has not bolted for the door, the group then celebrates an ancient rite with a man in a flowing white robe speaking of drinking blood and eating flesh. At this point, our otherness has become strangeness and the love and welcome of the gospel has been lost in the spectacle.

I told the church planter, "The answer is obvious. The reason why you have not grown past your ten original people is because you have been completely and utterly successful. You have reached everyone within driving distance who is comfortable worshiping in a garage, loves archaic language, glories in acapella hymns, desires to be slain in the Spirit while speaking in tongues, and hungers for the Eucharist. You have saturated the market and gained every possible convert in your mission field."

All of what I have described in their worship service finds precedent in the breadth of Anglicanism. From a contextualization standpoint, however, they carved a very small niche. What they did was not necessarily wrong, but it was surely ineffective in the larger mission. They had not taken into consideration the culture around them. So their choice was either to maintain that very unique identity and remain a tiny church with a chaplain, or to move to a more accessible expression.

This is an extreme example of under-contextualizing, but I hope you see the lesson. If we do not take into consideration how our expression will be interpreted by our surrounding culture and take steps to make what we do accessible, then even though we may be faithful to guarding the good deposit entrusted to us, we will fail in the equally important calling to reach the lost and make disciples of all nations.

Under-contextualization sometimes means we are full of pretense and smugness, rolling our eyes at the culture in which we live. If this is the case, your first step is repentance. Other times, under-contextualization is simply a carryover from a time when the culture was more acquainted with things of the church. In this second case, we approach mission as calling people back to what we think is familiar—forgetting that we are actually introducing them to something entirely new. In this case, you must realize that the current culture has very little memory of the church and even less memory of liturgical practice, so you must begin to think about how you should treat someone who is coming to you with very little previous knowledge and probably quite a bit of misunderstanding.

Over-Contextualizing

The ditch on the other side of the road is over-contextualizing. We err in this direction when we see the Anglican way as beyond the grasp of the people we are trying to reach and compromise its integrity to look more like the surrounding culture. At its worst, over-contextualized Anglicanism mistakes our breadth and freedom within the fences of orthodoxy and orthopraxy for having no fences at all. Anglicanism then turns limp and loses its substance, having the form of religion but not grasping the power of it, as Paul warns in 2 Timothy 3:5. In this case, our liturgy and way of life is no more formative or authoritative than marriage vows made by an unfaithful spouse. Even if done with the expressed hope of loving or reaching more people, compromising holiness and integrity has the opposite effect. When we fail to call the culture to the church, but instead close the gap between the two by rejecting aspects of church that may be offensive, we detach from the moorings of Scripture and become devoid of the life-giving Spirit.

Less severe than outright heresy, but equally poisonous, is when we treat the core aspects of our tradition as changeable or optional because we have a skewed view of mission, so that we are willing to discard anything to be effective. "Let's be as least strange as possible," is the motivation of those who would over-contextualize. I had a planter in the Deep South tell me that he did not baptize infants because it was divisive for his people since his culture was largely Southern Baptist. No, infant baptism is not optional for us as Anglicans, and this is lazy and fearful leadership. Our theology of baptism is not determined by its acceptability in our local culture. We lean on our formularies and the Articles of Religion, which states: "The Baptism of young Children is in any wise to be retained in the Church" (Article 27).

So, on a matter like baptism, our teaching, preaching, and discipleship should lead our people into a deeper understanding of the great joys that come with the sacrament and of how the authority of the Bible and our tradition shape what we believe. We do not flippantly disregard integral aspects of our identity for the sake of mission—this is fear or duplicity masquerading as missional awareness. It would be allowing the culture to dictate our identity, or over-contextualization. If some people will not be a part of your church plant because of a particular doctrine or practice, you must try to bring them to a point of understanding and acceptance, and if they will not or cannot come to that place, then you must be willing to release them. This is not a failure in mission. Quite the contrary, the mission of the church is to be a faithful witness of Jesus Christ—you cannot dictate the response of the people. We call for sinners to become more like Christ, not for the church to become more like sinners.

Knowing the Difference

Some planters who come to Anglicanism after a long background in other traditions may struggle with the nuance of knowing what is adaptable and what is not. Recall our discussion of Article 34. The instruments of accountability are the Scripture and the polity of the church. Take the liturgy, for example. I am going through great pains to show you that it is more than an aesthetic choice, but a foundational aspect of our Anglican way. You cannot rewrite it, tweak it, or rephrase it for the work of mission.

The words that are in the current Prayer Book were not written by one person. Those who give us spiritual oversight in the College of Bishops have put these words through communal curation, writing, revision, review, and finally acceptance for our use. We do not have the authority to change them even if we feel that wording things differently better suits our context. This is not bureaucracy; this is communal life. If we were allowed to rewrite at our whim, we would be circumventing communal discernment and the authority of our bishop, and we would be in danger of inadvertently forming our people with erroneous theology and Christian practice. To over-contextualize is to roll our eyes at the Scripture and the church, and at the vows we said while promising to submit.

I once visited a church plant and joined the planter and his small group of people for Morning Prayer. As we began the service, the planter said to his people, "I do not like how the Morning Prayer service begins with confession. I think it is a bit of a downer and starts us off on the wrong foot by talking about sin before I have even had my coffee, so I am going to skip that section." I politely asked if we could please begin at the beginning of the service.

Put simply, you cannot do this. Skipping confession would be detrimental to you and to the people who you are leading in worship. You cannot by your singular, uncaffeinated, sentimental whim disregard the scriptural pattern of worship found in our liturgy. Centuries of Christians have recognized our need to submit ourselves before a holy God through the admission of our sins and the reception of his grace. The Prayer Book is not a suggestion for the order of your service. It is the communally-discerned common worship of the church, and it is not for you to change.

The reason for my visceral response is because the liturgy is meant to hold us accountable to biblical teaching and ensure the proper formation of disciples. If you make this seemingly-simple change of omitting the confession, you are modeling significant error. You are taking a therapeutic view that sin is simply an annoyance and that the call for grace is only needed when we need to feel better about ourselves. You are bypassing the seriousness of our offense against a holy God who could justifiably send us to eternal punishment but instead has pursued us to the cross and the grave and offers us new life through his resurrection. The gospel is not a downer, it is glorious news! You cannot skip confession.

Am I overreacting? I do not believe so. The liturgy teaches sound doctrine and imitates godly life. If we change the liturgy or use liturgies outside of what has been deemed appropriate by our bishops, we are removing ourselves from the accountability of the church and can slip into error and unhealthy living. I do not think it overdramatic to say that approaching confession as serving your own emotional health, rather than recognizing the cosmic significance of your pardon through the atoning work of Christ, is denying the gospel itself.

The liturgy elevates the local moment from simply a morning ritual to an interaction with the triune God in community with the church visible, the communion of saints, angels, archangels, and all the company of heaven. Ours is to respond with thankful submission, not to flippantly disregard this holy moment on the authority of our personal feelings.

So are we left then with only one option for our experience of Morning Prayer that must be shared by everyone from Africa to America to Argentina? Yes and no. The wording and content of morning prayer is set by the version of the Prayer Book we are using. Music, tone, setting, atmosphere, and creative engagement are all up to you. You can share prayer requests aloud, write down your sins during confession, and then throw them away after the proclamation of your forgiveness, sing songs of lament or praise or freedom, remain quiet or shout for joy, dance or silently contemplate. There are many creative ways that stay true to the scriptural expression of the liturgy while allowing the local community to give it personal shape.

You may wonder if I am making too much of Anglicanism, bordering on idolatry. Shouldn't our primary concern be to uphold the truth of Scripture and the Christian faith, not perpetuate an Anglican way of being? Shouldn't we be keener to be effective in mission than to sustain a particular heritage? I will give you a hearty yes, with one important clarification: the entire purpose of the Anglican way *is* to ensure our faithfulness to a proper Christian faith.

Every person who is ordained to the priesthood in the Anglican church makes this vow: "I do believe the Holy Scriptures of the Old and New Testaments to be the Word of God and to contain all things necessary to salvation, and I consequently hold myself bound to conform my life and ministry thereto, and therefore I do solemnly engage to conform to the Doctrine, Discipline, and Worship of Christ as this Church has received them."[2] It is precisely *because* we believe in the authority of Scripture that we adhere to the church's way of being.

The reason for our structure, liturgy, sacramental foundation, and even our vestments or unfamiliar vocabulary is to guard, proclaim, and celebrate our saving God. To pit one against the other reveals an ignorance, or at least shortsightedness. Before you go hacking away at aspects of being Anglican, seek to deeply understand why things are done the way they are done, and why hundreds of millions of people for many hundreds of years have done it in this particular way. Please do bring fresh expressions to this timeless tradition. But as we explore how to bridge the gap between culture and Jesus, let us also be thankful that the essentials of

Anglicanism serve to keep our attempts at contextualization from slipping into compromise.

Clarity, Integrity, Accessibility, and Hospitality

Anglican contextualization can be summed up in four ideas:

1. **Clarity.** We must be clear on the fullness of the gospel, the wholeness of the Scripture, the mystery of the sacraments, and an Anglican way of understanding the nature and work of the church.
2. **Integrity.** Remaining clear about our identity, we must then at all times guard its integrity and not stray into personal preferences or people pleasing.
3. **Accessibility.** We must make what we believe and how we live as disciples of Christ free of unnecessary barriers to the culture around us.
4. **Hospitality.** We must have a real and caring desire for those outside of the church to be formed by our way of being. It is one thing to ensure our way of following Jesus is accessible, and something completely different to actually want people to take us up on the invitation.

Clarity and *integrity* are covered by what we've already discussed, so let's take a close look at the other two ideas.

Accessibility means providing entry points for those who wish to join in the community of Word and sacrament. An easy start is getting the words of the liturgy to the people in an easily-followed format. Teaching how to use the Prayer Book itself is vitally important, but that does not have to be forced upon a visitor the first time they witness a liturgical worship service. If we give the uninitiated a Prayer Book, a hymnal, and a service bulletin and ask them to follow us as we jump back and forth within and between the books, we might as well give them a unicycle as well. Whether through projector screens or printed materials, provide an easily-followed format for the liturgy. Make sure the aesthetic of how you display the liturgy communicates the ethos of the church. Design documents well; don't use dated fonts on a crowded sheet. If you do not know that Papyrus font is not going to provide the ancient-future look you are going for, or that Comic Sans should be used for absolutely nothing at all, you should probably outsource the design of your liturgy-sheet template. Make sure there are no mistakes in your projection slides and no backgrounds that call attention away from the words themselves. Making the liturgy accessible begins by getting it to the people cleanly so they can join in its corporate usage without being distracted.

Accessibility is also about teaching the liturgy. Passive instruction through your website and printed materials helps tremendously. A page on your website titled "Our Worship," with a general explanation of what the people can expect and what it means to worship in word and sacrament, works wonders to prepare visitors for what they are about to experience. By the door, we keep copies of a booklet titled *Why Do We Do That? Answers to Some Questions about Anglican Worship*. Like a catechism for liturgical worship, it gives answers to questions like: "What was your pastor wearing? Why do you call your pastor a priest? What is Communion? Why do some people make a sign of a cross on themselves?"

Accessible preaching should draw people more deeply into the Word written in the Scripture and visible in the sacraments. We devote so much of our time to liturgical and sacramental practice because we believe it is our corporate expression of the gospel. This means the exhortation of our preaching should often include an invitation to baptism and

Table fellowship as a part of worshipping community. Our sacramental life is made more accessible through preaching that explains its value as active and immediate participation in the glorious gospel.

Our teaching as well should explain and show how to apply the liturgy. If we teach our people about prayer, for example, we should teach a biblical understanding of prayer and train them in the use of the Daily Office. If we are teaching on eschatology, we should show how our participation in the Eucharist is a foretaste of the wedding supper of the Lamb. Making our Anglican way more accessible is to teach the what, why, and how of our life in Word and sacrament.

Hospitality is making people feel welcome as they explore this new life. Hospitality is an aspect of gospel proclamation. Following Jesus with a sacramental perspective should naturally lead us to an understanding that our actions of welcome are physical expressions of Jesus's invitation. Welcome does not mean we approve of everything our guest is involved with in life, nor does hospitality call us to rearrange our house according to the tastes of our guests. But hospitality creates welcome, and warm welcome gives credibility to the invitation given through Word and sacrament to come and be a part of the family of God. The life of Word and sacrament is not just a form; it is a way of being that longs for people to join us at the table—whether that table is in our home or in our church. From the moment people are received into our houses or into our sanctuaries, they should know the welcome of Christ.

Hospitality is both cross-cultural and counter-cultural, and is essential to contextualizing the invitation to a new life offered by Jesus. Even if our forms are initially strange, they are not scary when the people engaging in those forms are warm and generous. The beautiful communal life of the church and the gentle beckon of her people should make entering in easier for anyone trying to summon the courage. Simply treat visitors as guests: make sure they feel welcome and safe, make it clear where to go and how to get there, and give them options (rather than obligations) for their degree of social engagement. Above all, be sure they know you want them there.

The easiest way to pursue hospitality is to find people in your church who have a gift for it and let them loose. Empower those who naturally make people feel welcome. Let them think about signage, greeting systems, and the little touches that display not only our willingness to let others in but our desire for them to enter. Let those who smile well, give good (and discerning) hugs, laugh quickly, and take people's guard down be the first faces new visitors see.

As the planter or a lay leader in a church plant, you need to model hospitality in your home and encourage others to do the same. Hospitality is not only an attitude of greeting people to our public gatherings, but a way of life that extends the welcome of the family of God into homes and neighborhoods. In her book *The Gospel Comes with a House Key*, Rosaria Butterfield says, "Let God use your home, apartment, dorm room, front yard, community gymnasium, or garden for the purpose of making strangers into neighbors and neighbors into family. Because that is the point—building the church and living like a family, the family of God."[3]

Word and sacrament teach us that the Christian faith is more than simply believing. "Even the demons believe—and shudder!" (James 2:19). No, our faith should be shown by our actions. Hospitality embodies the gospel invitation for those who are far away to come and be brought near. If in the preciseness of your liturgical forms and the exactness of your sacramental theology you are more concerned with correctness than grace, or more attentive to formality than welcome, you have entirely missed the point of everything you are holding so dear. Sacramental hospitality says to the outsider, "Welcome. Things may be a bit different here, so let me show you around." Contextualizing Anglican worship is not so hard: simply give a warm welcome, a general orientation, a process for continued growth, and most importantly an introduction to the host.

A Case Study: Vestments

Let's run our learning from this chapter through the case study of wearing vestments (the robes and other clothes worn to denote role and office in the worship service). Put aside your own preference for a moment and operate under the assumption that there is legitimate Anglican expression in both high-church and low-church settings. So should you wear vestments or not? Let's walk through the question in six steps:

1. What does the Scripture say about vestments? They are neither commanded nor forbidden.
2. What does your bishop say? If he requires vestments, then you wear them. If he does not, then you have a choice.
3. To make this choice you must begin by gaining clarity on what vestments are, why they are worn, and how they impact the life of the church and the making of disciples. That way, you can decide on your practice with integrity. Then based on the latitude of your bishop and your own convictions and the discernment of any others who are leading the church plant with

you, and taking into account your cultural context, decide if you will wear vestments or not.

4. If you choose to wear vestments—whether you wear an alb and stole, a cassock and surplice, a chasuble, a clergy collar, or anything else—you should wear them with *integrity.* Wear them in the appropriate way for the purpose for which they are designed.
5. Proper contextualization then calls you not to assume everyone knows why you have on garments the people may have never seen before. You will under-contextualize if you wear them without explanation. Remember, you are being intentionally counter-cultural if you vest, so you need to make the reasons behind your vestments *accessible* and create an atmosphere that is *hospitable* to asking questions.
6. If you choose not to wear vestments, then you must find other ways to uphold the integrity of the Anglican expression of worship and emphasize the transcendence and holiness of the corporate worship gathering.

You may have very strong opinions about which choice is the proper one regarding vestments. That's okay. Part of the beauty of Anglicanism is the godly tension we share as a family. The point is that contextualization choices determine how we will interact with the culture and approach our mission. We can start from farther away from the culture and shock the people into exploring the mystery of faith, or we can start a bit closer and move them incrementally along. The terminus is the same. If you wear vestments, ensure that you leverage your obvious distinctiveness from the culture to call the people to the otherness of the gospel. If you choose not to wear vestments, you are one step closer to the culture so your accessibility takes less work, but now the challenge is to call people to a distinctly different life in a less distinct setting. They are two parallel paths to the same destination as we make disciples of Jesus through expressions of the Anglian way.

• • • •

Anglican contextualization is pursued through a sacramental mindset. We are not simply making aesthetic choices when we contextualize; we are striving to make sure that all our physical expressions are proper signs of the invisible gospel. Our contextualization does not only consider what is most effective for gathering a crowd, but also what is most faithful to the identity and purpose of the church.

Anglicanism is both unchanging and adaptable. It is appropriately rigid while simultaneously allowing for flexibility to serve the work of mission. It is concurrently God-centered and people-oriented. This mixed economy makes us well-positioned to bring the gospel and the ancient life of the universal church to every kind of community.

A Note to Non-Anglican Readers:

This chapter had a lot of Anglican-specific references that you may or may not relate to. The grid of appropriate contextualization (clarity, integrity, accessibility, hospitality) remains relevant no matter your tradition. What aspects of your traditions, beliefs, polity, ethos, and practices are important to gain clarity on? In what ways can the integrity of these things be upheld and where do dangers of inappropriate compromise lurk? What areas may need explanation or nuance to ensure they are accessible to the people visiting your church? How do you create an environment where people can ask questions and be allowed to be "in process" as they learn? Take specific care to look at your worship practices—what may be comfortably familiar to you, may be disquietingly odd to the unchurched. How do you shape your services in a way that honors God and respects your tradition but is invitational to others who hope to join your family?

CHAPTER 6

• • • •

The Anglican Way of Discipleship

The duty of the church is to comfort the disturbed and to disturb the comfortable.

— *Archbishop Michael Ramsey*

SUMMARY: The Anglican Way of discipleship utilizes practices rooted in the ancient church that impart knowledge, shape our affections, and provide rites of passage along the journey.

Church planting and making disciples are inextricable pursuits. The call to mission from the lips of Christ is, "Go therefore and make disciples of all nations, baptizing them in the name of the Father and of the Son and of the Holy Spirit, teaching them to observe all that I have commanded you" (Matthew 28:19–20). Much ink has been spilled elsewhere to prove this is a command not only for the first disciples of Jesus, but for all those disciples who would come after them. It is a commission for the life of the church.

This Great Commission leads us to ask, "How do we make disciples?" Thankfully, Jesus did not give a vague commission. He said to go and make disciples and then told us how disciples are made. First, their repentance and belief lead to their baptism into the church. Then, the newly baptized are taught how to how to live their new life of joyful obedience to Christ through their new family.

In contemporary Western Christianity we tend to separate evangelism and discipleship, as if "baptize them" and "teach them to observe all that I have commanded you" were two different commands. In the Great Commission, however, these actions together constitute one wholistic process of making disciples. Evangelism and discipleship are symbiotic—one is neglected at the peril of the other. Like ecclesiology and missiology, evangelism and discipleship are not sequential but helical. Evangelism necessitates discipleship, and disciples pursue evangelism and make more disciples, who are then sent out in evangelism. Paul taught this concept to Timothy saying, "what you have heard from me in the presence of many witnesses entrust to faithful [people], who will be able to teach others also" (2 Timothy 2:2). Disciples make disciples. Life begets new life.

Evangelism is not like catching fireflies. We do not grab converts, stuff them in a jar of disciples, and quickly put a lid on them. There is no lid to our jar. Making disciples is making missionaries.

If evangelism is seen as something done to the lost and discipleship something offered only to the found, there will be an ever-widening gap between these two groups. We must see evangelism as the first steps in making disciples who will be sent again to the lost. Discipleship is not separated from mission; mission is discipleship, and discipleship is for mission. New believers and mature believers alike should see the making of more disciples through loving, preaching, teaching, inviting, and baptizing as a normal function of their lives and the church of which they are a part.

Church planters can easily fall prey to a "phase" mentality. In the initial gathering phase of the church, they sometimes neglect discipleship for the sake of mission, and when the number of people gathered is deemed sufficient, they reverse the emphasis and neglect mission for the sake of discipleship. A church planter must look at the larger picture and find a way to develop a church community that is actively reaching out, building up, and sending out in perpetuity. Thankfully, our Anglican way of being is structured around this life of mission and discipleship.

Baptize Them: Discipleship and the Sacraments

Since church planting is inseparable from discipleship and Christ's command to make disciples includes the sacraments, it is important for you need to understand how the sacraments work to shape and form the people of your church. Again, Christ's outline of discipleship starts with baptism. This sacrament reveals that discipleship begins with grace and community. You are not saved by grace and then discipled by effort. My friend and fellow Anglican church planter Shawn McCain often says it this way, "Baptism shows us that, from the beginning, discipleship is not meant to be done by our own power, but through our participation in a grace already bestowed." We come to the water by grace, bringing nothing, offering nothing, meriting nothing. At the same time, we are not passive observers. We are called to actively participate in what God is doing.

Our baptismal liturgy shows this interaction of meritless grace and the call to take part in the process of discipleship. During the baptismal service, the candidate is asked clearly, "Do you desire to be baptized?"[1] There is no compulsion or manipulation. The question is simple and clear: Has the Holy Spirit awakened in you the desire for Jesus and to enter into his church? The candidate then articulates this desire through vows to reject the world, the flesh, and the devil. The candidate is asked if she repents and believes in Jesus, responding, "I do."

Up to this point, the questions have asked about the candidate's definitive response to the gospel. The structure changes upon reaching the final question: "Will you obediently keep God's holy will and commandments, and walk in them all the days of your life?" The response of the candidate is, "I will, the Lord being my helper." If the initial questions evoke a response of faith to what God has already done, then the final question recognizes our need for his continued action. We bring nothing to our baptism and we bring nothing to our discipleship. Calling the Lord our *Helper* here does not mean "assistant when it becomes too much for me to bear on my own." The word is one of the names of the Holy Spirit, the *paraclete*, the one who is called alongside. God is the one without whose help we have no chance to fulfill our vow. The goal of discipleship is not to be helped until we no longer are dependent upon God, but rather a continued lifelong participation in what the Lord is doing within us. Grace and the Holy Spirit are our help and our seals. The liturgy beautifully reveals the biblical truth that grace does not prohibit effort, but grace relieves the burden of doomed attempts at self-achieved justification and self-realized sanctification.

When the newly-baptized person emerges from the font blinking water from his eyes, the first sight he sees is the welcoming faces of his new family. The candidate is baptized into a life of following Christ, and that is meant to be lived with others who are doing the same. It is the role of the church community to work with the Holy Spirit to teach, protect, guide, and equip this new life. Therefore, we make vows as a local church during the baptism service when we are asked, "Will you who witness these vows do all in your power to support these persons in their life in Christ?" and we respond, "We will." This is a promise that should be taken very seriously. It is no less a binding vow than those we make when we say "I will" at the moment of our marriage. Discipleship is a community commitment.

This sacramental experience of discipleship continues in the Eucharist. In baptism we touch, see, taste, and feel the outward and visible sign of the inward and spiritual grace of new birth in Christ, and in the Eucharist we touch, see, taste, and feel the loving sacrifice of Christ that sustains us, strengthens us as a community, and offers a foretaste of our communal future hope.

We understand the sacraments to be means through which God bestows grace and instruments through which he strengthens our faith. The Lord works through the waters to renew us and through the bread and the wine to nourish us. So, being baptized and receiving the Eucharist are themselves acts of discipleship. Through the invitation of the church, which reflects the church's missional endeavors, we welcome the baptized to come by faith and participate in the meal given to us by Christ. We take our place at Christ's family table along with the community of the church as we inwardly receive what Christ provides. We are nurtured by the gospel.

Many see a pattern of the Christian life in the fourfold movement of the Eucharistic prayer (which is based on Christ's words from Luke 22:19 and 1 Corinthians 11:23–24): Christ took the bread, blessed it, broke it, and gave it to his disciples. This is how the Lord acts in us as well. He takes us by his grace, he blesses us with his Spirit, breaks us from our sin, and he gives us to the world. Our God is a God on mission, so it is no accident that in his wisdom he saw fit to give us sacraments that shape us for that mission.

Father McCain is a wonderful example of a planter who is seeking to form disciples through the Anglican tradition. In the communal life of Resurrection, South Austin, he intentionally weaves the sacraments (and sacramental rites) into the process of making disciples. He reminds his congregation how our sacramental life prompts us toward mission and equips us to go, using a framework of Welcome, Shape, and Send.[2]

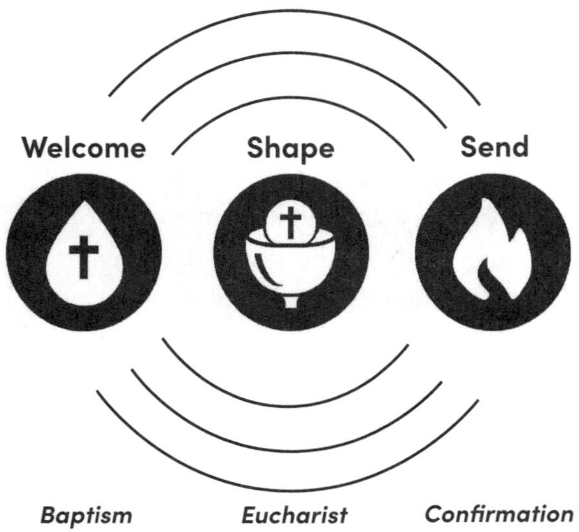

Courtesy of Resurrection Church, South Austin. Used with permission.

Welcome. The church is a place of welcome and introduction. The community invites unbelievers to hear the proclamation of the gospel and the claims of Christ, and to witness firsthand how gospel believers live as the family of God. When unbelievers are moved to join the family and respond to Christ's gospel invitation by repenting and believing, they are baptized. Here, the inward and spiritual grace of God that brings about their justification and new birth is shared outwardly and visibly with their family. Baptism is a rite of passage, marking the welcoming of the new believer into the church. The Anglican Catechism says, "I am born a sinner by nature, separated from God. But in Baptism, through faith in Christ and the gift of the Holy Spirit, I am made a member of Christ's Body and adopted as God's child and heir."[3]

Shape. As a natural part of family life, new believers are then shaped and formed in many ways through teaching, mentoring, study, and simply being a part of the church's shared life. Under the preaching of the church and shared study, the Word is imprinted deeply into the hearts of new believers. This inward communal shaping of the soul in sanctification is visibly experienced and strengthened by the working of God through participation in the family meal of the Eucharist. Again, we turn to the Catechism, which teaches, "As my body is nourished by the bread and wine, my soul is strengthened by the Body and Blood of Christ. I receive God's forgiveness, and I am renewed in the love and unity of the Body concerning sacraments of Christ, the Church."[4]

Send. But the believers are not simply meant to feast and be fat and happy at a closed Table. Rather, Christians are to bring others to the same family, same water, and same meal to which they have been accepted and saved. This means there is an intentionality in the church to send out new disciples as missionaries. Disciples are led through the process of catechesis and preparation and when they are ready, this missionary sending is marked by the commissioning service we call confirmation. Although confirmation is not a Christ-instituted sacrament the way baptism and the Eucharist are, it is a sacramental rite. The bishop lays hands on the Christian, prays for the anointing of the Holy Spirit, and commissions the believer for a life of continued discipleship and mission saying, "Now, these Candidates desire publicly to confess their faith in Jesus Christ as Savior and their commitment to follow him as Lord. They also desire the strengthening of grace through the laying on of hands, that the Holy Spirit may fill them more and more for their ministry in the Church and in the world."[5] Confirmation is sometimes referred to as "lay ordination" as the participant makes vows, is bestowed grace through the laying on of hands, and is sent out for ministry in the church and the world.

Discipleship progresses, which is why it is marked by these rites of passage that ensure discipleship is not an isolated or purely intellectual process, but rather a communal and formational journey in which God is an active participant. Father McCain describes this process as cyclical. He says, "In every changing age, cultural moment, and personal challenge, the invitation remains, 'How is God welcoming me into transformation, how can I cooperate with that shaping, and be sent with him for the sake of others?'"[6] McCain is making disciples simply by intentionally pursuing faithful Anglicanism, because discipleship is inherent and undeniable in our tradition.

I once heard Bishop Todd Hunter say that "The way of Anglicanism is ideally suited for making disciples—if that is what you want to make." In other words, all the gifts of the liturgy and sacramental church do not inevitably produce disciples as if an automated process. The church must have a missional impulse in all it says and does. It is possible to have the outward signs of discipleship without grasping their purpose or power. As a church planter, you must create a culture that sees the purpose behind all the beauty and order and function of the liturgical way: to glorify God and make disciples.

Teach Them: Discipleship and Catechesis

Thomas Cranmer, author and compiler of the Prayer Book, described the life of the new Christian as requiring three changes:[7]

1. **A new disposition.** We participate in a saving grace through repentance.
2. **A new direction.** We participate with sustaining grace in a life reoriented toward Christ.
3. **A new discipline.** We are motivated by love and grace, seeking to live in obedience to Christ.

Cranmer was instrumental in shaping Anglicanism during a pivotal moment of its history during the Reformation. He desired for us to realize that Jesus's instruction to "obey all that I have commanded" does not mean we are saved by grace through faith, baptized, and then left to our own efforts for discipleship. Rather, discipleship is a participation in continued grace as we are cut to the heart by the gospel and respond by gladly giving back to the Lord what he has given us: our lives.

One of the prayers for mission we pray during Morning Prayer reads, "Lord Jesus Christ, you stretched out your arms of love on the hard wood of the Cross that everyone might come within the reach of your saving embrace: So clothe us in your Spirit that we, reaching forth our hands in love, may bring those who do not know you to the knowledge and love of you; for the honor of your Name. Amen."[8] This prayer defines our mission as bringing people to both the *knowledge* and the *love* of Christ. Each of these aspects of relationship with Christ are required for a disciple to live obediently. Discipleship in our Anglican churches must therefore focus on both.

Knowledge of Christ

There is much for a new disciple simply to learn. Only this morning I attended a worship service, and a mother came to the Communion rail with her newborn child. The beautiful baby was just able to lift up his head and begin to look around. His eyes were like marbles as he took in every detail, every movement, every color, with the perpetual look of wide-eyed wonder that new babies have. He heard the liturgy and felt my touch as I blessed his forehead. The rhythm of the music vibrated his chest, and the people of the community smiled at him. In years to come this child, raised in the church, will learn everything from the feel of the cover of a Bible to the meaning of the ink on its pages and the truth they convey. He will learn how to see the world through the lens of Christ, how to live as a Christian, how to love as a Christian, how to celebrate and suffer as a Christian, even how to disagree as a Christian. He will learn theology and ecclesiology. There is so much for his new eyes and ears to take in and his mind and heart to grasp. Similarly, the eyes of new believers are just coming into focus and there is a new world for them to learn—to be discipled in.

Even the eyes of longtime church attenders are opened anew by continued discipleship.

J. I. Packer describes how Anglicanism functions to convey knowledge to the new believer:

> In England, the original form of the evangelistic ministry of Anglicanism for Anglican parishes—the form it took in the sixteenth century when the Prayer Book was put together, and the form it was still taking in the seventeenth century—was catechetical. The vision was to promote the parishioners' learning through an understanding of the substance of the children's catechism (contained in the Prayer Book), and through taking part regularly in the worship of Morning and Evening Prayer and the Communion service. In all these, the themes of sin, grace, and responsive faith are embodied, embedded, and expressed; all of it would ideally have been properly explained by one's clergyman. Thus, parishioners would grow into a living faith in Christ.[9]

Teaching and instruction have always been a part of Anglicanism. The 1552 children's catechism Packer referred to was further titled "An Instruction to Be Learned of Every Child Before He Be Brought to Be Confirmed by the Bishop." The catechism, which taught sound doctrine, along with the Articles of Faith, the Lord's Prayer, and the Ten Commandments, were required learning for anyone who wished to be confirmed in sixteenth-century England.

The children's catechism is a fascinating read. After the confirmand was prompted to describe the duty of the

Christian in life including such things such as, "Love my neighbor as myself. . . . Hurt nobody by word or deed. To be true and just in all my dealings. To bear no malice or hatred in my heart," the bishop says, "My good child, know this, that you are not able to do these things for yourself, nor to walk in the commandments of God, and to serve him, without his special grace, which you must learn at all times to call for by diligent prayer. Let me hear therefore if you can say the Lord's Prayer."

What a beautiful intermingling of the need for knowledge in the life of the disciple along with a dependence upon grace. Knowledge of righteous behavior is followed by a quick recollection of our need for grace, which is subsequently stated to be called for in prayer, where knowledge of the Lord's Prayer is essential. It's the circle of life—all of which is lovingly overseen by the church for support and safety.

The catechism is not simply for sixteenth-century minors. Today we have the gift of catechisms throughout the Anglican Communion including "To Be a Christian" from the Anglican Church in North America, written and compiled by a task force led by Packer himself. This catechism is a vital tool for teaching the knowledge of the faith. At Church of the Redeemer in Greensboro, North Carolina, where I serve, a one-year catechumenate course is required for membership where we use the catechism to instruct new and old believers alike in the doctrine and discipline of the church.

The need for catechism is displayed in the contrasting work of Anglican evangelists George Whitfield and John Wesley. Both men formed and spread Methodism, which began as a missional movement within the Anglican Church. Whitfield traveled the world and preached to more than ten million people, often bringing his hearers to tears—and more importantly to repentance and belief in Jesus. His gifting was oratory, however, not systems of discipleship. On the other hand, his friend (even through a lifetime of disagreement) John Wesley was a great preacher in his own right but he truly shone in organizational ability. Wesley would preach and then organize class meetings and societies for the ongoing catechesis and discipleship of the newly converted. Whitfield famously said late in life, "My brother Wesley acted wisely. The souls that were awakened under his ministry he joined in societies, and thus preserved the fruit of his labor. This I neglected, and my people are a rope of sand."[10] Using the same image, Wesley described his own ministry by saying, "Those who were desirous to save their souls were no longer a rope of sand, but clave to one another, and began to watch over each other in love. Societies were formed, and Christian discipline was introduced in all its branches."[11] The fullness of the commission is to make disciples by conversion *and* instruction in community.

In a church plant, we are midwifing the birth of those who convert to Christianity and then seeing about the task of raising them in the church. We do not want our church plants to be ropes of sand, so we must develop a clear pathway for discipleship and bestowing Christian knowledge. Utilize the catechism frequently in places like small group discussions, launch team training, leadership formation, evangelistic discussions, and many other situations. Do not be afraid of its initially-unfamiliar structure or of words the people may not immediately understand—that is why the catechism is a framework for discussion and explanation. You do not need to go to your local Christian bookstore to find discipleship curriculum; you have the catechism at your disposal. As you craft your approach to discipleship, focus less on being novel and more on returning to our roots.

Love for Christ

Discipleship is not simply transactional, however. It is not merely conveying knowledge about God, but inviting people to share a relationship with God. Knowledge is good, but on its own does not create deep relationship any more than learning to be happily married comes from reading a book on marriage—unless your affections are changed, the knowledge means very little. That's why discipleship is about shaping our loves and desires. "Rend your hearts and not your garments" (Joel 2:13), declares the Lord. "You will seek me and find me, when you seek me with all your heart" (Jeremiah 29:13). God does not want obedient automatons (not that obedience is possible without grace anyway). God desires us to delight in him as he delights in us. Our discipleship, therefore, should also be concerned with remodeling hearts.

The metrics for gauging success in leading others to love Jesus are harder to test than knowledge. There are no examinations to judge the process of sanctification. The Scripture tells us we will be known by our fruit (see Matthew 7:15–20). Galatians 5 distinguishes the works of the flesh from the fruit of the Spirit. These characteristics are indirectly proportional: if we participate in the Spirit's work to shape our loves we will have less sexual immorality, impurity, sensuality, idolatry, sorcery, enmity, strife, jealousy, fits of anger, rivalries, etc. (Galatians 5:19–21) and at the same time, we will have more love, joy, peace, patience, kindness, goodness, faithfulness, gentleness, and self-control (vv. 22–23). Discipleship must be a wholistic engagement of the life of the believer that stirs affection for Christ, which results in bearing good fruit.

In our church plants we need to shape affections so that our people are not simply striving to behave in a righteous manner, but hunger and thirst for righteousness. This affection is more caught than taught. Preaching should be exhortational. Our message should be inspirational, but with substance. The community should be welcoming and generous. Love in action should be our hallmark. We pursue what we love, so love for Jesus is the foundation of our discipleship.

Invitation and Initiation

Invitation to join the work of your church plant should be framed in a manner that does not simply ask people to be a statistic in your numerical growth, but instead is an invitation to join a community of people who long for the King and for his kingdom to come. Aidan Kavanagh says:

> The radical discovery of ourselves as the church is possible only in terms of Jesus dead and rising. Where this passage from death to life is continuously available to us in the conversion of people actually passing from death to life in him, and by him, and through him among his faithful people. Christian initiation is this passage. . . . Who does not know initiation does not know the church. Who does not know the church does not know the Lord. And who knows neither the church nor the Lord does not know the world as God meant it to be from before and always.[12]

Our church planting should involve invitation that leads to initiation through catechesis, baptism, Eucharist, confirmation, and sharing the ongoing communal church life of worship, service, and growth. In church planting, it is tempting to see people as commodities to be counted, but you must see them as souls that must be born anew in life everlasting and shaped to know the world as God meant it to be.

The way of Word and sacrament is a gift to this most noble endeavor. If you engage it consciously and pursue it properly you will be participating in the way of salvation. Having been justified, God's saving work continues in us as we learn to "live up to what we have already atttained" (Philippians 3:16 NIV), inviting our participation as we are taught, strengthened, and sent. Even more, throughout this entire process foreshadowed in the Eucharist and the liturgy, we are looking forward to the return of Christ and our glorification, when there will be a new heaven and new earth and we fully know even as we are fully known. Anglicanism introduces a way of communal discipleship that adds the arrow to the end of the line of our life, giving us direction and movement and setting us on a trajectory of glory. Discipleship as seen through the Anglican lens begins with gospel invitation, is marked by communal initiation, is rehearsed by sacramental participation, and will one day be fulfilled in Christ's consummation.

A Note to Non-Anglican Readers:

Your tradition most likely has a robust catechism somewhere in its history as well. I encourage you, before you go looking for a glossy-covered discipleship curriculum, to find a battered and torn copy of your catechism. Make sure it smells like an old book. Familiarize yourself with what you find there, then find ways to affectively bring it to bear on your current culture. Perhaps some of the rites of passage I have listed here do not exist in your tradition. You will then need to ponder how to provide a clear path for the development of disciples in your church, and how to corporately progress and growth on that journey. Bestow knowledge and shape affections. Finally, don't forget the importance of commissioning. Our rite of confirmation is a pivotal sending moment in the lives of our people—a time they prepare for in advance and remember for the rest of their lives as Christians. How will you gift your people with a similar incarnated moment of corporate support and sending?

CHAPTER 7

....

Missional Liturgy

Almighty God our Savior, you desire that none should perish, and you have taught us through your Son that there is great joy in heaven over every sinner who repents: Grant that our hearts may ache for a lost and broken world. May your Holy Spirit work through our words, deeds, and prayers, that the lost may be found and the dead made alive, and that all your redeemed may rejoice around your throne; through Jesus Christ our Lord. Amen.

— *Book of Common Prayer, Prayer for a Spirit of Evangelism*

SUMMARY: The structure, content, and practice of liturgy is missional by design, and therefore, should be a profound help to the church planter who longs to release the missional potential in his church and people.

One of the greatest gifts for mission and discipleship provided by our Anglican heritage is our liturgy. Anglicans believe that worship and the words and actions we employ in it are not merely expressive, they are formative. Our liturgy does not simply *articulate* how we feel, think, and therefore act, but actively *shapes* our feeling, thinking, and action. The oft-quoted phrase *Lex orandi, lex credendi*, which dates back to at least the fourth century, translates broadly as "how we worship is how we believe" and is sometimes expanded to include *lex vivendi*, "is how we live." Our worship is simultaneously the motivation behind, the equipping for, and the result of our mission.

This conversation regarding missional liturgy may shake up many preconceived notions. One sacramental church planter I know was asked, "Why would you want to plant a dead church?" The charge against liturgy is that its structure can be unwelcoming, its delivery droll, its language regarded as pretentious, its participants mindless, and its strangeness simply a bridge too far for visitors to a congregation. The argument goes that if the goal of mission is to attract people to Jesus and his church, then we need something more dynamic, contemporary, and easily accessible than our liturgy.

I do not deny that liturgy celebrated poorly—that is devoid of awe of God the Father, neglects the missional heart of the Son, and lacks the joyful presence of the Holy Spirit—is guilty of these charges. I do, however, disagree that the gospel of Jesus Christ, which announces our restored access to our Creator and bestows upon us the life-giving Holy Spirit, requires the addition of showmanship or dynamism to make it attractive.

There is no more exciting news than the good news of Jesus Christ. The gospel is sufficient to change hearts, minds, and the world, and it has been doing so for thousands of years. Our first concern should be how to properly proclaim the unadulterated gospel. God has chosen the church as his agent to bring the gospel to the world. We must not see our role as dressing it up to make it more attractive, but rather as giving pure local expression to the universal gospel through a community of people who have been transformed by it and are living in light of it. This is also the goal of the liturgy.

The gospel, not spectacle, should be what stimulates our minds and cuts our hearts. The liturgy is lifeless only when, through sin or error or apathy, it becomes derivative- an imitation of someone else's faith rather than an expression of our own. To only say the words of the liturgy and not share the faith they describe is like reading someone else's love letter. It may be beautiful, but it is not ours. The liturgy is meant to encourage its participants to experience the same passion that initially inspired those profound words to be written and, therefore, long to love Jesus equally as deeply. The liturgy is the church's love letter to Jesus, and it calls for the unbeliever to sign their name along with the all the saints as the sender. The liturgy invites the unbeliever and stirs up the disciple to love and be loved by Jesus.

Liturgy is the gospel in worship form, facilitating its proclamation, celebration, and exhortation. It is the embodied gospel: the beauty and participatory nature of the liturgy proclaimed by the church is a shadow of Jesus's beauty and his invitation to participate in his redemptive work as a part of his family.

The liturgy defines what a faithful church should look like. Benedictine monk Aidan Kavanagh calls the liturgy an enacted ecclesiology: "The liturgy is not some thing separate from the church, but simply the church caught in the act of being most overtly itself."[1] In other words, all that we are supposed to be as the church is expressed in our participation in the liturgy and should carry over into our daily lives—loving, worshipping, serving, repenting, rejoicing, washing, inviting. The liturgy is missional because it calls all people to repentance, belief, and baptism, and then forms them in the life of following Christ as a part of his body, the church.

The liturgy makes disciples. This chapter will walk us through six reasons why this is true.

1. The liturgy teaches us Scripture and sound doctrine.
2. The liturgy equips us to apply Scripture and sound doctrine.
3. The liturgy's beauty shapes our loves.
4. The liturgy models life in Christ.
5. The liturgy calls for action.
6. The liturgy provides sacred rhythms that define our story.

The Liturgy Is Didactic: It Teaches

At the heart of discipleship is Jesus, and we know Jesus through his Word—written, proclaimed, and visible. There is no getting around it: to be a faithful disciple of Christ requires learning, knowing, and following the Scriptures and "the faith that was once for all delivered to the saints" (Jude v. 3). The liturgy not only teaches us the content of Scripture, but also teaches us the importance of the act of reading Scripture. Listen to the beautiful words of Thomas Cranmer in the collect for the second Sunday of Advent: "Blessed Lord, who caused all Holy Scriptures to be written for our learning: Grant us so hear them, read, mark, learn, and inwardly digest them, that by patience and the comfort of your holy Word we may embrace and ever hold fast the blessed hope of everlasting life, which you have given us in our Savior Jesus Christ; who lives and reigns with you and the Holy Spirit, one God, for ever and ever. Amen."[2]

The Words of the Scripture flow throughout the liturgy. To give all the examples would mean reprinting the Prayer Book on these pages, but here are a few:

- Our salutation before prayer and at the opening of the Eucharistic prayer, "The Lord be with you" is the angel Gabriel's greeting to Mary in Luke 1:28 and echoes the words of Boaz in Ruth 2:4.
- The Kyrie, "Lord, have mercy," contains the words of the blind man in Luke 18:38.
- We proclaim, "Christ our Passover is sacrificed for us! Therefore, let us keep the feast. Alleluia!" at the Eucharist using the words of 1 Corinthians 5:7–8.
- The entire Lord's Prayer is read multiple times a day through the Daily Office and our Sunday worship.
- The Sanctus said at the Eucharist echoes the praises of the angels and archangels and all the company of heaven in Revelation 4:8 as they sing "Holy, Holy, Holy" and repeats the words of Psalm 118:26 as sung by the people on Palm Sunday in Mark 11:9, "Hosanna! Blessed is he who comes in the name of the Lord!"

In addition to the Scripture imbedded in the liturgy, passages from the Old Testament, the Psalms, the New Testament, and the Gospels are read throughout the day. Following the lectionary leads us to read the Bible cover-to-cover each year. If we pursue discipleship through the Anglican way, we should be saturated with Scripture. It should be ever on our lips, the very language we speak.

The liturgy teaches not only the words of Scripture, but also correct interpretation of Scripture through the teaching of sound doctrine. The essentials of the faith are clearly recited during every service by saying the Nicene or Apostles' Creed, and the rest of the liturgy teaches doctrine as well. Take, for example, the Eucharistic prayer of consecration:

> Holy and gracious Father: In your infinite love you made us for yourself; and when we had sinned against you and become subject to evil and death, you, in your mercy, sent your only Son Jesus Christ into the world for our salvation. By the Holy Spirit and the Virgin Mary he became flesh and dwelt among us. In obedience to your will, he stretched out his arms upon the Cross and offered himself once for all, that by his suffering and death we might be saved. By his resurrection he broke the bonds of death, trampling Hell and Satan under his feet. As our great high priest, he ascended to your right hand in glory, that we might come with confidence before the throne of grace.[3]

In this prayer the people are learning atonement theology, Trinitarian theology, redemptive history, eschatology, and much more. Yes, these words and teachings will require unpacking. This is why there is space required within the service for preaching, and further catechesis and discussion of the liturgy should be a part of our life together outside of the worship services. The liturgy provides the language to facilitate this community of dialogue and learning. It also empowers the laity by giving them the language to teach and explain the faith as well.

But as disciples we do not learn simply for the sake of knowing a lot of Christian facts. The Scripture tells us that knowledge alone tends to puff up rather than build up. The Bible celebrates the treasure of wisdom, which is knowledge properly applied to interpret life's events and respond with appropriate action. As Anglican C. S. Lewis said, "I believe in Christianity as I believe that the sun has risen, not only because I see it but because by it, I see everything else."[4] We form disciples to see the world through the lens of the Scripture and then act according to the holy truth of God. Our liturgical practice is immensely influential in this process. James K. A. Smith tells us,

> Discipleship and formation are less about erecting an edifice of Christian knowledge than they are a matter of developing a Christian know-how that intuitively 'understands' the world in the light of the fullness of the gospel. And insofar as an understanding is implicit in practice, the practices of Christian worship are crucial—the sine qua non—for developing a distinctly Christian understanding of the world.[5]

The Liturgy Equips

The liturgy is sneaky, however, because it can be a subversive teacher. It causes us to learn Scripture and doctrine when we do not even realize that learning is taking place.

What do you need to do when your plane is about to land? You return to your seat and make sure your seat belt is fastened and your tray table is in its full upright position. How did you know that? You have participated in an aeronautical liturgy. Veteran flyers know what to do because they have heard the same instructions over and over. As soon as the final approach is announced, they are sitting up straight with their seat belts fastened tightly across their laps and their tiny table folded up before they are even asked.

In the classic movie *The Karate Kid*, Daniel asks Mr. Miyagi to teach him karate. The first day Daniel comes ready to fight something, but Mr. Miyagi hands him two rags and a can of wax, telling him to wax his cars with a particular circular motion: "wax on" with circles from the right hand, "wax off" with opposite circles from the left. The next day it is "paint the fence," with brush strokes up and down. When Daniel complains he is doing chores instead of learning karate, Mr. Miyagi begins throwing punches at him. In a moment of muscle memory, without thinking, Daniel begins to block the blows with circular and vertical motions—wax on, wax off, paint the fence, paint the fence—and with wide-eyed astonishment Daniel understands that he has been learning karate all along. So it is with the liturgy. We are learning Scripture and doctrine and we may not even recognize the process until that knowledge is called upon in the Christian life.

Over time, the liturgy enables the words of the Scripture to so shape our hearts that Jesus seeps into our souls—godly action becomes natural and intuitive, the language of the Scripture becomes our primary vocabulary, holiness becomes our hermeneutic, and the life of the disciple is woven into our own life until the two become one.

In the process of planting multiple churches over the last two decades, I have had the honor of seeing a number of people come to the knowledge and love of Christ. I remember one new believer who was being shaped and formed in our church for a number of months. He came to me one day in a mix of frustration and excitement.

"I'm struggling," he said, "because I have such a passion for Jesus and I want to grow in my ability to pray, but I just can't seem to find the words."

I asked him if he could give me a specific example of something he was having a hard time articulating in prayer. "Confession," he said. He was eager to resist sin and pursue Christ, but praying "I'm sorry" didn't seem enough to him.

After assuring him that Jesus was pleased with his "I'm sorry" prayer, I made another suggestion: "How about, 'I confess that I have sinned against you in thought, word, and deed, by what I have done and by what I have left undone. I have not loved you with my whole heart and I have not loved my neighbor as myself. I am truly sorry and I humbly repent. For the sake of your son Jesus Christ, have mercy on me and forgive me that I may delight in your will and walk in your ways to the glory of your name. Amen.'"

He looked at me with the same look Daniel gave Mr. Miyagi. "Yes! And I know those words!" he said, "We pray them every Sunday."

These are the words of confession from the Eucharistic liturgy.[6] I sat down with him, and we walked through how to pray the Daily Office. Wax on, wax off, paint the fence, paint the fence.

Question: But isn't repetition boring? Will it not get old?

Remember, Anglicans believe that liturgy and worship are simultaneously expressive and formative. While the liturgy is employed by the Christian as an expression of faith, at the same time the Christian is being shaped by God through the liturgy in return. Again, we turn to the beautifully articulate James K. A. Smith who says:

> If worship is formative, not merely expressive, then we need to be conscious and intentional about the form of worship that is forming us. This has one more important implication: When you unhook worship from mere expression, it also completely retools your understanding of repetition. If you think of worship as a bottom-up, expressive endeavor, repetition will seem insincere and inauthentic. But when you see worship as an invitation to a top-down encounter in which God is refashioning your deepest habits, then repetition looks very different: it's how God rehabituates us. In a formational paradigm, repetition isn't insincere because you're not "showing," you're submitting. This is crucial because there is no formation without repetition.[7]

The Liturgy's Beauty Shapes Our Loves

It is one thing to go to an art museum and look at the pretty paintings. But when you go with someone who has studied painting and art history, when you witness firsthand their love for the craft and they take the time to explain the symbolism and importance of the pieces, your appreciation deepens and a whole new world of wonder opens to you. The corporate experience of beauty transforms paint on canvas into something that shapes your desires. You see a painted landscape like Monet's *Bridge over a Pond of Water Lilies,* and something is stirred in you that is greater than the sum of the brushstrokes. You long to go and stand on the bridge amidst the flowers and the reeds.

The liturgy is beautiful. The prose and poetry are meant not only to instruct, but also to arouse. They shape not only the head through proper instruction, but the heart through the experience of beauty. Take, for example, the opening explanation before the confession of sin in the service of Morning Prayer:

> Dearly beloved, the Scriptures teach us to acknowledge our many sins and offenses, not concealing them from our heavenly Father, but confessing them with humble and obedient hearts that we may obtain forgiveness by his infinite goodness and mercy. We ought at all times humbly to acknowledge our sins before Almighty God, but especially when we come together in his presence to give thanks for the great benefits we have received at his hands, to declare his most worthy praise, to hear his holy Word, and to ask, for ourselves and on behalf of others, those things which are necessary for our life and our salvation. Therefore, draw near with me to the throne of heavenly grace.[8]

In this prayer we are lovingly addressed as beloved ones, reminding us of our identity in Christ. This sets the tone for the exhortation to confession that follows. The basis for the invitation to confess and be forgiven is rooted in the teaching of Scripture, subtly showing us that all aspects of our faith should be similarly grounded. We are then taught by example that our posture before our heavenly Father is humility and obedience. We are reminded of the infinite goodness and mercy of God and his prodigious grace in offering us forgiveness of the grave offense of our sin. We are instructed how to reflect on God's blessings and are called to public prayer both for ourselves and on behalf of others. And then there is the invitation that should prick our hearts: "Draw near with me to the throne of heavenly grace." The invitation is overt and heard with the ears on our heads, but also more profoundly felt with the ears of our heart. We feel it: "I want to go there."

This is an invitation to actually stand on the bridge at Lily Pond, to enter into the painting, to not only talk about grace but to receive grace, respond to grace, and experience grace. "Draw near with me" structures the prayer corporately so we find, to our joy, that we have others to share our laughter and awe. The aesthetic—the preciseness of the language, the building crescendo of the invitation, the loving tone—does more than inform us. It beckons us.

Of course, one can attend a Morning Prayer service and miss all of this. The words can be said in rote recitation. The experience of the moment can be lost. We can pray Morning Prayer with the anxieties of the coming day or the sin in our hearts plugging our ears to the profound invitation being laid out before us—just as we may look at a Monet with a shrug.

We come to know the Jesus described in the liturgy when we stand where the writer stood and gaze upon our beautiful Savior, surrounded by a community of those we love and have loved. Our experience of the liturgy will be forever changed as its immense beauty brings us into the greater beauty of Jesus Christ.

Astoundingly, this beauty is not meant to be bottled and kept in the confines of a sanctuary. Through the liturgy and sacraments, it crashes into our everyday life.

We want to be surrounded by art for one of two reasons: either to see what cannot be seen elsewhere or to see the ordinary in extraordinary new ways. Anglican author Tish Harrison Warren captures this idea in her book *Liturgy of the Ordinary*: "The psalmist declares, 'This is the day that the

Lord has made.' This one. We wake not to a vague or general mercy from a far-off God. God, in delight and wisdom, has made, named, and blessed this average day. What I in my weakness see as another monotonous day in a string of days, God has given as a singular gift."[9]

The liturgy invites us to notice Christ in every moment. Praying the Daily Office in our homes and workplaces allows us to resist the pull of self-serving or the compartmentalization of church life and "real" life. The liturgy brings the words of Scripture and the person of Christ into our everyday reality, showing that beauty is not held captive by the masterpieces in galleries but can be found everywhere Christ is found. The liturgy shapes our loves so that the desire of our heart is to see every aspect of the world redeemed to match the beautiful truth of God as revealed to us in his Scripture.

The church is not an art gallery. The liturgy is not meant simply to be gazed upon, but to be acted upon. It is not meant to be kept behind glass bound by location in a church building, but rather to inspire and equip us to take the gospel to the world. Our liturgy is not a realized eschatology. As Augustine says, "We ought not to want to live ahead of time with only the saints and the righteous."[10] As the liturgy shapes our desires through the words of the Scripture, it should not evoke in us a desire to retreat from the world, but to bring the beauty that we know to a world that so badly needs it. We have seen the beauty, now let's go make the rest of the world look like it.

. . . .

These first three reasons liturgy makes disciples—because it teaches, it equips, and it shapes our loves—sum up so much of a church plater's task. What do you desire for the people of your church plant? Do you not want to see people whose hearts and minds are shaped by the beautiful truth of Jesus and then live lives of awe and wonder and service, not limited to attending services but striving to impact their communities with the redemptive love of Christ—people who have the equipping, motivation, and courage for the work of mission? Of course you do. Let the liturgy help shape their minds and desires as you gather, build up, and send out.

Question: But isn't liturgy too cerebral, too intellectual, or too full of strange words?

The liturgy is full of words, some of them familiar and some not, but like artistic masterpieces they are meant to stretch us. Language shapes our perception of reality, both teaching us new truths and reminding us of truth we have forgotten, adding new life to what has become normal and ordinary.

I am writing this chapter while on sabbatical and staying with friends in Kailua, Hawaii. As I type I am a hundred yards from one of the most beautiful beaches in the world. Azure waters along the soft white sand blend into a wine-dark sea beyond. Rugged volcanic mountains covered with a dark carpet of jungle greenery jut upward as if great fingers peeled away a crooked strip of sky. Countless palm trees dance in the breeze. It is truly one of the most idyllic places on earth. At lunch with local friends today I remarked on how I was constantly amazed at the stunning beauty in which they get to live. One of them said, "You know, I've been here for decades. After a while you just don't see it anymore."

This can be true for the Christian faith as well. What once twisted our gut with amazement over the person and work of Jesus can fade. Our church-planting work is to call unbelievers to new life and also to wake up the Christian sleepers who need to be reminded of the beauty of the gospel. The liturgy provides reminders to breathe deeply of sweet ancient air and be startled into the alertness of the hopeful.

The collect for Tuesday of Easter week reads,

> O God, who by the glorious resurrection of your Son Jesus Christ destroyed death and brought life and immortality to light: Grant that we, who have been raised with him, may abide in his presence and rejoice in the hope of eternal glory; through Jesus Christ our Lord, to whom, with you and the Holy Spirit, be honor and glory, now and for ever. Amen.[11]

Never would I pray like this out of my own wit. It would take me longer to craft that prayer than to pray it. I can pray this prayer with thankfulness that someone else gave the proper words to express my longing. This specific prayer is prayed both during Easter week and on the occasion of Christian funerals, making the resurrection a reality for all of our life experience. What a gift the liturgy is to our work of church planting as we seek to enliven a love for Jesus in our communities!

The life of the Christian comes with new words to describe our new reality, and new words need explanation—especially ancient Christian vocabulary. For example, if you do not explain when you say to someone, "Please go to the narthex where you will be assimilated into the church," they will think they have been abducted by their new reptilian overlords.

However, if you consider ecclesiastical language too lofty to use, you will rob new disciples of the new language they need to describe their new life and new worldview. It is taking the silver crayon out of the box. So I do not fault you if you initially roll your eyes thinking *narthex* sounds pretentious, and instead call it the foyer, but I pray you will look more closely. The narthex of a church is different from the foyer of your home. It does not lead to a place of recliners and TVs, but to a sanctuary of worship of the Triune God. We mustn't tamp down the transcendent into the mundane.

In his astounding trilogy, The Song of Albion, Anglican fiction author Stephen Lawhead tells of the adventures of an Oxford student named Lewis Gillies who is magically transported to a different world called Albion. This world is of such beauty that Lewis has trouble describing, or even truly grasping, what he is experiencing. Soon Lewis begins to learn the language of this new world. He states that as he learned the proper language, the world itself became more beautiful. He says,

> I think this had to do with the language itself: there were no dead words. No words that had suffered the ignorant predation of a semiliterate media, or had their substance leached away through gross misuse; no words rendered meaningless through overuse or cheapened through bureaucratic doublespeak. Consequently, the speech of Albion was a valued currency, a language alive with meaning: poetic, imagaic, bursting with rhythm and sound. When the words were spoken aloud, they possessed the power to touch the heart as well as the head: they spoke to the soul.[12]

So it is with the valued currency of the liturgy of the church. The richness of Christ, the multi-faceted jewel of the gospel, and the immense proportions of the hope of redemptive history deserve a language that is "poetic, imagaic, and bursting with rhythm and sound." The expression of our faith must not be limited to the laconic, prosaic, or simple.

"Use your words," we tell our young children when they are frustrated. But before they can use them, they must learn them. It is the same for the children of God. What better lexicon can be given them than the words of God himself? The liturgy gives us the words of Scripture to express our hearts and to interpret our world. What may seem strange at first will later be understood as the perfect descriptor of our new faith.

The Liturgy Models Life in Christ

The liturgy shapes our way of being even in its structure. The structure of the liturgy is what the architecture of the Metropolitan Museum of Art in New York City is to the art it contains. The Met is imposing, with soaring pillars and arches bending to invite you to the beauty within. The building is designed to guide you so you can see all it has to offer. The architecture of the liturgy makes the communal use of Scripture accessible and walkable and properly displayed. Its order provides a model for the life of the disciple.

Opening Acclamation. The first words we hear in any of our liturgical services are not words of welcome or greeting to the people. No, the first acclamation that rings in the sanctuary on Sunday blesses God: "Blessed be God: The Father, the Son, and the Holy Spirit and blessed be his Kingdom now and forever. Amen." God is the primary audience of our worship service. This action of looking to God before the people both sets the tone for the service and models the proper priorities of life.

Holiness and Grace. We then hear our need for grace even in the act of coming to worship a holy God, as we pray the prayer for purity, recite the summary of the law, and call out our need for mercy in the Kyrie, which culminates in praising God for his goodness in answering our prayer as we sing the "Gloria in Excelsis." Our liturgy, like our life of discipleship, does not begin with our list of demands or our résumé of importance. It begins with humility and repentance in light of God's holiness and thanksgiving for God's grace.

Proclaiming, Hearing, and Responding. We then hear the Word read in the Scripture and proclaimed in the sermon. Just as we must in our Christian life, the liturgical structure then turns to our response to the Word: we confess our faith through the Nicene Creed and we commune with our Lord as we pray together in the Prayers of the People.

Confession and Pardon. The presentation of the gospel that is rife throughout the first part of our Eucharistic service should move us to repentance, so as we have been convicted by his truth, we then have the opportunity to repent through the Confession our sins and to receive life-changing assurance of our pardon in the Absolution. Then follows the Peace where, as the gospel is not just about reconciliation with God, but also with one another, we offer greeting and forgiveness to each other as we prepare to come to the table of unity in the Eucharist. Out of a heart overflowing with gratitude we model our generosity as we give at the Offertory.

Feasting and Foretasting. The climax of the service comes when, as a community, we gather at the Table of the

Lord in the visible gospel of Communion. In the Eucharistic prayer, we are reminded of the story that shapes us through a summary of redemptive history and a recounting of the sacrifice of Christ that has brought us to this family meal. Through the priest, we hear Christ's invitation to his feast even as we look forward to the great hope of its future culmination in the wedding supper of the Lamb where we shall see our Lord face to face.

Joyful Sending. Our feasting in Communion is accompanied by songs of praise, and then, giving thanks for what the Lord has done, we ask him in the post-Communion prayer to "send us out to do the work you have given us do, to love and serve you with gladness and singleness of heart." With this prayer still wet on our lips, we hear the comforting words of blessing in the Benediction to remind us that as we go out in mission Jesus will be with us always until the very end of the age. With praise and a rousing final dismissal, we are sent out rejoicing in the power of the Spirit to love and serve the Lord.

Next week, after six days of serving Jesus in the world, we come again in the same way and in the same cycle we gather by grace, hear the Word, respond to the Word proclaimed, are filled by the Word visible, and are sent out for a week of service with the assurance of Christ's blessing. Each week we rehearse the life of the disciple. Each week in corporate worship we recite and participate in the gospel. Every day in the Daily Office we do the same. This repetition, this constant reminder of who God is and who we are in light of his gospel, lays the foundation of our new church plant and shapes our identity for the missional life of the church. Our discipleship and mission through the liturgy are holistically communal, physical, spiritual, emotional, and active.

Question: But isn't the liturgy only for older people? Don't the young people want lights and lasers?

The same generation that we claim is saturated with a shallow technology-driven perspective and will need the new and flashy to feel connected, is the generation that is buying John Coltrane and Miles Davis on vinyl for a more authentic way of experiencing a higher culture. They are dumping their automatic coffee machines and making coffee through pour-overs or in a manual French press. They have all used a microwave and realize that faster is not always better. They carry all the flash they need in the devices in their pockets. They are searching for a timelessness, a transcendence, a realness, that is rooted in something deeper, truer, and bigger than themselves or the gleam of the culture. God has placed this need in their hearts, and the liturgy and sacramental way of being speak directly to this longing as deep cries out to deep. Our liturgy makes us poised to reach this generation for Christ.

This does not mean the entertainment-driven megachurches are all going to drain into our liturgical churches and the young lost will come running to your church plant like the opening of a new Chick-fil-A. Most people are not consciously aware that they need or want what we are providing, and when first exposed to it many find the tangible presence of the ancient unnerving for reasons they cannot immediately articulate. Like the crackle of the vinyl for the uninitiated, liturgy and tradition can seem like something that we should have left behind in our societal progress.

The antidote to this lingering, anxious ambivalence is for your church to tangibly live what it proclaims in the liturgy. The people we are trying to reach have been fooled by gimmicks and are bombarded with marketing of products and services promising a better life now. They come testing to see if the call of the church and the allure of the liturgy are any different. Will they deliver, or is this another empty promise? Your vibrant, communal life brings credibility to our ancient practice in the eyes of a modern person as you show that this is not unthinking, ignorant tradition. When others witness the experiential and deep community of formation created by liturgical practice, what previously had seemed outdated or foreign will feel like a new discovery of a well-kept secret. Prove the words of the liturgy to be true with the actions of a generous and loving community. "Be doers of the word, and not hearers only, deceiving yourselves" (James 1:22).

However, the liturgy itself tells us that its recitation is not the end goal: "We pray, give us such an awareness of your mercies, that with truly thankful hearts we may show forth your praise, not only with our lips, but in our lives, by giving up our selves to your service, and by walking before you in holiness and righteousness all our days."[13] Liturgical practice is counter-cultural. It subversively challenges many unconscious assumptions of the culture, calling people to reject the ideas that bigger is always better, newer is more advanced, trendy is authoritative. This transition takes time for discovery, observation, acceptance, appreciation, and spread.

The Liturgy Calls for Action

The liturgy is not meant merely to be observed. Again and again, both subtly and overtly, through proclamation, exhortation, and example the liturgy calls for responsive action. Those who do not yet believe are beckoned to repent, believe, and be baptized. Those who are followers of Christ are called to an enlivened faith that results in worship and mission. Take, for example, the words of absolution in the service of Morning Prayer:

> Almighty God, the Father of our Lord Jesus Christ, desires not the death of sinners, but that they may turn from their wickedness and live. He has empowered and commanded his ministers to pronounce to his people, being penitent, the absolution and remission of their sins. He pardons and absolves all who truly repent and genuinely believe his holy Gospel. For this reason, we beseech him to grant us true repentance and his Holy Spirit, that our present deeds may please him, the rest of our lives may be pure and holy, and that at the last we may come to his eternal joy; through Jesus Christ our Lord. Amen.[14]

The presentation of the gospel as a call to repentance and the assurance of forgiveness is grounded within the life of the church. Its intended result is lives that are active in pleasing God, pursuing holiness, and living in hope until the return of Christ. The liturgy does not leave the newly-repentant sinner confused as to what happens next.

The very fact that the liturgy is experienced in community is inviting. Those who come and witness a gathering of people sharing intimacy with God and one another will long to be a part of such a number. Jesus said the world will know that we are his disciples by the witness of how we love one another (John 13:35). If our loving community proves our status as disciples, the liturgy defines what a disciple is and does, and reaches out on mission to invite the uninitiated to join this new life.

The Liturgy Provides Sacred Rhythms That Define Our Story

When I was growing up, I loved the movie *The Last Starfighter*. Discontented with his seemingly aimless life, Alex Rogan finds escape in playing an arcade game called *Starfighter*. After he beats the high score of the game, aliens come and take him away revealing that *Starfighter* was actually a training simulator to recruit pilots in their intergalactic war. Alex goes on to save the universe (sorry to spoil it, but I believe the statute of limitations has expired for movies from 1984). Alex's mundane life became full of meaning and purpose, and I wanted that too. I remember concentrating on games like *Space Invaders*, driven by my conviction that when I was the top player a government vehicle would pull up in front of the house to ask my help in defending the earth against the hidden alien threat. Not that I needed much motivation to play video games, but now I also had moral justification to tell my mom that I couldn't do my chores because I was training to save the world.

Stories are how we understand our reason for living. If our career is our story, then our priorities and actions are ordered to advance that narrative. If our existence is only for the pursuit of pleasure, then we find value in binge drinking, sex without commitment, or shopping on Amazon. Our understanding of our story determines what thoughts, actions, pursuits, and morals have meaning and purpose to us.

The liturgy sets the interactive story of Christ at the foundation of our shared lives. We progress through the church calendar each year remembering and reenacting the events of the life of Christ. We do not simply observe the calendar, we live it.

The church calendar is meant for us to make the story of Christ our own. We remember what he has done and shape our lives in response. Advent gives us a reason to live with expectation as we look back to the time before the first coming of the Messiah, and to engage in preparation as we look forward to his coming again. Christmas celebrates the incarnation of Christ and calls for us to investigate how Christ comes into our lives and how we incarnate his gospel. Epiphany follows the growth of Christ and recalls the events that began his public ministry, as we are called to grow as disciples and minister to the world. Lent mirrors the time of Christ in the wilderness, reminding us of the depth of sin and calling us to repentance. Holy Week celebrates the passion of Christ, calling us to be crushed by the price he paid in his sacrifice on the cross, mourning his death, and bursting forth in resounding joy over his victory in the resurrection. We are then called to live as Easter Christians, with our reality formed entirely by our new identity in Christ—the old has gone, the new has come! We follow Christ through his ascension, heightening our awareness of his abiding presence at the right hand of God. Then we are filled by the Holy Spirit at Pentecost. As we recall the power that descended upon the disciples from on high and their response in bold and passionate mission, we are empowered for our call to the same mission today in our communities. Ordinary time invites consistency in our shared life so we do not see our story only as a series of mountaintops, but rather as a long obedience in the same direction: eager in service, longing for the return of Christ, but content in his grace.

People today are starved for story. Our culture tells them to throw off tradition and family and put on an ambiguous freedom. This life without substance necessitates distraction, which is why we cannot get our faces out of our screens. The hollowness of our existence also makes us search for a cause that brings meaning to our lives, which is why there is so much passion around politics.

We are looking for the true story of human history—why we are here, how we should live, and where we are headed. The story of Christ gives us substance by showing us how intentionally God created us, and how much our Father values us and has pursued us through the Son. We have an identity as members of the church. We have a purpose, participating in Christ's redemptive work in the world. We have hope and a trajectory, as we long for the coming of Christ and the continuation of our story with our Creator in the new heavens and the new earth. The liturgical calendar shapes our understanding of time and our place within it by orienting our stories around the story of Christ.

Through our liturgical structure, the gospel story saturates our every moment. On a macro level, the church calendar moves us through seasons. On a micro level, the Daily Office constantly calls us away from false narratives that easily distract us.

The fictional story of *The Last Starfighter* triggered my imagination as a young boy, convinced me that a greater conspiracy was afoot, and transformed regular playing of *Space Invaders* into a story I knew was progressing all around me. How much more then can the true story of redemptive history, carried along by the power of the Holy Spirit, arouse our passion for liturgy, life, worship, and mission.

Enfold the life of your church plant into the great story of the church calendar. The church calendar is often one of the most easily accessible and least threatening ways of introducing a rhythm of life. Help remove a sense of isolation by introducing the church calendar as a way of connecting the story of your new church plant to the ancient and ongoing work of Christ.

Laying a Liturgical Foundation

One of the most common questions I am asked by new planters is how to introduce the liturgy to a group of people who have no liturgical background. Not only are we inviting people to invest in the mostly foreign enterprise of starting a new church, but we are also introducing what is often a new way of being the church. One day their lives are seemingly predictable, and the next they are being challenged to walk through a wardrobe into a land where they are a domestic missionary accompanied by a robed cleric who is teaching them ancient communal recitations. It can be a shock to the system.

Give the people time and space, as this concept may be quite new. Give them explanation—but even more so, show them a need they perhaps didn't know they had. As Antoine de Saint-Exupéry is purported to have said, "If you want to build a ship, don't drum up the men to gather wood, divide the work, and give orders. Instead, teach them to yearn for the vast and endless sea." Your goal as a missionary is to evoke in your people a longing for Jesus. The liturgy then becomes something they hunger for because it both elicits that longing within and assists in their pursuit of the one for whom they long.

Start slow, perhaps with regular Compline or Evening Prayer. Take the time to answer questions about liturgy. Show how the liturgy helps us apply the Scripture to our work of church planting—how it is an enacted ecclesiology, revealing how we live out the Scripture's definition of church. Teach the practice of the Daily Office and challenge individuals to try it for two weeks and then come back and discuss the experience with you. Explain the church calendar and how we revolve our lives around the story of Christ.

If your people do not yet trust the liturgy, they at least trust you, so use the relational equity you have with them to allow you to guide them into liturgical practice. When you gather an initial group, study the Scripture and show how the liturgy gives you the ability to use the words you have studied in corporate worship. Your patience is worth the effort, for you are building a lasting foundation in your church plant for the sustained and focused work of mission and discipleship for years to come.

Liturgy is a gift to the mission of the church and the work of church planting. The practice of liturgy presents a clear vision to your people of what you are planting and how you are planting it, since the purpose of both the liturgy and the church is to proclaim the holiness of God, shape the hearts and minds of the people of God, and invite others to join the community. Recognizing the importance of the liturgy in forming and shaping disciples and your church planting work, I encourage you to be informed and intentional in your liturgical practice so that your church and those who are raised up under your care may perfectly love God and worthily magnify his holy name through Christ our Lord.

A Note to Non-Anglican Readers:

In your tradition you may not have an equally overt liturgy as we do on the Anglican Church, but you still have a liturgy. The structure of your worship service, what you choose to include or exclude, the particular phrases you use, the themes you stress—it is all liturgy. Liturgy is unavoidable. So, the question for you is how to leverage liturgy to properly form your people and praise your God. Think through how you will be intentional in letting the Scripture shape your communal life and how you can create rhythms that provide a sense of sacred time. Even if you don't use the Prayer Book in your services, how can you pay more attention to crafting good liturgies that utilize the Scripture for use in worship? How will your worship teach your congregation and help them see the beauty of Jesus? How can you ground your local planting work in the great story of Redemptive History? Finally, search your heart for places where you are tempted to dress up the gospel to make it more culturally palatable rather than trusting that the gospel in its pure unadulterated form is more than capable of changing hearts and lives.

CHAPTER 8

....

Preaching in Word and Sacrament

Give me one hundred preachers who fear nothing but sin, and desire nothing but God, and I care not a straw whether they be clergymen or laymen; such alone will shake the gates of hell and set up the kingdom of heaven on Earth.

—*John Wesley*

SUMMARY: Preaching the pure Word of God is essential to the work of church planting. Preaching in such a way that is both faithful and missionally effective requires reflection on both the office and the message.

Anglicanism places preaching the Word alongside celebrating the sacraments as the two pillars that carry the very definition of church. Put simply, if you are not preaching the pure Word of God, you are not planting a church. Preaching is the primary vehicle through which God has chosen to proclaim the good news to the lost. The New Testament is rife with preaching and church history continues the theme.

Anglicanism has a history of powerful and effective preachers. Of course, we share the history of the church catholic and look primarily to Jesus and the apostles for the example of the finest preachers. We also claim leaders like John of Antioch, nicknamed Chrysostom meaning "golden-mouthed," who said, "I cannot let a day pass without feeding you with the treasures of the Scriptures." Anglican bishop Hugh Latimer was one of the standout preachers during the English Reformation, and many others have followed their example throughout our history, such as George Whitfield, Charles Simeon, and John Stott. To this day, all three orders of ordained leaders in our church (bishops, priests, and deacons) take vows to preach faithfully as part of their call to ministry.

Thomas Cranmer, in his introduction to his first Book of Homilies, states, "The Word of God, which is the only food of the soul, and that most excellent light that we must walk by, in this our most dangerous pilgrimage, should at all convenient times be preached unto the people, that thereby they may both learn their duty towards God, their Prince, and their neighbors, according to the mind of the Holy Ghost, expressed in the Scriptures."[1] He goes on to say that poor preaching is dangerous, for without good preaching we cannot "avoid the manifold enormities which heretofore by false doctrine have crept into the Church of God" and, "great inconveniences might arise and ignorance still be maintained."[2] The same is true in our church plants. We must reflect on our preaching—both the office and the message—with great care. More than church attendance is at stake, but the very souls of those we have been called to reach.

The Office of Preaching

The office of preaching must be well-considered before one takes up this mantle. Hugh Latimer said, "This office of preaching is the office of salvation." He continues, "For St. Paul saith, 'It hath pleased God to save believers by the foolishness of preaching (1 Corinthians 1:21).' How can men then believe but by and through the office of preaching? Preachers are Christ's vicars."[3]

The word *vicar* comes from the same Latin word that gives us *vicarious.* Latimer is saying that Christ speaks to his people vicariously through the preacher. This means preaching is no trivial pursuit, nor one to be approached frivolously. If we recognize that we are speaking the very words of Christ to the people as if Christ himself were speaking to them, "God making his appeal through us" (2 Corinthians 5:20), and if our hope is that as the lips of Christ move so do our lips move, we should tremble in fear! Who can stand under such a weight? If the preacher is Christ's vicar and the preacher's office is the office of salvation, this responsibility cannot be taken lightly. There is no room for haughtiness, or lack of preparation, or negligence in prayer. Those who are qualified for this task are made so only by their deep recognition of their own dependence upon the same grace they will be preaching to others.

Former Archbishop of Canterbury Donald Coggan said of preaching, "Here is the miracle of the divine economy, that between the forgiveness of God and sin of man stands the preacher. That between the provision of God and the need of man stands the preacher. That between the truth of God and the quest of man stands the preacher. It is his task to link human sin to forgiveness, human need to divine omnipotence, human search to divine revelation."[4]

I daresay that with such significance placed upon the office of preacher, we must consider it greater than our calling as a church planter. I am not suggesting we hide behind long sermon preparation to the neglect of the many tasks of church planting, but I am reminding planters that the purpose of preaching is not growing your audience—it is delivering the pure Word of God. Spirit-filled preaching does often draw a crowd, as the quote popularly attributed to John Wesley says: "Light yourself on fire with passion and people will come from miles to watch you burn." But while faithful preaching is of utmost importance to planting, and the skill of the preacher matters, I want to dispel any notion that preaching is merely part of a formula for attracting a crowd. In fact, faithful gospel preaching sometimes has the opposite effect.

Much of modern Western church planting is presumed at its core to come down to entertaining communication, excellence in music, and effectiveness in advertising. There is a coolness factor, a hunger to be the "it" church of the moment that wows with its creativity and singularity and is quite often centered around the charisma and communication skills of the preacher.

Many who enter into church planting in the West dream of the big stage, the face mic, and the large crowds of listeners. The Anglican way tempers that celebrity impulse. Anglican priest and poet George Herbert said the preacher should seek to be known not as "witty, or learned, or eloquent, but holy."[5] Latimer said the preacher must "beware of vain-glory and only seek to edify and to profit their audience as Christ did."[6]

So yes, preaching is of extreme importance, but the preacher should not be the star of the show. That is reserved for the person of Christ. Engaging in liturgical worship helps guard against this danger.

The gospel is proclaimed multiple times throughout the liturgy and is seen visibly in the sacraments. The Word of God is read at length. The people pray directly to the Author and Sustainer of their faith. The preacher's role is to be part of a greater whole that pushes the hearer to the Savior, not to solely carry the burden of the worship service. This is why preaching holds a prominent place within the structure of the liturgy, but is not its sum total. It is the preacher's joy to know that the pressure for the proclamation of the Word is not his alone.

In practice, I have seen Anglican churches where the liturgy is truncated to fit within the shadow of the sermon and I have also seen the sermon reduced to a piddly, vapid, insipidly useless thing that simply must be endured in order to get back to the liturgy. Both approaches are unhelpful at best, and surely not in line with Anglican thought and practice. Word and sacrament, liturgy and preaching, should all be highly valued and given their proper place. In synergy, they are a formidable force for presenting the gospel.

Preaching inevitably draws some attention to the preacher, but the duty of the office of preacher should be to place Christ firmly in the sight of the people. It should be Christ that draws the crowd or, sometimes, dismisses them as he did in John 6 when he did not give the people the loaves they desired, but invited them to know him as their source of true life. The crowd may come simply for the sweet bread of entertaining communication, but that bread will never be sufficient. The preacher must help the people realize that what they truly require is Christ, for as Peter testified in John 6:68, they can go nowhere else to receive the words of eternal life.

So, church planter, if you are entering into this task because you long for the big stage, or if your secret strategy for growth is simply to awe people by the prowess of your preaching, you must reconsider planting a church. You will not preach them in. Better preachers than you have tried. Crowds are fickle, just ask Jesus. If you gather them only by force of your personality, or your entertainment value, when you are no longer sufficient to give them what they want, they will turn on you. Preaching is not the place for celebrity. You cannot keep them coming through an endless stream of creativity and one-upping your previous sermon. It will be too much for you. It will burn you out, and it will never be enough for your people.

Still, I have rarely seen a successful church planter who was not a good communicator of the gospel. Preaching deserves significant preparation in study, prayer, and holiness of life, and those who engage in it should be given double honor, as 1 Timothy 5:17 says. I want to both elevate your consideration of the office of preacher and encourage you to realize that, although the sermon may be your most recognizable missional task, you are not the only preacher in your church. Through the liturgy, preachers of the past join their voices with you, and through the sacraments, the pure Word of God you have proclaimed is visibly seen and participated in. Preach well, preacher. Take up the mantle with significant consideration, and know that you are not alone.

The Message of Preaching

Preachers should be one-trick ponies. We must echo Paul and resolve to know nothing except "Christ and him crucified" (1 Corinthians 2:2). Although some preachers are gifted with eloquence, humor, or fervor, these attributes must not be the full substance of the sermon. Whatever methods are employed, the message must remain the same: the death and resurrection of Jesus. This is what Paul says is "of first importance" (1 Corinthians 15:3).

It is tempting in church planting to lean toward preaching sermon series on "Health in Your Marriage" or "How to Raise Happy and Healthy Children." I will not dismiss these choices out of hand, but I challenge you that health in marriage and raising kids or anything else on which you preach must be explained in light of the death and resurrection of Jesus—or you are not preaching a Christian sermon. I cannot overstate the point that every sermon must return to the crucified Christ, the need of the sinner to repent and be baptized, and the call for true believers to mature in their faith. This is the substance of every New Testament sermon and must be the central exhortation in each of ours. All roads lead to the cross and the resurrection.

I am a fan, perhaps an armchair amateur historian, of British naval history. I have always been intrigued by the leaders, the conflict, the strength, and the courage seen in the ships of the Napoleonic age. I find a good analogy for preaching in the story of the HMS *Pickle.*

In October 1805, the British met the combined fleet of the French and Spanish in battle off the coast of Spain near Cape Trafalgar. Napoleon hoped to use this fleet to invade England. In an epic battle, the British fleet led by Admiral

Lord Nelson decimated the enemy, destroying twenty-two opposing ships without losing a single British vessel. England was saved, but the battle was not without its cost. The hero Lord Nelson died after being struck by a sniper's bullet.

Small compared to the great ships of the line, the schooner HMS *Pickle* was not able to engage in the actual battle of Trafalgar. She was, however, the swiftest ship in the fleet and was therefore dispatched with all haste to bring the glorious and tragic news of victory to England. After a harrowing nine-day sail through a tremendous gale, *Pickle* made port at Falmouth, England. Her commander, Lieutenant John Lapenotière, then took the dispatches in hand and rode with such fervor that he made the journey, which normally took a week, in just thirty-seven hours after changing horses nineteen times. He delivered the news to the admiralty, and within hours it had reached the king and the people.

Nelson's flagship, the HMS *Victory*, is still with us today, and is the longest continually-commissioned warship in the world. The *Pickle*, however, was lost three years later after stoving in her bottom when she ran aground on a reef.

Preachers are the *Pickle*. We merely carry the great news of a saving victory and even the death of its hero (and in our case his resurrection) with great eagerness. Even if, in the end, we finish our task broken in our service, the victory will endure. We proclaim triumph. We announce safety. We herald freedom and the defeat of our enemies—Satan, sin, and death. We did not win the battle ourselves; the victory belongs to Christ. We simply proclaim it with our preaching.

We are compelled to great exertion by the news we bring. We preach with haste and fervency while enduring hardship and trials. Our recognition of the great news we carry, our zeal in getting it to the people, our bursting lungs as we share this secret of victory that belongs to the people—these make the message all that much more alive and urgent.

After announcing the great news, however, there are questions of details and tactics and next steps and logistics. So enters the work of teaching and instruction that follows the great announcements of preaching. The people have been saved at great cost and they ask, just as they did of Peter on Pentecost, "Brothers, what shall we do?" (Acts 2:37). The answer is the exhortation to repent, believe, be baptized, and subsequently be devoted to the apostles' teaching. Preaching, in whatever style, should be heralding the victory of Christ.

Our Preaching Must Be Biblical

One of the greatest Anglican preachers was John Stott, longtime rector of All Souls Church in Langham Place and leader in global evangelicalism. Stott said of preaching that all true Christian preaching is expository preaching. He was not referring to a particular style. He said, "To expound Scripture is to bring out of the text what is already there and expose it to view."[7] So style can vary, but all preaching should be based on the Scripture. All preaching is biblical, or it is not preaching. There is no room for showing inspirational clips from Disney movies, leading a dialogue, or simply telling cute stories. Anglicans preach from the biblical text—as should all Christians—for the Word of God is truly "profitable for teaching, for reproof, for correction, and for training in righteousness" (2 Timothy 3:16).

Our Preaching Must Be Catholic

Anglican preaching, like all true preaching, is catholic in that we teach no new thing. We are stewards of the faith as this church has received it, and witnesses to the work of

Christ. I love that in most of our liturgical services the Nicene Creed follows the sermon. Its placement there allows for the confession of faith by the people in response to the Word proclaimed, and its serves as accountability for all that the preacher has just purported to be truth. We can preach no better word than that which the Nicene Creed summarizes. Preaching is not about laboring to bring some new innovation, angle, or approach. Rather, it is to faithfully carry on the tradition of those who have preached before. You're a church planter, so you are innovative and entrepreneurial. Not here, you are not. Here the innovation of your content is restrained by faithfulness, even as your appropriate creativity in communication is encouraged.

Our Preaching Must Be Instructional

Although there is a difference between preaching and teaching, there is a profound overlap in the two disciplines. New Testament preaching recounts the actions of Christ and the truth of Scripture, and brings thought and behavior under the sovereignty of Christ. Our preaching is not simply for the stirring of emotions, but for the mind as well. Hopefully, your church plant is reaching the lost while simultaneously strengthening the found. The instruction of your preaching plays a significant role in both tasks, and each requires depth in your preaching. Bishop Latimer, our consummate guide in this chapter, said, "The preaching of the Word of God unto the people is called meat [that is solid, daily food]: Scripture calleth it meat; not strawberries that come but once a year, and tarry not long, but are soon gone; but it is meat, it is no dainties."[8]

Do not underestimate the biblical illiteracy of our day, nor how much people misunderstand the gospel, the church, and what it means to be a disciple of Christ. Paul's instructions to Timothy describe well our current task:

> I charge you in the presence of God and of Christ Jesus, who is to judge the living and the dead, and by his appearing and his kingdom: preach the word; be ready in season and out of season; reprove, rebuke, and exhort, with complete patience and teaching. For the time is coming when people will not endure sound teaching, but having itching ears they will accumulate for themselves teachers to suit their own passions, and will turn away from listening to the truth and wander off into myths. As for you, always be sober-minded, endure suffering, do the work of an evangelist, fulfill your ministry. (2 Timothy 4:1–5)

Timothy is called to be ready to preach and instruct even in the midst of opposition and suffering. So is the call to preaching in a modern church plant.

You cannot assume knowledge in your listeners, nor should you be surprised at opposition. You are not only inviting people to the feast, but you are also teaching them about each dish and how to use the utensils. If you are going to use a strange theological word, explain it. If you are going to reference another story in the Scripture, summarize it, since many people in your church will not be familiar with even the most basic of biblical stories. If you are going to tell them that Paul said something, tell them who Paul is. They are more familiar with Paul McCartney than Paul of Tarsus. Simply say, "Paul who was a leader in the early church and a missionary, and who wrote much of the New Testament said . . ." In your preparation, listen in advance to every word as both a believer and an unbeliever might hear them.

When you preach in a church plant, you are setting the tone and DNA for the future shape of the church. You must preach and teach to both gain trust in your ministry leadership and to set expectations for the life of the new church. You must establish the Word of God as its foundation and chief arbitrator. You are also teaching your people how to listen to the Word of God preached and inwardly digest what they hear. Preach into life the vision of the church to be the church as described in the Scripture. Do not be afraid to preach the unadulterated Word of God, and never compromise the Word of God for the sake of growth.

Our Preaching Must Be Exhortational

Preaching is also in part about the stirring of emotions. All Christian preaching should be exhortational. Our preaching should be a call to action: repent, believe, and be baptized. The goal of our preaching is transformation. We desire to see the people cut to the heart by the gospel and respond with vigor.

Charles Spurgeon, known as The Prince of Preachers, described the preaching of George Whitfield during a revival in Ireland: "He preached on, now thundering like Boanerges [son of thunder], and then comforting like Barnabas [son of encouragement], and the work spread, and no tongue can tell the great things that God did under that one sermon of Whitfield. Not even the sermon of Peter on the day of Pentecost was equal to it."[9] Oh, that there were more Whitfields in our day! We must preach boldly with passion, challenge, and comfort. We must lay upon the people the heavy weight of their sin, that they may know the joy of its release through the grace of Christ. They must know the succor of the Lord and the scandal of the cross. We preach for change with words of power, of pleading, and of peace.

Preaching in a church plant, or in any other pulpit, you must always preach as if unbelievers are in the room. If you do not prepare your sermons with the unbeliever in mind, your people will wonder if it is safe to invite their unbelieving friends since you do not preach to anyone but Christians. I have also committed and witnessed the mistake of the preacher realizing too late that there are visitors in the congregation and attempting to change the sermon on the fly to suit the potential unbeliever. This never turns out well and usually results in awkward and forced exhortation.

To preach for conversion and discipleship you must prepare your sermons each week with application that answers, "So what?" After all your exegesis, lashing, comforting, humor, and passion, what does this Scripture mean for the believer and what does this Scripture mean for the unbeliever? In fact, it is an effective homiletical tool to answer these questions explicitly: "So, what does this mean for you if you are a believer? Here is how you apply this truth of Scripture . . ." or "Here is what I hope you take from this message today if you are not yet a believer in Christ . . ." Never assume that you are always preaching to only Christians, or your assumption will become a self-fulfilling prophecy.

Our Preaching Must Be Contextualized

Jesus, the master of all preachers, was particularly adept at bringing the great truths of God to the people in a way they could understand. Put aside for a moment the parables he purposefully meant to be enigmatic. Jesus spoke clearly about fishermen and shepherds and farmers. He chose a language, a style, and content that was meaningful to the people in first-century Israel. This has been the duty of the preacher throughout history.

In a sermon preached in front of King Edward, Bishop Latimer recalled how he had previously failed to appropriately consider his preaching when asked to preach to Edward's father, King Henry VIII. Latimer said to Edward, "I would desire your Grace to give me leave to discharge my conscience; give me leave to frame my doctrine according to mine audience: I had been a very dolt to have preached so at the borders of your realm, as I preach before your Grace."[10] What those in the country needed to hear and how they needed to hear it was different from in the royal court. What Latimer referred to as framing our doctrine according to our audience is what we would now call contextualizing.

Contextualization does not mean preaching only what people want to hear. Contextualization means speaking in the language of the people—not confusingly above their heads or insultingly below their intellect, but in a way that grabs their ear in order to bring the unchanging truth of the gospel to the changing culture in which we live. Kings and country squires, urbanites and suburbanites, college professors and the illiterate, people of all races and socioeconomic status and geographic locations all need the same gospel of Jesus, but preachers must do the work of communicating it appropriately.

Who are you preaching to in your church plant? How does the gospel speak to the hopes, dreams, sin, and celebration of the culture you are in? What are contemporary examples of shepherds, fisherman, and farmers in your city or town? Do not write the sermon in your head or craft it to impress your former homiletics teacher. How do you properly convey the renown of Christ and the urgency of the gospel to the ears he has given you to speak into?

Answering these questions will take some trial and error. I have preached all over North America and in many locations throughout the globe. Certain rhetorical strategies, attempts at humor, examples, metaphors, and specific points of application work powerfully in some locations and fall flat in others. Even accents and vocabulary can be barriers. The difference between preaching in the military setting of Fayetteville, North Carolina (the location of my first church plant) and suburban Atlanta (where I planted next) was like preaching in two different worlds—words that made military men want to take the hill made soccer moms quite uncomfortable.

You will make mistakes as you contextualize to your community. You will be a dolt like Latimer, but keep preaching and remain diligent in contending for the truth of the gospel.

Our Preaching Must Be Dependent

No matter our skill, experience, or passion as preachers, we cannot force conversion or transformation. Even Paul himself was ineffective in some cities and saw great harvest in others. Salvation is ultimately God's work. Latimer said preachers can "do no more but call; God is he that must bring in; God must open the hearts. . . . God must work, God must do the thing inwardly."[11] Our preaching must come from an abiding love for Christ and a hunger for those who do not know him—in order to introduce the two. Before we turn these passions loose on the crowds, however, we must first take them to the Lord in prayer. Our preaching preparation must not only be structured through study but founded on prayer to ask God to move mightily through our preaching. You will never convert a soul through a witty turn of phrase unless that wit is saturated in the Holy Spirit and carried along by his power. Hear me, because you will forget in the busyness that is church planting: preaching is inseparable from prayer.

• • • •

As a church planter, I pray that you will become a student of the craft of preaching. Learn at the feet of the greats who have gone before and currently carry the torch. You will find in all the shining stars of preaching a deep love of Christ and an intimate knowledge of Scripture. Both flow from these preachers effortlessly, because they spend so much time with each. You will see also that these preachers are fearless. Latimer was burned at the stake for his preaching, but he was a preacher to the last. As he was lashed to the stake back-to-back with his friend Nicholas Ridley, it is reported that he said, "Be of good comfort, Master Ridley, and play the man; we shall this day light such a candle by God's grace in England as shall never be put out!" Although I pray your preaching does not end on a lighted pyre, I do pray that through your bold, faithful, and fearless preaching of the Word you will light a bright candle in your community.

A Note to Non-Anglican Readers:

I believe that most of this chapter should translate to other traditions without much explanation, although depending on the place of the sacraments in your church, you may need to adjust some of what we have discussed here. In the end, however, the Word is universal in its truth, and our proclamation needs emphasis, care, boldness, and prayerful preparation no matter our denomination.

CHAPTER 9

. . . .

The Efficacy of the Sacraments

Since the sacraments are a means of God's grace, it is God who is the chief actor in the sacraments and not we. Grace, in and through the sacraments, is his gift, his favor shown to us.

— *Bishop John Rodgers*

SUMMARY: God is actively at work through his sacraments. For this reason, the sacraments should be central to our mission work.

Ruby was a glorious Southern Black woman. Mid to late fifties, she was short in stature but quite round in the middle. She liked to describe herself as "comfy." Ruby smiled all the time, and she had a small gap between her front teeth that seemed to act as a joy pressure valve so that if she got too giddy some of the happiness could escape through the opening before her head exploded in a shower of mirth. If she found something funny, first she'd start to whistle through that little dental portal, and then she would throw her head back and her whole body would convulse as she filled the room with raspy howls that echoed off the walls. If you could get her going in a public place, people all around would turn to stare, but they couldn't help but smile. She could laugh better than anyone I have ever known.

Ruby was our neighbor when my wife and I first moved to Fayetteville, North Carolina, to plant a church. Karen and I were in our early twenties, both blond, and quite Caucasian. Ruby called us her "little White friends." We spent a lot of time together.

Our friendship began simply as we were trying to get to know our neighbors and went over to introduce ourselves shortly after we moved in. Ruby invited us into her small home, and we sat in her living room and talked. That first day we spent a couple of hours just "visiting," as we say in the South.

These visits became more frequent, and we learned that Ruby hadn't been a part of the church since she was a child. Oh, she believed in Jesus, and she'd tell you that quickly, but she couldn't really tell you what that meant. So Ruby started to come with us to our worship services in our brand-new church plant. She'd ride in with us two hours before the service started to help get things ready, or she'd just sit there and talk with us as we worked.

Ruby wasn't sure if she had been baptized. She thought she probably had been but didn't have any recollection of it. Now she was hearing about this new, immediate, deep, ancient faith we were teaching. She was happy to serve, sit, and listen, but she shied away from deeper discussion about repentance, belief, and baptism. At the Eucharist each Sunday she sat on the front row and smiled and waved at everyone with that infectious, beautiful smile she had. By the time folks reached the front to receive the sacrament, they were beaming. Ruby was contagious. But she never came up front herself. Until one day she did.

I had preached a normal sermon that Sunday as I had every week for the six months Ruby had been coming with us. I don't remember it being particularly spectacular or passionate—just simply exegeting the Scripture and presenting the gospel. Sermon. Creed. Prayers of the People. Confession. Absolution. Peace. Doxology. Eucharistic Prayer. "These are the gifts of God for the people of God." Then there was Ruby standing first in line with her hands out.

Now, I didn't know what to do. I was twenty-two years old. I had only been ordained a matter of weeks. I learned in seminary that baptism is required before coming to the Table of the Lord. I knew that. Ruby knew that. We didn't know if Ruby had been baptized. What should I do? Tell her no and sit her down? What would happen if I gave her Communion? Would she burst into flame? Would *I* burst into flame? But clearly something was happening here. And she thought maybe she was baptized, right? So, in a moment of spontaneous decision, I sort of turned my head slightly to the side, tossed the bread into her outstretched hands, and leaned back in case she ignited or withered away like a vampire in the sunlight. But she didn't. She wept. She ate that bread with deep sincerity, received the chalice, sipped the wine, and started to whistle. Her pressure release valve was activating. But instead of laughing she cried.

She wailed like only a robust, beautiful, Black, Southern woman can wail. It filled the room. It reverberated off the walls. She continued to moan and cry throughout the rest of the service, so I had to yell to lead the post-Communion prayer and give the Benediction. Remember, I was twenty-two and pretty inexperienced. I was not sure exactly what was happening. Was the bread slowly eating its way back out of her unbaptized stomach? Do I acknowledge this now or wait until later? I had visions of her looking at me like a son of Sceva and saying, "I know Jesus and Paul, but who are you?" and I'd be run out of the church plant naked and bleeding.

We sang the final song (loudly, to be heard over the continued wailing), and after I dismissed the people, I went and sat down next to the still-weeping Ruby. After removing a wad of soaked tissues the size of a softball, I took her hand. "Ruby," I said, "it seems like the Lord might be doing something in you right now."

Please refrain from being in awe of my brilliant observation.

I'll never forget what happened next. She looked at me very sternly and suddenly stopped crying. She turned toward me and said, "Dan, I've heard you preach over and over again about Jesus, and you did a good job." *Thanks*, I thought. She continued, "But today something happened. It was that food!" She yelled it again, "That food! When you gave me that food and I put it into my mouth, something changed in me. I don't know what it was, but I'm different now. The words you have been saying started making sense. Jesus is real now."

I was stunned. God had worked through the feeble preaching of a kid in his early twenties, and actualized the Word proclaimed through the Word visible. The mysterious presence of Jesus in the Eucharist had filled Ruby with a certainty of the promises of his salvation. Ruby and I prayed together. We talked about repentance, and she prayed for Jesus to forgive her sins. She asked him to fill her with his Holy Spirit. She wept and laughed. Other people from the church plant joined us and we prayed, and wept, and laughed together. Not long after that we conditionally baptized Ruby, which is a provision in the Prayer Book where if it is uncertain whether or not a person has been baptized, they can be baptized again by inserting the phrase "If this person has not been previously baptized, we baptize you . . ." She went under the water and came up sputtering and laughing.

Soon Ruby started to invite her friends and family. On any given Sunday in our small, new church plant amongst the mainly White congregation you would see a few rows of beautiful Black faces dressed in big hats, brightly colored dresses, and zoot suits with pocket squares fanning themselves during the service. Ruby's family moved a year or so later, but the story of her conversion through Word and sacrament and Spirit left an indelible mark on our church, on me, and of course on Ruby's life.

As church planters, there are several things we can learn from this experience:

God Works through the Sacraments

Anglicans believe, as have the vast majority of Christians throughout all of history, that the sacraments are more than just a public profession of faith and a memorial meal. We believe God is actively at work through them to affect the recipient. The sacraments are not simply moments of human action, but also of divine initiative. Put another way, the sacraments are a *means of grace*, meaning an instrument through which grace is bestowed. Grace is not simply celebrated, it is given. William Tyndale, most prominently known for his Bible translation, said, "The sacraments which Christ ordained preach God's Word unto us, and therefore justify and minister the Spirit to them that believe."[1] Something mysterious happens at baptism. We don't know how it works in the cosmic order of things, but somehow a washing of the soul takes place. The mysterious presence of the Lord in the Eucharist works to sanctify and empower the believer. God is at work through the sacraments in the life of the believer.

Because God Is Working, the Sacraments Are Central to Mission

God is redeeming the world. The church is God's agent of that mission. The sacraments have been given to the church by Jesus himself. So, follow this reasoning: if mission is what God is doing, and God is doing something efficacious through the sacraments he gave to the church, then isn't it logical that the sacraments advance his work of mission?

Jesus said he "came to seek and to save the lost" (Luke 19:10), and this is the mission the church carries on. Anglican evangelist Michael Green taught that the word *saved* is used in the Scripture in the past tense (I *was* saved from the penalty of sin), the present tense (I *am being* saved from the power of sin), and the future tense (I *will be* saved from the presence of sin).[2] Theologians call this *justification* (the one-time work of Jesus on the cross forgives and cancels our all our sins), *sanctification* (although our sins are forgiven, we are still sinners, but the Holy Spirit is at work within us making us holy), and *glorification* (when Jesus returns sin itself will be destroyed). Salvation is both complete and a continuing activity. The sacramental life of the church reflects this reality.

PAST	PRESENT	FUTURE
Saved from sin's **penalty**	Being saved from sin's **power**	Will be saved from sin's **presence**
Justification *One-time* cancellation of sin	**Sanctification** *Ongoing* growth in holiness and victory over sin	**Glorification** *Still-to-come* total destruction of sin
Baptism	**Eucharist**	**New Heavens & New Earth**

Baptism is the sacrament of justification. We are baptized only once because justification is at once complete. In baptism we die to sin, Jesus washes us clean, and we experience resurrection to a new life as we emerge from the waters. This new life is lived as a part of the people of God, sharing in the life and mission of the church. Just listen to the charge we give to the newly baptized in our liturgy: "We receive you into the fellowship of the Church. Confess the faith of Christ crucified, proclaim his resurrection, and share with us in the royal priesthood of all his people."[3] The first word of the church upon welcoming the dripping-wet new believer is a call to mission—confess and proclaim!

Something mysterious and beautiful has taken place in the moment of baptism. I do not know the details of the timeline to say when justification has actually taken place. Was it when the person confessed and believed? Was it in the waters of baptism? This is an unimportant chicken-or-egg question that is easily put to rest by understanding that God is not bound by our perception of time and space. What we see in the Scripture is that justification is inextricably bound to baptism. In the first Christian sermon ever preached, Peter reveals that a proper response to the gospel is repentance and baptism (Acts 2:37–38). Or read Paul when he says, "We were buried therefore with him by baptism into death, in order that, just as Christ was raised from the dead by the glory of the Father, we too might walk in newness of life" (Romans 6:4). You could also read Colossians 2:12 or 1 Peter 3:21 to see that in the Scripture God connects justification and baptism—and so should we. God acts in the waters of baptism. If mission is introducing people to God, and if discipleship begins with a personal and corporate relationship with God, then let's immerse people in him.

The *Eucharist* is the sacrament of sanctification. We routinely return to the communal Table of grace to "proclaim the Lord's death until he comes" (1 Corinthians 11:26). We see his broken body in the bread, we taste his poured-out blood in the wine, we receive him by faith into our very being, and we share it all as the unified church. This is the gospel visible. He has not given us a mission as the church and then left us to our own devices. He is present with us in the Eucharist, actively strengthening us and advancing us in the process of sanctification and the work of mission. Thomas Cranmer said:

> Our savior Christ hath not only set forth these things most plainly in his holy Word, that we may hear them with our ears; but he hath also ordained one visible sacrament of spiritual regeneration in water, and another visible sacrament of spiritual nourishment in bread and wine; to the intent that as much as is possible for man we may see Christ with our eyes, smell him at our nose, taste him with our mouths, grope

> [that is, grasp] him with our hands, and perceive him with all our senses. For as the Word of God preached putteth Christ into our ears; so likewise these elements of water, bread, and wine, joined to God's Word, do after a sacramental manner, put Christ into our eyes, mouths, hands, and all our senses.[4]

Together the sacraments point to our future glorification. Part of the grace bestowed in the sacraments is for hope and perseverance in our mission work. What greater encouragement can there be than a rehearsal for the wedding supper of the Lamb! As the baptized believers gather for Communion, we see a foretaste of the heavenly banquet where we will one day rest from our labors, gathered around the throne in the new heavens and the new earth, as our defeated enemies of Satan, sin, and death are no more. In his institution of the sacrament on the night of his betrayal, Jesus looked backward to the salvific events of the Exodus, he looked around at the current moment of shared community, and he looked ahead to the promise that what was then being shared in part would one day be "fulfilled in the kingdom of God" (Luke 22:16). When we share the Eucharist in our churches, we stand at this same intersection of God's faithful past deeds, his current abiding presence, and his guaranteed future promise of glory. The sacraments give us a wonderful sample of the prize toward which we are striving to take hold. In light of these future truths, Paul tells us to "encourage one another with these words" (1 Thessalonians 4:18).

The sacraments are not arbitrary commands from the Lord. They were given as gifts to the church for the edification of his people and the pursuit of mission.

The Sacraments Call for Faithful Response to the Gospel

Proper response to the proclamation of the gospel is required. On this, the Scripture is clear. Romans 10:8–13 tells us that the heart and the mouth play a role in confessing and subsequently receiving salvation. First Corinthians 11:17–34 shows us that taking part in the sacraments without faith brings not the joyous communion we have described, but rather brings condemnation and has disastrous spiritual and physical repercussions. Whatever your understanding concerning how one comes to the point of conversion—predestination, prevenient grace, human decision—is not my concern at this moment, but the Scripture is clear that there is a requirement of a faithful response to the gospel that includes repentance, belief, and baptism before one enters into the church and receives salvation.

This is why we do not employ the Communion bread as an evangelistic tool. In other words, we do not give the bread to those who have not yet come into the church through baptism. It is also why we fence the Table as a part of our liturgy. Before the congregation is invited to take part in the Eucharist, the celebrant tells the people that the Table is open to any baptized believers in Christ and invites any unbelievers or those who are not baptized to come forward to receive a blessing. This is intentionally exclusive. Entering into the church must be done through the door God has ordained: baptism. If we are not willing to submit to his will even at the beginning of our life with him, have we truly yielded our life to him at all?

But we fence the Table with hope for the unbeliever as well. We want them to know that their exclusion is their own choice, for God has offered them the invitation of grace if they would receive it through repentance, belief, and baptism.

I like to fence the Table by saying this: "This family meal is open to anyone who is a baptized believer in Jesus Christ. If you are not yet a believer or you have not yet been baptized, I encourage you to come forward with your arms crossed and we will give you a prayer of blessing instead. If you are not comfortable with either one of those options, we encourage you to stay right where you are, but please know that we long for the day that you will come to know this Jesus that we know and share in this meal that we share."

As church planters, we want those who do not yet belong to long for the gospel and for the community of the church, and we want them to hear that God and the church long for them as well. It would be disingenuous and harmful for us to allow those who do not yet belong to Christ to feel as though they have the full benefits of the church of Christ. We want them to know that their lack of belief and baptism is keeping them away from the glories of Christ and his earthly family, so that they will be moved to desire faith and baptism in order to know Christ and be a part of the people of God. The Eucharist is for unbelievers a sacrament of their unbelief—an outward and visible sign of their inward and spiritual separation from God. Just as the sacrament strengthens Christians in their life in Christ, the Eucharist reveals to non-Christians what is absent in theirs. In this way, the sacraments are efficacious in both their giving and their withholding. This is a point worth remembering even when in our church planting we are desperate for growth.

In one of the churches I planted, there was a three-year-old girl named Anna who began to ask her mom if she could share in the bread at Communion. Her mom was hesitant.

"She's so young, she doesn't understand Communion," the mother told me.

I looked at her and asked, "Do you? Because it is certainly a mystery to me."

The mom continued to voice her concerns as Anna was a bit rambunctious. "What if she comes with a bad attitude? What if she won't stand still?"

I have to admit I was enjoying this a bit as I said to her mother, "Do you always come with a good attitude? Is your soul always still when you receive the Eucharist?" After this good-natured chastising, she nodded her head in amusement and understanding. But she still did not answer her daughter; instead, she placated her by telling her that she could take Communion when she was four.

The day came when Anna turned four. Her mother had hoped that Anna would forget, and she hadn't said anything on their way to worship that Sunday. When their family came to the front for Communion they knelt together. As I was serving the bread I came to Anna and I looked to her mother for approval, but she shook her head no. I said a prayer of blessing for Anna and served her family.

Anna began to yell, "Bread! I want to eat the bread! I want the bread that everyone else has. I'm four! I'm four now!" Her plea was not that of a spoiled child demanding a treat, but of extreme disappointment in being left out. Her mother attempted to pick her up and carry her away from the communion rail, but Anna wrapped her arms and legs around the balusters and clung there screaming "Please, can I have the bread!? I'm four!"

The congregation had, of course, noticed the commotion and were watching with rapt attention and smiling faces. I placed my hand on the mother's shoulder and I asked her if she would give me permission to serve Anna the bread. She agreed and I placed the piece of bread in her daughter's hand. I will never forget; her puffy red eyes matched the color of her red pig tails as I said to her, "This is the Body of Christ, broken for you." She smiled and ate the bread and skipped back to her seat holding her mother's hand.

I stepped to the center of the aisle and addressed the congregation. "My prayer for you, church" I said to the watching crowd, "is that all of you would long for Jesus with even half the passion of this little girl." In the desire for the sacrament, we see a desire to be part of the community of the church.

The sacraments create longing and call for decision. Will you enter the water? Will you come to the Table? Our church planting is meant to create more moments of decision, to offer more people the opportunity to be brought near. As people come to be a part of the church plant, you are asking them to make a choice to take part in the communal life of the new local church. For Anna, the bread was something bigger than just not having something to eat; it was about being part of the family. For Ruby, when she received the bread, the Word of God became real, and she longed to come deeper into the church through baptism. The sacraments are the door to our church plants.

The Missional Efficacy of the Sacraments Is Embedded in the Life of the Church. Therefore, the Sacraments Are an Essential Part of Church Planting

Let us review: God works through the sacraments, so they are central to the life of the church. The church (our ecclesiology) leads to our missiology, and both inform our methodology. So if you are planting a church, the sacraments are an essential part of your life and work. You must consider deeply the place of the sacraments in how you are pursuing church planting. How will you teach these things? How will you introduce the sacraments to the life of your new church? How will you prepare converts in the early stages of your church plant for the sacrament of baptism? In what ways does your local cultural expression integrate with your celebration of the sacraments?

I encourage you to buy a chalice early in the life of your church and take the opportunity to show why this cup is important, how it is a sign of the community to come, and how it serves to unite your people and your work around the saving grace of Jesus Christ. These things and more are important aspect of your thoughts on planting.

We Only Set the Table

Article 26 of the Thirty-Nine Articles of Religion names the source of the sacraments' efficacy as the work of Christ, not the power of the minister. It beings with the explanatory title, "Of the unworthiness of ministers which hinders not the effect of the Sacrament," and it explains that it is not the holiness of the celebrant that makes the sacrament efficacious, but rather the action of Christ.

This is important for our understanding of mission, salvation, and sanctification within our church plant setting. The sacraments serve as a visible reminder that no matter how hard we work as church planters, our efforts cannot save—but we can bring the lost to the one who can. Just as we prepare the waters for baptism so people can come and be washed, and we set the Table for the Eucharist so people can come and eat, church planting provides the conduit through which people can be introduced to Jesus Christ. In 2 Corinthians 11:2, Paul describes his planting work by saying, "I betrothed you to one husband, to present you as a pure virgin to Christ." We do not save, we present. The sacraments ground the effectiveness of planting in the redemptive work of God rather than the entrepreneurial gifting of the planter. God is actively at work in your church plant, not simply a passive observer or judge.

It is exhausting to carry the burden of mission on our own shoulders, and while surely we relate to Paul when he says he feels "the daily pressure on me of my anxiety for all the churches" (2 Corinthians 11:28), we must remember that God is the primary actor in our church planting work. Rather than asking God to bless our mission, it is much less burdensome to see ourselves as participating in God's mission.

Something mysterious happens in the sacraments that is purely God's initiative, working in the heart. Sometimes our role is just to be faithful in administering them and get out of the way. This is not to say that we do not have further significant responsibilities in educating, training, caring, preaching, and all the other aspects of the life of the church; what I am saying is that the sacraments remind us that just as the sacraments are merely normal water and food unless the presence of God is at work through them, so are all the other activities we do in the name of the church. No matter how good your teaching is, how creative your communication is, how loving you are as a pastor, how talented your musicians are, you cannot by our own efforts save a single soul or create one disciple. So bring your best, work your hardest, and prepare diligently, since God's work deserves the best we can bring. But always remember that although your sweat is sweet in the eyes of the Lord, he does not need your toil to save the world; he's already taken care of that. So, relax and come to the Table. Then also remember that you are setting the Table for those who are not yet here, so go and take the invitation to the world.

A Note to Non-Anglican Readers:

Admittedly, this chapter is steeped in Anglican sacramentology. How you interact with this content depends significantly on your approach to the nature and function of the sacraments. Clearly, Anglicans are not Memorialists, but neither are we at the other extreme end of the spectrum that would say that salvation is delivered only through the sacraments. We are somewhere in the middle combining influences from Calvin, Luther, and others, recognizing the need for both divine action and personal faith. It is what we call the Anglican Real Presence—we know that God works through the sacraments and grace is bestowed, but how that is accomplished we are content to say is a mystery. Wherever you fall on this continuum, I pray that you will be challenged by what we have explored together in this chapter and spend time contemplating the role of sacraments in your church plant.

Part 3

How Do We Plant?

CHAPTER 10

• • • •

Sacramental Church Planting

In this way does God make known his secret purpose to his Church: First he declares his mercy by his Word, then he seals it and assures it by his sacraments. In the Word we have his promises; in the sacraments we see them.

—*John Jewell, On the Sacraments*

SUMMARY: We must see our church planting as sacramental in nature. Our purpose in planting is the same as that of the sacraments—to be a physical sign of the gospel of grace, a means by which people can receive that grace, and a tangible assurance to our communities of the redemptive work of God.

Thus far our journey together has been some part ecclesiological, missiological, and liturgical. In this chapter we begin to shift our thinking a bit more methodological. I want to show how many of the themes we have been discussing directly impact our philosophy and approach to church planting. This discussion of methods is not meant to be exhaustive. I am aiming more for an introduction or a sampling of ways to apply what we have so far discussed. I pray that this section will intrigue you and motivate you to seek further training and study.

In engaging in our methodology, I first propose that we begin to see church planting itself as sacramental. It is not novel of me to expand the idea of something being sacramental beyond the two sacraments ordained by Christ. The church has often seen other works of God and activities of his people as having sacramental characteristics. Besides the evidence of the five sacramental rites, John Calvin said in his *Institutes* that the word *sacrament* "embraces generally all those signs which God has ever enjoined upon men to render them more certain and confident of the truth of his promises."[1] So, in saying that church planting should be pursued sacramentally is to say that our purpose in planting is the same as that of the sacraments, which the catechism defines as "an outward and visible sign of an inward and spiritual grace. God gives us the sign as a means whereby we receive that grace, and as a tangible assurance that we do in fact receive it." So, if our church planting is sacramental, it should be:

1. a sign
2. a means of grace
3. a tangible assurance

Physical Signs of the Gospel

The English Reformers emphasized *similitude* in the sacraments: Christ chose the particular physical signs because of their symbolic likeness to the spiritual truth they represent. Augustine said it this way: "If sacraments had not some point of real resemblance to the things of which they are the sacraments, they would not be sacraments at all."[2] We submerge in the waters of baptism due to its similarity to death and resurrection, washing and rebirth. For Communion, we use bread and wine due to their similarity to the body and blood of Christ and how they nourish our physical bodies as Christ's body nourishes our souls. Also, both the grain and the grape had to die to give us life through their sustenance just as Christ gave his life so that we may live. Of all the items that the Lord could have chosen, water, bread, and wine were not arbitrary selections—they are effective because they are similar to what they represent in form and necessity for life.

In the same way, there must be similitude in our work of church planting. Our concrete actions in the work of planting have no value unless they bear great resemblance to the truth of the gospel we are proclaiming. Therefore, in sacramental church planting we put great effort into ensuring that our planting work itself is a visible sign of the gospel we represent.

Let me give you a few examples of how our church plants can be physical signs of the gospel.

Integrity in Leadership

The ways in which the leadership of the church plant thinks, speaks, behaves, and makes decisions should all mirror the character and purposes of Christ. Although we remain sinners, we must strive under grace to ensure our motives and actions are pure. The church does not hold a place of trust in most Western communities anymore, in part due to the misbehavior of her leaders. In this culture of cynicism and suspicion we must be physical signs of Christlike integrity. Be above reproach in all things, including relationships, sexuality, social media, finances, and the truthfulness of your communication. Explain things well. Handle conflict appropriately. Be a witness of the purity and truth of the gospel. Just as Ruth learned the goodness of the "God under whose wings under whose wings [she came] to take refuge" (Ruth 2:12) through the goodness and generosity of Boaz, so should we as church planters be a sign of the character of the God we serve to those who the Lord would bring us.

Eating Together

Find ways to eat well together even outside of the sacrament of the Eucharist; have people in your home, share life together. The Bible makes a point to show that the earliest church gathered corporately and for meals together outside of the weekly worship service: "attending the temple together and breaking bread in their homes, they received their food with glad and generous hearts" (Acts 2:46). These activities correlate. As Schmemann said,

> Centuries of secularism have failed to transform eating into something strictly utilitarian. Food is still treated with reverence. . . . To eat is still something more than to maintain bodily functions. People may not understand what that "something more" is, but they nonetheless desire to celebrate it. They are still hungry and thirsty for sacramental life.[3]

When you eat together you let the joy of your dining room table or community park picnic table point toward a greater Table—with its promises of hospitality, community, and provision. I have found that sharing meals is by far the most effective means of evangelism in which I have engaged throughout my life of church planting. Eat well together around the grill and you will eat well together around the Communion Table and later at the Lord's banquet.

How You Go about Mission

We should reflect on all our means for gathering, strategizing, advertising, and organizing, making sure they are signs of the gospel in how and why we engage in them. We do not gather a crowd in our plants by Easter-egg drops from helicopters. Yes, that's unfortunately been tried. Nor do we depend on slick advertising like the card I once received in the mail for a new church plant that stated "This ain't your grandma's church!" with an orange call-out explosion in the corner that read "Free gift for first 100 families!" I'm not sure what they had against my grandmother, nor do I know why the gospel would only be given to the first 100 families, but I am certain this is not the type of missional methodology I'm hoping for in a church plant. We should instead create methods that embody the heart of the shared meal and the gathered community.

As an example, in the planter training we share, my colleague, Molly Ruch, recommends what she calls "elbow events" in which you create a place for people to be able to interact with one another side-by-side as opposed to either gathering as isolated spectators or forcing awkward vulnerability too quickly. Wine tastings, art events, service projects, etc., are all events where people can share an activity or experience something meaningful safely alongside one another. Another elbow event employed by many a church planter is homebrewing—boiling, brewing, bottling, consuming are an unassuming shared activity that provides a shared activity and deepening relationship. These types of events are invitatory with a trajectory of depth. There is a beckoning and a pastoral patience that echoes that of the Eucharist. Dropping thousands of Easter eggs from a helicopter draws a crowd based on shallow entertainment. And that's it. No invitation to further depth. No call to ease into relationship. The only choice from here is continued entertainment to keep the crowd, or a bait and switch in which the entertainment stops for an abrupt moment of religious seriousness in which the gospel is presented.

Jesus does not do parlor tricks to gather a crowd. His miracles and his actions were purposeful. Looking again at John 6, he did not hand out free bread as a way to grow the number of the crowd, but as a sign of God's ability to provide for them. He turned away the crowd who would gather only because of the free snacks. Jesus said to them, "Truly, truly, I say to you, you are seeking me, not because you saw signs, but because you ate your fill of the loaves. Do not work for the food that perishes, but for the food that endures to eternal life, which the Son of Man will give to you" (John 6:26–27). Let us consider our missional efforts in such a way that we are not simply filling stomachs. Let us resist the temptation for flashy outreach and instead ensure our methods are a physical sign of the gospel invitation of Christ. In many ways our methods are our message.

There are many other ways for us to be physical signs of the gospel, this chapter is by no means exhaustive. The point is that we engage our planting work through the lens of the sacraments so that we hold our methods accountable just as Christ was particularly thoughtful in how he instituted the sacraments in such a way that they serve as physical signs pointing to a greater reality.

A Means of Grace

Your church plant should not simply be a physical sign of the gospel, but a means whereby the grace of Jesus can be received. We don't just point to grace, we give it. "Grace" in this sense should be understood as the blessing or favor of God. Grace then is manifested in many ways, the chiefest, of course, is the salvific grace of forgiveness of sins through Jesus Christ. For those that enter into the depths of his saving grace through repentance and belief, the sacraments bestow a grace for the nourishment of the soul. God, however, does not withhold his grace only for the saved. There is a common grace experienced by all humankind. John Murray defines common grace as, "every favour of whatever kind or degree, falling short of salvation, which this undeserving and sin-cursed world enjoys at the hand of God."[4] Anything that hinders sin, brings about restoration, stirs up the gifts of God in his creation, or provides a glimpse of God's goodness are examples of common grace. Our church plants should be places in which saving grace is received through Word and sacrament and places where we serve tastes of common grace that we pray will lead to others receiving Christ's ultimate salvific gift.

Preaching

I will remind you here that we must engage in preaching in a way that bestows grace. Paul said, "How then will they call on him in whom they have not believed? And how are they to believe in him of whom they have never heard? And how are they to hear without someone preaching?" (Romans 10:14). Your preaching plays a role in the process of salvation. Preach for conviction. Preach for encouragement. Preach for conversion.

Prayer

Bestowing grace is not something that we do, it is something God does through us. Therefore, we must build our church plant on prayer. Hear how Paul speaks to the Colossians, "Continue steadfastly in prayer, being watchful in it with thanksgiving" (4:2). He then asks them to pray for his mission work and he describes Epaphrus as "always struggling on your behalf in his prayers, that you may stand mature and fully assured in all the will of God" (4:12). Paul planted churches through prayer, built his church planting team around people of prayer, and exhorted his church plants to be diligent in prayer. Prayer unleashes grace. May we find ways to struggle for our people in prayer, praying for their missionary efforts, and may we pray that God would bestow his grace upon our communities in ways that will lead to salvation. How will you ensure that your church plant is a praying church? How will you disciple your people in prayer?

Service

Common grace is bestowed in the physical ways we serve our community. Whether we are refreshing a mural, building a Habitat for Humanity house, participating in social reform, or cleaning up a dirty highway, we are bringing blessing. When, as a church plant, we partner with ministries already organized or find new and creative methods to reach those in need, we bring grace to those whom our world sees as least, the last, and the lost. Assisting our schools through tutoring, mentoring, and volunteering; being good neighbors as we bring their trashcans back from the road for them; fostering children; the list is endless of ways that we can bring grace through physically serving the people of our cities and towns.

We do not do these things simply to grow our church plant, rather we do these things to be the people of God who have experienced grace and who now spread it. Of course, we want to be intentional in our evangelism and always ready to give an answer for the hope that we have, but we also need to recognize that people often receive saving grace only after being assured that Jesus, the grace-giver, is both real and good through experiences of his people showing his unmerited favor. As Peter tells us, "Live such good lives among the pagans that . . . they may see your good deeds and glorify God on the day he visits us" (1 Peter 2:12 NIV).

So much changes when you see church planting as a means of grace, but this is a shift in thinking that you will have to help create in your people; it is not normal in our churches. As you gather your launch team, consider how you will help them see the extent of what God wants to accomplish through them. Show them that this planting work is for those who are not yet here.

Tangible Assurance

Our God is good and he is near. Our ultimate goal for our church plants is that through our words and our deeds we can reassure our hurting and cynical communities that this is true. Our service in the community; our maturity in temperance, perseverance, strength, and self-control; our reputation with our neighbors; the depth of our love for one another—all of these things and more seek to serve as a tangible assurance that that God is indeed present.

"How is this different from being a physical sign," you ask? Assurance is more than just providing evidence; it is about eliciting trust. We will make major strides for the gospel in our communities when believers and unbelievers alike trust that we believe deeply and our faith has made us different from the world in tangible ways. Our hope is that our neighbors can say, "I don't know if I feel that God is here, and I'm struggling intellectually with whether God is real. What I do know for certain is that the people of that church have made a difference in the lives of the people of this community and they are a people of deep faith." This is what Acts described as the church "having favor with all the people" and the result of that trust was that "The Lord added to their number day by day those who were being saved" (2:47). If we earn the trust of our communities by being a tangible assurance of the truth of the words of Christ, some with then allow us to walk with them to the waters of baptism and the feast at the family Table.

We are also a tangible assurance of the grace of God to our own people. When they doubt, when they fear, when they do not have any strength left, they can be assured of the grace of God because he has given them the gift of the church plant to which they belong. You, planter, by moving to their city to start a church that is now giving them hope, are an answer to prayer and a tangible assurance of the presence of God in their lives. Well done.

The sacraments are such a gift to you as a church planter. If you teach these truths to your people and give them the lens to see all that we do as having spiritual truth and physical expression, if you show them that God wants to use them to bestow his grace, if you cast a vision for your church as a tangible assurance of the gospel, the sacraments allow you to reinforce and rehearse these aspects of your common life every week. The people who begin to gather around the idea of planting this church will immediately begin thinking about

Sunday worship and steeples. Instead steep them in the sacraments. Give them a sacramental framework to understand why we will choose to do certain things and avoid others according to their efficacy as a sign, a means of grace, and a tangible assurance. I trust that you have creative ideas for your church—I pray that the sacraments both embolden and appropriately constrain that creativity as you see your church planting work as sacramental.

A Note to Non-Anglican Readers:

Even if you differ in your sacramentology, these truths are equally valid for your church planting ministry. You still must ground your physical planting work in the spiritual truths you profess—even if you do not use sacramental language. Consider how you will gauge the wisdom, propriety, and effectiveness of the methods you choose for mission. How will you help your people see the cosmic significance of church planting and why the way you do ministry is profoundly important to the message you are bringing? Overall, how will you build trust with your community that brings awareness, credibility, and accessibility to the gospel of Jesus Christ?

CHAPTER 11

....

Who Should Plant?

I pray God to send a few people with what the Americans call "grit" in them; people who when they know a thing to be right, will not turn away, or turn aside, or stop; people who will persevere all the more because there are difficulties to meet or foes to encounter; who stand all the more true to their Master because they are opposed; who, the more they are thrust into the fire, the hotter they become; who, just like the bow, the further the string is drawn, the more powerfully will it send forth its arrows, and so, the more they are trodden upon, the more mighty will they become in the cause of truth against error.

— *Charles Spurgeon*

SUMMARY: It is important for anyone who is entering into the work of church planting to go through a process of communal discernment and assessment. God can use anyone he chooses to plant a church, but there are certain characteristics that are common among church planters. Part of this discernment process is also examining our motivations behind our planting.

Church planting does not happen on its own. Outside of the person of Christ, the person with the most influence on a church plant is the church planter. Like a rudder on a ship, the planter has the ability to point her bow in a proper direction for safe travels to the desired destination—or to put her in dire peril. The smaller the ship, the easier to steer or to capsize. It is important, then, to have the right person at the helm who has proper skill on the tiller and clear navigational ability.

Switching metaphors, if churches are planted, the gardener is important. I have recently started a small garden in my backyard. I had no idea how much goes into gardening until I engaged in it. I had to gain new construction skills in making raised beds and trellises. I have read books and watched countless videos to learn how to prepare the soil, plant seeds properly, prune correctly, and water appropriately. I am now an amateur agricultural botanist. I also built a pipe watering grid that connects to an app and waters the garden according to the weather forecast making me a bit of technical engineer. My garden is constantly under attack from weeds, disease, pesky insects, and lumbering groundhogs who will maddeningly take one bite out of a tomato and toss it away. So I have become a trapper and pellet-gun sniper as well. I blame this last part on Adam and Eve.

My point here is that even with my small garden, I need the proper knowledge and skill to do this work. I also need the proper motivation or else I will not persevere through the sweat and frustration. I need to be willing to put in the labor. I need the courage to face down rodents of unusual size, and the tenacity to keep at it. The life of the garden depends on my head, my heart, and my hands.

Church planting is similar in that it requires a broad set of skills and knowledge, the willingness to learn, the wisdom to know when to get help, the boldness to offer yourself to the community, the courage to defend against attack, and the tenacity to keep going when planting gets frustrating. This work is not for everyone.

I am often asked, "Can anyone plant a church?" Have you read the Bible and seen the people that God chose to do his work? It would be quite presumptuous for me to tell anyone that God cannot work through them if he has chosen in the past to work through that group of murderers, adulterers, whiners, and villains. God can do what God wants to do. However, in his great wisdom, God has typically wired those whom he would call to church planting to match the requirements of the calling. There are many types of people who plant churches—men, women, introverts, extroverts, rich, poor, white-collar, blue-collar, old, young, varying ethnicities—but there are certain characteristics that, with few exceptions, are found in every successful church planter.

I will say that many more people can plant if given proper supporting structures. There are some who have such natural charisma and profound spiritual giftedness that they seemingly can plant a church by accident. They stop at a red light and, somehow, by the time it turns green they have formed a launch team from the five surrounding cars. They are natural planters who seem to instinctually know the proper next steps to pursue and the pitfalls to avoid. These people are very rare (and I still think they need assessment and training). There are other people who are wired and gifted in ways that do not even remotely match the specific needs of planting. Without miraculous intervention, they could not plant a church if you gave them a hundred people and half a million dollars. They may be profoundly gifted in ministry, but not right for church planting. Most people are in the middle. They would struggle to do the work on their own, but with help and support could be healthy and effective church planters in the right situation. I'll discuss a few of these support systems now and more later when we talk about the role of the diocese in church planting.

The Need for Assessment

It is impossible to properly discern our own calling. The work of church planting is a communal work, and the community should be a part of the assessment of potential church planters. Even Paul and Barnabas submitted to prayers and wisdom before they were sent out by the church. It is absolutely necessary for every potential planter to go through a formal process of church planter assessment. This is important: the goal of assessment is to discern the right *person* for the right *place* at the right *time*; all three of these aspects of assessment are vital. Assessment does not only look at the makeup of the planter, but also his fit in the place where he hopes to plant, and the appropriateness of planting at that particular moment in his life. The process, usually under the authority of the diocese, includes written answers to questions of ministry experience, personality makeup, relational health, and personal devotion—plus surveys of the planting location. The process culminates in discernment interviews with trained assessors with the planter and his spouse.

Almost every church planter I know feels they are the exception to this process because of their uniqueness and profound giftedness. Hear me clearly: you are not an exception, you are not a snowflake, you are not above communal discernment. Even profoundly gifted natural planters should go through assessment. I even encourage people who have already successfully planted a church to go through assessment again before they plant another church. If I plant a third church, I will ask to go through a formal assessment process. Even though I have spent twenty years in church planting and have worked with dozens of other planters, and am writing a book about church planting, I would want assessment before I would plant again. People change, locations are different, situations are not the same. Assessment helps us enter into the work properly.

Formal assessment is a gift to help potential planters gain an accurate picture of their own competencies. It also allows others to ask us good questions we would not think of on our own. Assessment is not about whether the candidate is worthy enough to plant a church, or none of us would pass. Assessment is inviting the community to speak into our situations, point out potential pitfalls, root out besetting sins, encourage where they see strength, and advise where they see weakness.

Assessment is extremely important for the planter's spouse. The planter has been dreaming of the plant, reading all the planting books, having conversations with other leaders and planters—eating, sleeping, and breathing church planting. The spouse, on the other hand, is often only hearing things secondhand. In an effort not to discourage the excitement of their mate, they many times leave their own fears, worries, anxieties, and questions unstated. During assessment interviews, spouses are lovingly engaged, asked encouraging questions, and allowed space to communicate their own thoughts. Many planters are quick talkers and fast movers who can accidentally leave their spouses behind. Assessment closes that gap and, sometimes for the first time, helps the planter and spouse begin to work as a team.

The Need for Training

You also need training before you plant. In the more than twenty years I have spent in and around church planting, I have seen hundreds of church plants and I can tell you that Anglicans have a terrible recent history of sending out unprepared church planters. Like assessment, many planters feel they do not need training; they have this figured out. But I can assure you: you don't know what you don't know, and you don't know how what you do know will work in a ministry you have never done. You have been to church, and you have served in church leadership, but this is not the same. I don't want an electrician to work on the wiring of my house if their qualifications consist of many years of using a light switch. School him, train him, certify him before he burns down my house. The same is true for church planting. You will either learn in advance through training, or on the job by making significant mistakes when you plant—but in the second option you may burn down your church plant in the process. I know I am being slightly dramatic, but as someone who has been around this work for a long time, I know that the work of church planting seems obvious in our imaginations but is quite complex and difficult in reality. I would much rather have you learn in a safe, enjoyable, communal environment than on your own in ways that can hurt you and others.

The Need for Coaching

Finally, even after you are approved through assessment and have been prepared through training, you need coaching when you plant. A coach is not your buddy who has planted before and has agreed to help you when you need it, nor a volunteer clergy person who has studied planting. Those are friends and mentors. They are vital to you and your work, but they are not coaches. A coach is someone who is trained and paid for their time and expertise. Your coach will help you apply what you learned in training to your current situation, assist you in creating a strategic plan, and hold you accountable for actually pursing that plan. When I coach planters, we talk through their current obstacles and objectives and discern what strategic actions need to happen next. Then I ask them, "When do you want to have that completed?" I put a date on my calendar and follow up with the planter to see if that task has been accomplished. Coaching keeps you on track, gives you tangible accountability, and provides someone who can walk you through real-world church planting. Paying for your coach should be part of your fundraising plan. I have had a coach for many years, and still do to this day.

Qualities of a Church Planter

What are we looking for in a potential church planter? Assessment and discernment should be broken down into five areas: calling, character, competency, capacity, and chemistry.[1]

Calling

Calling can feel arbitrary, as it is difficult to define and to measure. Do we *feel* called or do we *know* that we are called, or some combination of both? In my opinion, there are three aspects to discerning our calling: prayer, community, and time.

1. First, we pray. A lot. Asking God to either increase or remove our sense of calling to a particular endeavor. We fast and read the Scripture.
2. When as an individual we feel a sense of growing confirmation, we take our thinking to others in concentric circles, starting with those closest to us in our family and local church. With confirmation at that level, we move to more formal discernment and assessment.
3. The time it takes to work through a proper process allows a calling to be hardened into a conviction or revealed as a fleeting notion.

An important aspect in this process is submission. Your individual sense of calling must be validated through the community. This does not mean a bureaucratic process, but a legitimate process of discernment. And the answer may be no, or not at this time. Calling finds its source in God; he is the one who calls. But God usually speaks to his people through his people. We are given the gift of community to help us decide if the thing tugging at our hearts is a divine commission from God or a crazy manifestation of an overactive digestive system. Don't go into an assessment process feeling that the answer is already confirmed in your heart, instead be open to hear what the Spirit is saying through the church.

Character

Your calling can be derailed by a lack of character no matter the quality of your competency. When the pressure of church planting turns up the heat, the cracks in our character reveal themselves. If you are prone to anger, you will get angry. If you are greedy, or fearful, or manipulative, it will show under the duress of planting. None of us are without flaws, and we are all dependent upon grace, but we need help to become aware of our particular vices and to make sure we are engaged in proper healing and accountability to mitigate their dangers. Church planters must exhibit a high degree of integrity because it will surely be put to the test when they are in the midst of the challenge and isolation of church planting.

Competency

Not everyone is equipped with the proper skills needed for church planting. Much can be gained through training, but some skills come from internal wiring or experience. Different contexts for planting also require different skills. For example, planting a church in conjunction with a mother church requires subtly different competencies than a parachute-drop plant. Or planting a church in an ethnically-diverse urban area will need a different kind of planter than planting in a more monolithic suburban setting. But most of these differences are more a matter of emphasis than a completely different skill set, so it helps to broadly define the competencies required by the vast majority of planters.

In the 1990s, Charles Ridley conducted research on the common characteristics found in successful church planters.

He then turned his findings into a profile for use in church planter assessment. His seminal work has served as the basis for most church planter assessments that have followed, including those that I have helped create for my diocese and the province. Ridley articulated thirteen desired attributes for church planters:[2]

1. Visioning capacity
2. Intrinsically motivated
3. Creates ownership of ministry
4. Relates to the unchurched
5. Spousal cooperation
6. Effectively builds relationships
7. Committed to church growth
8. Responsive to community
9. Utilizes giftedness of others
10. Flexible and adaptable
11. Builds group cohesiveness
12. Resilience
13. Exercises faith

Most of these qualities are self-explanatory and probably not surprising. For our discussion of Anglican planting, I would add a few more. First, the potential planter must be a good communicator, possessing the ability to winsomely and boldly proclaim the Word of God in preaching and teaching. Second, the planter must also show an understanding of the sacraments and their function in mission. Finally, I look for the catholicity of the planter—the candidate's willingness to engage in the work of church planting with creative fidelity that honors the bishop, the Anglican way, and the doctrine and discipline and worship as this church has received them. We are, after all, planting Anglican churches.

Capacity

Church planting requires the ability to balance a wide range of responsibilities at the same time. I want to see candidates who are not easily overwhelmed and do not get flustered in the face of multiple complicated tasks. A capacity to handle risk without being reckless and the ability to adapt to the unpredictable are important as well. I look closely to see evidence of the gathering capacity of the potential planter. If you are going to plant a church, have you shown an ability to conceive an idea, gather people to it, execute the plan, and see it multiply? Finally, I look also for the capacity to multiply. Our hope is not simply to plant one church, but to plant churches that plant churches and to make disciples who make disciples.

Chemistry

Another important aspect is a candidate's fit. First is his fit with people—do people like being with him? Church planting is a people work, and a planter must love people. I am not suggesting the candidate has to be extroverted or charming or beautiful; I simply want to see if he loves people and people enjoy his presence. Secondly, is the candidate a fit for the location in which he is hoping to plant. This is not a test of the attractiveness of the location (who wouldn't want to plant in a town of welcoming people next to a beach?). We are looking to see if this particular planter is right for this particular place. How well does the location resemble other places he has lived and flourished? How familiar is the planter with the culture, socioeconomic implications, education level, etc. of the area where they will be planting? Finally, what is the planter's fit in that particular diocese? Do the two line up theologically and in significant areas of Anglican expression? For instance, a low-church evangelical should have good conversations with the leadership of an Anglo-Catholic diocese if he is thinking about planting a church in their diocese. Even if the candidate is not a fit for a particular diocese, this does not mean multiple dioceses cannot work together with the planter on a plant in that geographic location. But the questions need to be asked and the answers explored in advance before the planter gets trained, raises funds, quits his job, uproots his family, and relocates to plant. Else, what could have been a healthy discussion often results in conflict and compromise that leaves everyone involved discouraged and weakened.

Improper Motivations to Plant

I have had conversations with dozens of people who were in the process of discerning whether or not they should plant a church. They are usually (and quite rightly) concerned with the how-to of planting and whether they personally have what it takes to do this work. I make it a point to ask them a question that takes some of them off guard: "Why do you want to plant a church?"

In the concern of "can I do this?" and "how do I do this?" we sometimes do not stop to ask the fundamental question of our motivation for planting to begin with: "Why am I doing this?" If we don't engage this work for the proper reasons, we will not pursue it in proper ways.

Although there are many wonderful reasons to plant, which we have already covered, there are also a number of horrible, no-good, very bad reasons. I am about to share with you some of the more common misplaced motivations

I have encountered over the years. I want to help you examine your heart as you approach this work. I am going to be very honest with you in these paragraphs, and I pray that you will be honest with yourself. Remember, however, that grace abounds. You will most likely find the taint of some of these motivations in your life, because you are a sinner whose sanctification is not yet complete. No ministry is devoid of sinful motivations. If only those who are completely pure in motivation were allowed to plant, we would have absolutely no church planters.

What is important is that, although some of these wrong motivations exist in us, we are (1) not primarily driven by them, and (2) we are constantly striving through the Spirit to die to ourselves and live for the glory of Christ. So, as you find echoes of these things in your desire to plant, do not feel as though you are disqualified out of hand. It is possible you will find in this list the true motivation of your heart, so that you decide that you should not plant a church. It is very likely, however, that you simply need to work through some issues through prayer and in conversation with those who will be overseeing you in this process. Consider these items for evaluation to bring about clarity and repentance.

Improper Motivation to Plant: You Need a Job

It is not sinful to need a job, but it is unwise at best to go into church planting as a last resort because you cannot find anything else. In this new Anglican reality that we live in, ministry jobs are at a premium. We often have more leaders than established paid positions. Often, new seminary graduates or seasoned ministry veterans who are between positions are told that there are no positions available, so fully believing that they are called into full-time Christian ministry, they feel (or they are told) that the only option they have is to try and start something new.

The problem is that in this case church planting often becomes a means to a paycheck. Although we may couch it in theological or churchy language about mission and reaching the lost, our true desire is to create a comfortable position that pays us well. Our goal becomes an office, consistency, the normalcy of a regular church service, and the predictability of the chaotic life of the local church. If our primary motivation to plant is simply to create a job for ourselves, we are planting to eventually get comfortable. But this should not be our aim as church planters. We are perpetual missionaries. We are striving to take the gospel to the ends of the earth, beginning with the local community in which we have been placed, and there will be no end to that task during our lifetimes unless Jesus returns. If the glory of Christ, the making of disciples, the reaching of the lost, and the expansion of the church do not make your heart beat faster, please do not plant a church.

It is not wrong to desire a paycheck to feed your family. In fact, it can serve as a big boot that will get you moving and working hard. But church planting is a calling. If you do not have the proper passions or skills, this is not the endeavor for you. You will cause damage to others and yourself. You will begin to see people as a commodity and a source of revenue. You will be tempted to grow your church at all costs and employ unrighteous methods to do so. You will be tempted to compromise to keep people, and therefore will avoid conflict and confrontation. You will be tempted to preach a gospel that tickles the ears rather than breaks the heart. You will be tempted to plant this church through the wiles of your own flesh, and in so doing you will plant something dysfunctional and unhealthy.

Yes, it is proper to consider the financial implications of planting and to make a plan. It is wise to count the cost of planting on your life. The question is, are you so hungry for the glory of Christ and broken by the state of the lost in your community, that you are willing to risk greatly to pursue them? Only that kind of passion will carry you through the long journey of planting. Simply needing a job and planting out of desperation won't do it.

"But I am called to ministry," you tell me. Perhaps, but that does not necessarily mean you are called to church planting. Church planting is not a default ministry to fall back on when other positions are not available. God will provide other avenues for you to serve.

I want to be careful here because many of us, including me, initially began church planting reluctantly, and I do not want your reservations to give you an excuse to get out of this if the Lord is calling you into planting. Perhaps the Lord has closed all other doors because he has called you to this work even if it is not your first choice. Having financial concerns at the outset, or entering into planting hoping that your efforts will blossom into a healthy large parish with you as the rector, do not mean that you have improper motivations. You don't have to be jumping for joy as you set out to plant, fully confident in your calling and competency. You may in fact be trembling in fear, sweaty with anxiety, and soaked in a sense of inadequacy. In fact, I kind of hope you are. What I am speaking against with such length and force is those who would slop into this work without conviction, passion, or preparation simply for professional or economic reasons. Those folks, although often unintentionally, hurt themselves and their hearers.

Improper Motivation to Plant: You Think You Can Do Church Better

When I was newly married and before my wife and I had children, I had some strong opinions about parenting—strong, uninformed, and, as it turns out, incorrect opinions. One evening after leaving the home of a family who had invited us over for dinner and watching their children be picky over their food, I distinctly recall saying to Karen, "My child is not going to eat only chicken nuggets and pizza." I pontificated about how children try to control their parents by refusing to eat anything other than their favorites and how parents just get lazy and give in. My future kids were going to eat whatever I put in front of them.

Despite what I was certain were my keen observational skills and exceptionally profound twenty-year-old wisdom, after having kids I learned that parenting is in truth a lot more difficult when you are actually doing it. It is easy to bring commentary from the outside. In my house today we do fight the good fight of food, sometimes successfully and sometimes not. But I will admit we eat our fair share of pizza and nuggets.

Don't plant a church simply because you think you can do it better. You've seen the ineffectiveness, the conflict, and the misplaced priorities of the local church. Maybe you serve on a staff and constantly roll your eyes behind the back of the senior pastor. Maybe you are a lay leader and you have a list of things that you think need to be done differently based on your vast experience in the pews. Listen, I believe we need to continue to reform the church, and I have a strong stream of the prophetic in me that desires us to no longer accept the status quo of dysfunctional church life and return to the commands of the Scripture. I am in full agreement that there are many things in the church that need to be fixed or done in new ways. However, often when we correct these things, we simply create other issues. When you actually have the reins of a church in your hands, you are going to find that some of those leaders you thought were completely inept had more wisdom than you realized.

Don't plant because you can do it better. Plant humbly. Plant knowing you need oversight. Plant valuing the wisdom of those who have been in this longer than you. We continue to discuss creative fidelity in this book, and to explore where we can bring new ideas and gifts to the mix. But when you enter into dreaming about planting, knock yourself down a notch or five, and ask more questions than you bring answers.

Improper Motivation to Plant: You Think You Know What You Are Doing

You do not have this figured out. I don't either. I had a conversation with a clergyman who was about to plant for the first time, and he told me he was not coming to my church planting class because he had been in ministry for twenty years, and (with a smirk) he said he figured he could handle this. His church never got off the ground. I'm not saying that if he had come to my class he was a sure bet for a successful church plant. Neither are you by reading this book. The problem was not the class, it was his attitude. Just because you have borne great fruit in other ministry endeavors does not mean you will in church planting. Church planting has a breadth and complexity that makes it different from much other ministry work. Your experience in ministry will be invaluable, but there are new skills you will need as well.

Also, every church plant is different, and we constantly need to study, learn, and get input from others. Even after planting multiple times and decades of study, the churches I planted were in no way guaranteed successes. We struggled in many areas, and there were many times I did not know what the next step should be. There were times I was scared and confused or angry and frustrated. There were other times when our perfectly-designed strategy fell flat, and still more moments when the worst decision I made bore fruit for the work. We need each other, we need teachers, and most of all we need grace and the power of the Spirit. Don't plant because you think you've got it all figured out and it can't be that hard. You don't, and it is.

Improper Motivation to Plant: You Want to Be in Charge

Few would admit this one—it sounds too unholy. Type A, alpha leaders are often drawn to church planting because it can seem like an opportunity to have control without those pesky other people and their annoying opinions. I am purposely overstating this, but if you are a leader, you have thought this in your heart. If we are honest, we admit that church planting could seem to be an opportunity to grow our own little fiefdom within the kingdom.

We must die to this. Church planting is a people work, and if you are making disciples of people, leading people, and living in community with people, they will and should have their thoughts and opinions. I know that you know that, but let us all examine our hearts to see if we have the proper balance of submission and authority. Let's make sure we recognize that we are primarily servants to both Christ and those he has given us. As William Wallace says to us,

"You think the people of this land exist to provide you with position. I think your position exists to provide those people with freedom."[3]

Furthermore, we must remember that it is not our church we are planting, it is Christ's church. We are stewards and watchmen. Don't plant your church, plant Jesus's church. I'm not saying anything new here. I'm simply encouraging us to examine of our hearts and repent of our usurping tendencies.

Improper Motivation to Plant: You Simply Want to Preach More

This one can cut deep. You are on a pastoral staff somewhere and you do not get the number of chances you would like to enter the pulpit and address the masses. You have something to say. If you know the gospel, then yes you do! I pray that you do have a hunger to preach! It is the way God has chosen to soften hears, confront sin, and break pride. It is an honor to be able to preach the unadulterated Word of God with vigor and passion!

Church planting will give you the opportunity to preach more, but only after a long while of having no one to listen to you. You had better be ready to preach to the fifteen people who show up one Sunday in June after you have already set up the sound system, Communion Table, nursery, greeter's area, and fifty chairs—thirty-five of which remain empty. Creating a platform for your preaching is not the end goal for this church planting work.

Improper Motivation to Plant: You Think It Is Sexy, Cutting-Edge, and Radical

When I first started planting in the early 2000s, there were not nearly as many resources available as there are now. Church planting has become much more common (praise God!), and more and more denominations and individuals are seeing its importance. Many church planting innovators have been featured in glossy Christian magazines or online stories and have become influential Christian leaders. Great. Honestly, that is great. But friends, this work is usually unsung. Most of us will not speak the conference circuit; we will just grind out the work. This work is not really even cutting-edge and radical. Every church in the world was at one time a church plant, so this has been going on for quite some time. Do this work because you are passionate about it and called to it, not because it is currently also a fad.

Improper Motivation to Plant: You See Yourself as an Entrepreneur

Honestly, the word *entrepreneur* just makes me itchy. I was in a breakout session at a major church-planting conference, and the leader of the class began his teaching by saying, "When you are a church planter you are primarily an entrepreneur and secondarily a pastor." I almost threw up on my shoes. I categorically disagree. If you are ordained, then you are first of all a priest (or pastor) in God's one, holy, catholic and apostolic church. You are secondarily called to an entrepreneurial ministry in his name. This is God's church and planting is done primarily through his power. Yes, there is skill involved and many of the needed skills and attributes are shared by both planters and business entrepreneurs (risk tolerance, vision capability, financial organization, etc.). The image of the entrepreneur in the modern Western world, however, is one of bootstrapping and winning at all costs. It is very focused on the entrepreneur as the center of the wheel. I do believe that the primary indicator of the survivability of a church plant is the proper church planter, but not in the same self-promoting, inwardly-focused way as it is for business entrepreneurship. Maybe we could use a phrase like "God-centered and Spirit-dependent humble ecclesiastical entrepreneurship," but that seems a bit clunky. My point is that just because you have started a business does not necessarily mean you can start a church. Business entrepreneurs can be close friends and wonderful advisors to you, but understand that what you are doing is a very different undertaking. Don't watch *Shark Tank* to learn how to plant a church.

Improper Motivation to Plant: You Are a Person Who Needs Constant Change

I've run into folks who say something to the effect of, "I'm a person who needs change. I don't like a lot of the same ol' same ol'." There is definitely a lot of excitement in church planting, but you need to see planting as a marathon rather than a sprint. Maybe even a marathon with hurdles. Yes, there is change, and there are many decisions to be made, and I too like that part of the work. I would have a hard time in a gentle country parish. But we also need to realize that this is going to take a long time.

A lot of planters get itchy feet around year three. They start to think about planting somewhere else or wondering if they can stick with it, and they begin looking at more established positions. That's because the romantic first couple of years are when you are discovering the dream for the new church, and the first new faces begin to live that dream with you, and the initial tangible expressions of the dream in a weekly service are formed. It is fun to find a new place to meet, to purchase all the equipment, and to move a small group from your home to a rented facility. Such times are nervous and giddy. Then it becomes a grind when you realize that you have done this so many times you are beginning to recognize individual chairs and there is no end in sight. Year three is the push-through year when it is tempting to leave, but things are still too young and will fall apart if you go. Yes, it can be exciting, but church planting is a marriage, not a fling.

Improper Motivation to Plant: You've Already Planted the Church in Your Head

In Bill Easum and Jim Griffith's short book, *Ten Most Common Mistakes Made by New Church Starts*, number three is: "A love affair with one's fantasy statement blinds the planter to the mission field."[4] In other words, you've already planted your dream church in your head. You might even have bylaws written, a logo designed, and a sketch of your first service in crayon on your fridge. I have heard people say to plant the church that you would like to go to. I don't necessarily disagree with this, nor do I think it wrong that you have dreamed about the future of this church (in fact, that is one of the most fun aspects of this work). The problem is, this church is not for you. This church is for your mission field. Now, the closer your preferences and perspectives line up with the mission field you are in, the better fit you are going to be, but there will always be differences. You must learn to contextualize to the community in which you are planting. You must also be ready to adapt and pivot as necessary. You cannot plant the fictional church that's in your head.

Improper Motivation to Plant: You're Inspired by Stories of Fast-Growing Church Plants

The problem with watching TV home improvement shows is that we begin to think we can do what they do ourselves, at home, on a thousand-dollar budget, in two days. The reality is that they do not include the hours of sweaty work on TV. It all seems easy when packed in a thirty-minute block. I promise you, it was not that easy in reality. If we try this at home, we will spend more, hurt more, and argue more than we had planned, and then live six months without sheetrock.

When you read or hear a story of a church plant that has seen tremendous success, it is very much the same thing. The vision is exciting, the difficulties are mentioned for dramatic effect, and the final product is revealed so you can get teary-eyed. I know, because people have written stories about work I've done, and because I've written many stories about church planters.

It is impossible in a thousand-word article to give a real picture of planting. It would not be a good read to tell of the hours the planter spent weeping on his bedroom floor. It would be inappropriate to tell of all the interpersonal conflict he endured. There is not a pull quote of his wife asking him what in the world he has gotten his family into. The timeline is compressed so that multiple months of desperate labor are summed up in a sentence like, "After spending a season of reaching out into the community, the plant began to see some growth." I promise you that to the planter who falls into his chair in exhaustion week after week, the "season of reaching out" felt like a long and cold winter.

I love to tell church planter stories. I want to give glory to God for the work he is doing. I want to honor the heroes of church planting who do this difficult work, and I want to inspire others to take up this mantle as well. Just be realistic. You'll gain more from hearing what those church planters don't say, what ended up on the editing room floor as too explicit for public consumption. I hope one day I get to hear and tell your story, and watch you as you smile knowingly while you listen.

Improper Motivation to Plant: You Are Mad at the Episcopal Church (or the Anglican Church of Canada, or the Methodist Church, or Evangelicals, or the Megachurch, etc.)

If you are not familiar with the story of Anglicanism in North America, I will sum it up simply by saying that the Episcopal Church USA and the Anglican Church of Canada were the dominant Anglican expressions in their respective countries for a long time. Both, however, removed themselves from the moorings of Scripture and the Great Tradition to move into a place of active heresy—similar divisions continue in other traditions as well. Now, the Anglican Church in North America has formed to be an authentic, biblical, historic Anglican witness on this continent. In this process of breaking and reforming, many relationships have been strained or broken and a lot of anger still exists (some righteous and just, some not so much). Perhaps you relate to this story in your tradition.

If you are planting a new church simply to "stick it to" the local Episcopal (Methodist, Presbyterian, etc.) church you left, please don't plant. You cannot define yourself by what you are against. We plant churches not out of an anger against heresy, but out of a loving reflex to the good news of the gospel. Planting an angry church is unhealthy and unsustainable. ("Welcome to our church. The first thing you need to know is who to be angry with.") Pray for and love your enemies, and plant a church for the glory of Christ and the sake of the lost.

You also cannot define what you are planting as simply a refreshed version of what you came from. What I mean is that some have left the Episcopal Church not for the sake of the gospel, but rather as a response to moral and political issues. Our faith is not primarily a faith of morality, sexuality, or politics, and it was not only these things that were skewed in the Episcopal Church. Likewise, the trouble with the megachurch is not only a weak ecclesiology, and the errors in greater evangelicalism are not simply its public image. We don't plant out of a rejection of where we've come from. Either you are planting a church for the sake of the gospel, or you have too small a reason for wanting to plant something new. This is going to be costly for you. You are not planting an Episcopal church with better morals and politics. You are not planting an anti-megachurch. You are not gathering "ex-vangelicals." You are involved in the redeeming work of God in the world, not fixing a broken misuse of a storied tradition or correcting an entertainment-driven worship culture, and that is an important change in perspective.

The Most Important Paragraphs of This Chapter

By my own merit, I am not qualified to plant or to write about planting. I have many of these bad motivations in my own heart. I have made terrible mistakes. I struggle with identity, trust, and patience. I get tired. I get frustrated with people, and with the process of planting, and with God for not moving in the way I have told him to move.

Church planting is hard work. It can be soul-wrenching. It is emotionally, physically, relationally, and financially draining. Sometimes I dream of swinging a hammer for a living so I could start the day with instructions and a quota then end the day with something tangible to look at. Maybe roofing would work—then I could see what I had done by lugging sacks of asphalt up a ladder, beating nails into wood, and cutting out flashing. It would be hot and dangerous, but it would be simple and measurable and able to be completed.

When I mix these together—my inadequacies, compounded by the tremendous difficulty of church planting—I get a caustic reaction with some flashes of anxiety, fear, and depression. And I am not alone. I have hardly spoken to a church planter who has not had moments when he wanted to quit, either because of the enormity of the task or his powerful realization of his own insufficiency. But here is the amazing truth: I would not want to be doing anything else.

Whether a lead planter, or leading an established church that plants other churches, in church planting, I see the grace of God powerfully present. Our Father is so gracious. By our own merit we have no right to consider the work of planting; we are completely dependent upon his grace as lavished upon us through his Son—and that is precisely what qualifies us for this role. My friend, listen to me: I love church planting because I see the grace of God powerfully change lives through his gospel, and I see that most personally in my own heart. This reality will be true for you as well. God does not need your work; he wants your soul, and through you, the souls of many others.

Do not be discouraged by this list of improper motivations. Instead, be realistic. Be challenged. Be humbled. Fall to your knees in recognition of your need for grace—but do not be discouraged. I love that Jesus frequently said, "Peace be with you" to his disciples after his resurrection. These guys were ashamed, afraid, and confused. Jesus was in essence telling them to take a breath, lower their heart rate, and relax—because he was with them. It is no accident that his final statement of the Great Commission, in which he said "Go!" to the disciples and to us, that he will be with us when we do.

Church planting is the most exciting, invigorating, tangible example of the ongoing work of God in this world that I have ever been a part of. As planters, rectors of church-planting churches, bishops of church-planting dioceses, or laity giving of ourselves to start a new local church, we are living out the continuing work of the book of Acts. We are in a long line of bold missionaries, surrounded by a great cloud of witnesses. I know it is hard. Terribly hard. I know that it can be overwhelming. But it is worth it. I invite you into this adventure if the Lord so calls. You will never be the same.

A Note to Non-Anglican Readers:

I don't feel there is too much to translate here. Some examples are specific to Anglicanism, but I'm sure there are comparable examples in your tradition. Are there characteristics or competencies that planters in your tradition need to have? Have you experienced other examples of improper motivations in your tradition that I have not listed here? We all share in this same need for assessment, discernment, training, and coaching in this work of planting.

CHAPTER 12

....

Planting in Sacred Order

Anglicanism has always been pastoral, always concerned with making Christians . . . and then shepherding them. That concern is there in the ordinal of the Prayer Book. The minister is ordained, first and foremost, to find Christ's sheep and then to walk with them as a shepherd, leading and guiding them from the beginning of their spiritual lives right through to the end.

—*J. I. Packer, Heritage of Anglican Theology*

SUMMARY: Governance and church structures, when properly understood and pursued, can be engines for the work of church planting. On the contrary, if bureaucratic and improperly focused, these same structures can be a barrier to effective mission. This chapter explores the role of polity structures in supporting church planting and the role of church planters in the polity structures.

You may have noticed by this point that Anglicans like order. Whether in our liturgy or in our organizational structures, we like a place for everything and everything in its place. In Genesis 1, when the Spirit hovered over the deep and tamed the chaos, all the Anglicans breathed a sigh of relief. Clearly, Paul was prefiguring the Anglican way of being when he said that "God is not a God of confusion but of peace" (1 Corinthians 14:33). Perhaps counterintuitively, our emphasis on order is not meant to come at the expense of organic mission.

My writing spot is in our sunroom overlooking our garden. My small garden is full of life: lush greenery vining and sprouting at all angles, brightly colored flowers, healthy red tomatoes, yellow squash, butterflies, bees, and even a chipmunk or two. But there is also structure: beans are growing up trellises, tomatoes are tied to stakes, peppers are leaning against bamboo rods. The whole garden is contained within three raised beds covered by a grid of pipes that provides irrigation. The structure brings greater health and life to my garden, without which there would be less healthy fruit.

John Finney says the Anglican church is a blending of the Roman (structured) and Celtic (organic) ways of being. He calls this a mixed economy, saying, "We need a mix of both Roman and Celtic forms of ministry. We need the stability of the parish system, but we need also the freedom and ability to experiment of the entrepreneurial evangelist."[1] This mixed economy is difficult to maintain. There is always a pull either toward over-structuring, which squashes innovation, or toward under-structuring, which leads to chaos. For Anglicanism to be effective in the work of church planting it must carefully shape an organizational culture that holds this tension. On a diocesan level, we must give planters structure for faithfulness and room for flexibility. On the local level, planters need to introduce the right amount of structure at the right time so as to avoid two pitfalls: collapse through disorder, or strangulation through bureaucracy.

The governance and ordering of the church is called our *polity*, from a Greek word meaning "citizenship or government." Anglican polity involves the laity and a threefold order of clergy in bishops, priests, and deacons. It is grounded in the local congregation (led by a priest), the jurisdiction of the diocese (led by a bishop), and the unification of the local dioceses within the larger province (led by an archbishop or primate), which is then in relationship with other autonomous provinces through the Anglican communion (with the Archbishop of Canterbury serving as the convener and First Among Equals). Although leaders have been set apart through ordination to give particular oversight to these spheres of organization, the laity are equally as valuable as any deacon, priest, bishop, or archbishop.

It is important to note that whereas our polity system is hierarchical to a certain degree in that the bishop has significant authority in the diocese and a rector has spiritual authority within his congregation, we are primarily conciliar and synodical. This means significant decisions are not made unilaterally from the top down, but rather in counsel as we come together as the church in local bodies, diocesan gatherings, and provincial assemblies.

Also important to Anglican polity is the principle of collaboration with subsidiarity. This means we desire to work in unity with one another in partnership for the gospel on as large a level as possible, but individual decisions should be made at the most local level possible. This principle keeps us from turning into a faceless conglomerate with a disconnected hierarchy. The role of the larger body is to serve the local body where direct ministry takes place in the streets, offices, shops, houses, and schools of local communities. This philosophy has direct bearing on our church-planting conversation, for the entire structure of Anglican polity is meant to bring the weight and strength of the combined missional efforts of the Anglican family in support of the local church planter.

Perhaps most important is that our organizational structure is not based on managerial principles; our polity is an attempt to organize the church according to the Scripture itself. Archbishop John Whitgift, late sixteenth-century archbishop of Canterbury said, "The substance and matter of government [of the church] must indeed be taken out of the Word of God and consisteth in these points, that the Word be truly taught, the sacraments rightly administered, virtue furthered, vice repressed, and the church kept in quietness and order."[2] Although the English Reformers stopped short of saying that an episcopal form of government (*episcopal* means "having bishops") is a required mark of the true church, the language of many of our Anglican formularies speak very strongly to the biblical roots of our system of polity. The preface to the 1662 Ordinal begins, "It is clearly evident to anyone who diligently reads both the Holy Scriptures and ancient Authors, that from the Apostles' time these three Orders of ministry have existed in Christ's Church: Bishops, Priests, and Deacons." This is a strongly worded phrase.

What organizational structures are referenced in the Scriptures? The Greek words *diakonos* (deacon), *presbyteros* (priest or presbyter), and *episkopos* (bishop) are used throughout the New Testament to denote church offices. These servants, elders, and overseers are charged with giving order to the church—or as the apostle Paul tells Titus, himself a leader under Paul's authority, "This is why I left you in Crete, so that you might put what remained into order, and appoint elders in every town as I directed you" (Titus 1:5). The ancient church carried on these same offices as evidenced in an early second-century letter from St. Ignatius in which he says, "everyone must show the deacons respect. They represent Jesus Christ, just as the bishop has the role of the Father, and the presbyters are like God's council and an apostolic band. You cannot have a church without these."[3] As with everything else, Anglican polity strives to carry on church governance as described in the Scripture and lived out in the church history.

Church planting requires such nimbleness that, on that surface, a robust system of order and structure may seem restrictive. In actuality, I have found this to be far from the truth if those in the polity system understand why the system exists.

Appropriate order brings focus and precision to the work of planting, as a barrel does to a bullet. Our polity system is intentionally restraining, but in a healthy way. Restraint keeps us from going where we should not go. Like rumble strips and guard rails on a highway, our polity warns and corrects us when we get off track and keeps us from careening off a cliff. The road between the rails is broad, with plenty of room for innovation and diverse expression, but we are checked when we head toward danger.

Our polity is not merely corrective, however; it is also meant to be supportive. The typical picture of a church planter is that of a lone wolf on a personal journey who must live off his resourcefulness and tenacity. But isolation and rugged individualism are not healthy conditions, nor is it the model shown to us in the Scripture.

You will need to explain this approach to polity to your people as you start your new church. The combination of having a hierarchy, the upside-down nature of that hierarchy as chief servants, and our focus on conciliarism, is all biblical. Jesus teaches the upside-down leadership principle in

Matthew 20:25–28, "You know that the rulers of the Gentiles lord it over them, and their great ones exercise authority over them. It shall not be so among you. But whoever would be great among you must be your servant, and whoever would be first among you must be your slave, even as the Son of Man came not to be served but to serve, and to give his life as a ransom for many." And we see conciliarism modeled in places like the council at Jerusalem in Acts 15, and in Galatians 2. But this can be new, confusing, and suspicious to those used to other forms of ecclesiastical government or who only know secular models of polity. A hierarchical approach to better serve the people, authority that does not oppress, and a balance of structure and freedom—these may be novel to most of your people whether they are new believers or new to an Anglican church. It is important then, for both you and your hearers, that we look at each aspect of our polity in order to define the work of each within church planting.

Deacons

Deacons are a widely misunderstood group. Our earthly infatuation with power has led us to neglect this profoundly important office due to its focus on service. I truly believe we need to raise up an army of deacons for the health of the church and the work of church planting. We need faithful servants who are not consumed with the oversight of the church but are free to pour into the lives of the people without distraction. Deacons are the dirt-under-their-nails workers who are daily on the front lines of ministry.

The origin of the order of deacon is described in Acts 6. The apostles were overwhelmed by the organization of the process of distributing food to those who were in need. They were being pulled away from their duties of preaching and teaching, saying, "It is not right that we should neglect the word of God in order to wait on tables" (Acts 6:2 NRSV). This is not a snarky response as if serving food was beneath them or of lesser importance. Rather, because the apostles so highly valued the people, they were concerned that either the people or the ministries of preaching, teaching, and evangelism would be neglected. The apostles were at capacity, and it was too much for them to do it all.

The solution was to "pick out from among you seven men of good repute, full of the Spirit and of wisdom, whom we will appoint to this duty. But we will devote ourselves to prayer and to the ministry of the word" (v. 3). Thus, the office of the deacon (from *diakonos*, which means "servant") was born, set apart to give specific leadership to the area of service. Its quality, competence, and devotion were exemplified as Stephen, one of their number, testified with astounding courage, biblical knowledge, and love of Jesus before his martyrdom.

As the church spread beyond Jerusalem, Paul, the overseer of many church plants, gave instructions regarding those who should qualify for this role in 1 Timothy 3:8–13. Continuing throughout church history, deacons have played an important role in the church that was greater than simply organizers of service.

The diaconate is the first role of any ordained person and, as the saying goes, "once a deacon, always a deacon," for no matter if later ordained a priest or consecrated a bishop, clergy never cease to serve. In the fifth century, John Chrysostom spoke to this truth by pointing out that Paul's instructions in 2 Timothy 4:5 for Timothy to fulfill his "*diakonia*" came after Timothy was clearly a bishop—since he's one who lays hands on to ordain in 1 Timothy 5:22.[4] Christians are forever servants, and deacons embody that role.

To briefly describe the role of the deacon and apply it to church planting, we turn first to the Anglican ordinal. Here are the words that commission the new deacon: "It belongs to the office of a Deacon to share in the humility and service of our Lord Jesus Christ, for the strengthening of the Church, which is his body. You are to read the Gospel and proclaim Christ at all times through your service, to instruct both young and old in the Catechism, and, at the direction of the Bishop or Priest, to baptize and preach."[5]

This exhortation is inherently missional. A deacon's service is meant to "proclaim Christ at all times" so those who do not know him may come to the knowledge and love of him and those who do belong to him will be awakened in their faith. The deacon is also charged with the task of catechesis to create deep and mature faith in the people of the church.

The deacon is not simply to be the all-other-duties-as-required person in the church. The deacon is not junior-varsity clergy. The diaconal office is a full and equal order for the purpose of proclaiming Christ at all times and strengthening the church through humble service.

In church planting, deacons serve many roles. One such function, which I have a particular heart for, is older deacons who support younger planters. Young, energetic church planters are a gift, but they can also be a liability. Trust me, I have been one. Their stress and panic needle can go from overconfident to weeping in a corner over one ill-attended event. Assuming the lead planter is a priest, the presence of a senior priest can sometimes create confusion in the leadership structure. Older deacons, however, bring steadiness and consistency while not vying for authority—that's not their role—but supporting, encouraging, and loving. The wisdom and experience that comes with age allows the deacon to stay calm and get things done when new and unexpected obstacles come along that may derail the younger planter.

I remember the time, in my first church plant, when I walked into our rented space on Palm Sunday and the water heater had rusted through the bottom and was actively flooding the entire building. Frantic, I called our deacon, Vance Tyson, and he calmly told me to turn off the water valve on the heater to shut off the flow. There was no shut-off valve! So I called him back, and he calmly told me to walk to the street and find the main shut-off under a cover. The hole was full of fire ants! So Vance said, "Give me a minute, I'll be right there. You don't worry about it. Go get ready for the service." A few minutes later I was inside in bare feet with my pantlegs rolled up, reviewing my sermon and setting up the Communion Table, while Deacon Vance was kneeling outside pulling mounds of squirming fire ants away from the shut-off valve with his bare hands. He turned off the spewing water, came inside and said, "Well, it needed to be done, and I didn't have anything else, so my hands had to do." That's a deacon.

Vance, first as a lay person and later as a deacon, served the church as one of my closest friends. Truly, that church would not have been planted without him. Neither the church nor I would have survived. He hosted multiple dinners with his many contacts in the area to introduce them to me and the church plant. He was my chief confidant and defender. His humility and wisdom saved me from a lot of grief. At twenty-two, I was so young when I became the lead planter of that church that many times when I would do anything bold or innovative that challenged people's expectations, it was interpreted as the ignorance of youth. As the more senior voice, Vance heard many complaints about me, and he would reassure people that he trusted my leadership. They would often times go away mollified, if not satisfied. Then, sometimes, Vance would come talk to me in private to bring gentle correction or a suggestion. Vance was the stability the church needed as I buzzed around with my missional thoughts and made many mistakes. When my first son was born, we gave him the middle name Vance.

I have also witnessed deacons serve as the primary gatherer of the initial group that will eventually form a church plant. Their ordination brings a sense of institutional credibility to their invitation, and their gifts and training are such that they are well suited for this work. To bring people to the table to even discuss starting a new church requires someone who quickly earns trust. We are inviting people to gather in a small group with other people they may not know for the purpose of engaging in a very foreign, risky, and intimidating endeavor. Deacons, in their humility, wisdom, and hearts of service, bring an experience of calm and confidence to this fragile time.

Bill Arnold is one such deacon. In his late sixties when I met him, Bill had spent the majority of his life in high-dollar sales, and is a salesman at his core. When I first arrived outside of Atlanta, Deacon Bill drove my wife and I around the community. He had a fact or story about nearly every building we passed: "That's the largest Kroger grocery store east of the Mississippi. The president visited that restaurant in 2002 while passing through town. That's where I get my hair cut and the barber there is the greatest I have ever seen. There are two hundred homes being built in this new subdivision being marketed to young families. This county has won the award for best parks and best school systems multiple times." He knew the people and the place.

Bill gathered lists of people from his town who had visited Anglican churches in nearby cities and he cold-called every one of them. Then he heard that a church planter (me) had just finished his work in North Carolina and was discerning next steps, so he called me and asked me to consider if the Lord may be sending me to the Atlanta area. A few months later I moved my family, and we began planting a church in suburban Atlanta. Deacon Bill became my biggest supporter, cheerleader, protector, confidant, and caregiver. Bill was rough around the edges, could talk the ear off a corn stalk, and there were times when after a life of custom business suits his robes of humility seemed tailored for someone else, but he was one of the best examples of a deacon I have ever met. His efforts laid the groundwork for the church I had the honor of joining him to plant.

The diaconate is not only for the older and wiser—the young and wise make great deacons as well. Young deacons bring vitality to the church. Their mere presence gives a sense of forward trajectory and a feeling that this church is here for the long haul. They bring strong backs and helping hands to the work, sharing the load of caring for people and helping bear the weight of organizational logistics. In Acts 6, the deacons took on food distribution. In modern church planting, their waiting on tables often takes the form of overseeing the process of setup and teardown for public worship, event planning, and making personal visits. Deacons are also able to give extra time to some people who require added attention at a particular moment, making sure the person is ministered to while allowing the church planter to remain focused on leading the larger body.

Another important note to mention is the extreme value of women deacons in church planting. Currently, most lead church planters are male. With this being the case, women called to the diaconate are a particularly profound gift to a church plant. Ordained or not, women present a different perspective, gifting, and credibility that brings fullness to the body of Christ. Women deacons publicly personify the value the church places on women in leadership and service. Women deacons reach segments of the population outside of the church that are difficult for men to reach, and build up the church from within to be stronger and richer through their unique perspective. May the Lord raise up for the church an army of gifted women deacons!

Church planters should salivate over having deacons in their churches. Every planter is healthier and every church plant is better for having one or more people with particular training and giftedness who are set apart for the work of service in the church.

Priests

In most Anglican dioceses, priests are our primary planters. This makes sense since priests are the shepherds of local congregations and have gone through significant preparation. A sacramental church needs an ordained planter. Often, a group of laity might come together to begin building the foundation of a church plant, but soon a gifted and prepared priest will need to join the work to bring leadership through Word and sacrament.

The title *priest* is derived from the Greek *presbyteros*, meaning "elder" (not as in age, but in office). At its base level, the office of the priest is the head of a local congregation under the authority of the bishop and in council with lay leadership. Being a church planter does not change the office, it simply nuances the function. We do not take vows as church planters, we take vows as priests.

We turn again to the ordinal to define the office of the priesthood. The bishop reads the following to those being ordained:

> You have heard, during the Church's discernment of your vocation and in the Holy Scriptures themselves, how weighty is this Office to which you are called. I now exhort you, in the Name of our Lord Jesus Christ, to be a messenger, watchman, and steward of the Lord. You are to teach, to warn, to feed, and to provide for the Lord's family, and to seek for Christ's sheep who are in the midst of this fallen world, that they may be saved through Christ for ever.[6]

Notice the three duties of the priest mentioned in that exhortation: messenger, watchman, and steward. We will examine each.

The Priest as Messenger

The call to be a messenger is a prophetic office. A king's messenger carries the king's message wherever the king sends him. The message is not his own; the messenger is a steward of someone else's message. The priestly messenger is to bring the Word of God to the world. Paul tells Timothy, "Do your best to present yourself to God as one approved, a worker who has no need to be ashamed, rightly handling the word of truth" (2 Timothy 2:15). A faithful messenger must be precise and complete, bringing the entire message, not a summary or only the parts that will be well-received. We are to bring the whole counsel of God to the people—reproving, rebuking, and exhorting, "with complete patience and teaching" (2 Timothy 4:2). Regardless of whether we are called to planting or not, we are called to guard the good deposit entrusted to us (2 Timothy 1:14), proclaim the kingdom of God, and teach about the Lord Jesus Christ "with all boldness and without hindrance" (Acts 28:31).

The call to be a messenger is also a missionary office. The message we bring is a message of invitation and of harvest. We should expect not merely to shepherd well those who are within the walls of the church, but to gather those who are without. Listen to Charles Spurgeon preaching on 1 Corinthians 3:6–9:

> I think some churches forget that an increase is expected from every field of the Lord's farm, for they never have a harvest or even look for one. The people come together and take their seats on a Sunday and listen to sermons—that is, when they do not go to sleep—the sacraments are celebrated, a little money is contributed, a few poor folk are relieved, and affairs crawl along at a snail's pace. As to affecting the whole village, or endeavoring to bring the surrounding population to Christ, I do not think it has occurred to some churches to attempt it—and when certain warmer spirits seek to bring sinners to Jesus, the older and more prudent folks fetch wet blankets and use them with very great effect so that

> every sign of enthusiasm is damped down. Brethren, such things ought not to be. I conceive that if there were no Christians in England but the members of our baptized churches, these would suffice for God's great designs of mercy, if they were once awakened to real labor. Alas, the loiterers are many, but the laborers are few.[7]

That was 1881, but it could just as easily be preached today. The priest serving as a church planter has a primary calling to build a church that defies Spurgeon's observations, awakening the congregation and gathering the lost. We must model evangelism ourselves, as Anglican priest George Whitfield reportedly said, "God forbid that I should travel with anybody a quarter of an hour without speaking of Christ to them." As messengers, we must also exhort others to engage the world. In the milieu of church planting with its vast and diverse demands, we must not lose sight of the priestly calling of the messenger, and the metric of our success should not be stability and comfort, but success in missional endeavors. What is the use of planting if we are not harvesting?

The Priest as Watchman

A watchman must have eyes for both opportunity and danger. The priest is to guard those under his care. You must be concerned for the spiritual, physical, and relational health of your people, for both wolves from without and disease that festers within can destroy the work of your church plant.

The priest-planter is on the lookout for a diversity of threats ranging from heresy to those who would prey on the people of your church. The priest must guard the pulpit and every platform that teaches the people to make sure that what is taught is sound in doctrine and application. The priest must also make sure he works with the proper leadership in the church and diocese to set up proper systems of safety to guard against physical, sexual, or emotional abuse, and to protect against theft and embezzlement. These overt threats are the more obvious to guard against.

There are also much more subtle threats like fear, an attitude of scarcity, or a gentle inward turn that leaves you vulnerable to focusing all the energy of the church toward those who are already there.

I worked with a small church plant that had been plateaued for years. In consulting with them, it became clear that a handful of older women who had been very close friends had firm control over the church. It was a boutique church meant to serve them and their families, all others be damned. This group of genteel Southern women had run off more people than were currently attending on Sundays. The chair backs in the sanctuary had plaques affixed with dedications—mostly from one of these women to one of the others: "Given by Sue Smith in thanksgiving for Jane Baker." "Given in honor of Sue Smith by Jane Baker." And so on.

My bishop asked me to work with this church, visiting regularly for a few months and training their leadership to see if we could get the church-planting work turned around. Halfway through my time of working with them, discussing much of what is contained in this book, even with my attempts at patience and winsomeness, one of the women had enough. She asked me with deep frustration, "Well, if you were the rector of this church, what is the first thing you would change?" I told her I would get a screwdriver and take all the shiny brass plaques off the backs of the chairs.

"But those are our chairs! We gave them!" she said, aghast.

"That's the problem," I said. "If they are your chairs, they are yours to take home and sit in them, but if this is God's church and these are God's chairs, they are meant to seat those whom we bring in through mission. Those chairs, this church, are meant to serve the mission of God, not the designs of a private social club."

That blessed them. The silence that followed seethed with anger. The priest must be a watchman for the death spiral of a church plant turning inward.

A watchman must also not be afraid. If a watchman is afraid, he will either be blinded by fear and see nothing at all, or he will see threats in every shadow where none actually exist. The first capitulates, avoiding conflict and turning a blind eye to areas that clearly need his attention. The second is overly confrontational or passive-aggressive, and can become manipulative or spiteful. The author of Hebrews reminds us, "We can confidently say, 'The Lord is my helper; I will not fear; what can man do to me?'" (Hebrews 13:6). David reminds us, "Be strong, and let your heart take courage" (Psalm 31:24). Fear is dangerous in church planting.

When I had the opportunity to work with a group of churches in England, one of the rectors told me he had fewer than ten people in his 150-year-old church. After hearing about what is required for missional engagement he said, "This is all so very new. What if I introduce these ideas and my people leave?" All ten of them? Is that truly a threat? Although every soul is important to God and even the fall of a single sparrow does not avoid his attention, we cannot sacrifice the pursuit of mission out of fear masquerading as pastoral concern. Jesus loved the ninety-nine, but he did not pander to them. He left them to seek his lost sheep who are in the midst of this fallen world, that they may be saved through Christ forever. A better concern might be what happens if these ten people stay. Apparently, they are not currently full of apostolic vigor. They were all capable people, and they must be shaken awake—or if this fails, disbanded as to not give false witness to the nature of the church. That church either needs a revival or a funeral. Shock it and see if we get a pulse.

You too will be tempted to make decisions out of fear—fear of financial constraints, fear of people leaving, fear of failure. You have taken vows to be a watchman. Let neither fear nor arrogance guide your decisions.

As a watchman, you must also handle conflict. There will be conflict in your church plant. If you avoid it or run from it, you give it time to metastasize, and it will be a much bigger issue in the future. Handle conflict head-on, with both truth and grace. Conflict avoidance undermines your church's confidence in your ability or willingness to create a safe environment. Be encouraging and diplomatic as needed, and firm and corrective when called for. Many of the problems and schisms I have seen in church plants can be traced back to a lack of willingness on behalf of the leadership to courageously engage in working through conflict.

To be a healthy watchman, you must not only notice threats, but victories as well. It is easy as a church planter to want to fix what is broken and develop what is lacking. We can accidentally become taskmasters of ourselves and our people, downplaying success and consistently pointing out failure. I often fall into the trap of growing things but not rejoicing in the harvest. I will bring in vegetables from my garden and set them down only so I can go back out and pick weeds. A lot goes wrong in our church planting, but a lot goes right as well. We need to take the time to celebrate, to feast. Be on the lookout for your tendency to only notice the work that needs to be done while neglecting to give thanks for what has already been accomplished.

Finally, our role as the watchman inherently brings both urgency and hope. The psalmist declares,

> I wait for the Lord, my soul waits,
> and in his word I hope;
> my soul waits for the Lord
> more than watchmen for the morning,
> more than watchmen for the morning.
> (Psalm 130:5–6)

We are ever watching for the coming of Christ, which produces a missional exigency and expectation. There is a more at stake here than filling a room for a worship service and calling it a church; there are souls in the balance. The imminence of the return of Christ should hurry our steps. This fire within us does not consume us, however, because what we watch for is not a deadline that will leave us grieving over what we were unable to accomplish. Instead, it is a finish line when all we've hoped for will be fulfilled and we rest at the wedding supper of the Lamb, gazing along the table at all those we have had the honor of introducing to Jesus. Then, and only then, will our vigil on the wall be complete. Remember this image, and be encouraged when church planting seems too much to take.

The Priest as Steward

These churches, these people, our office—they do not belong to us. We are merely stewards. They are not for us to do whatever makes us most comfortable or is the least amount of risk. Our God is a God of mission, and the role of the priest is to steward the church plant over which he has charge to be an effective part of that mission.

You will face a tension: Knowing your first duty is to plant a church in which the pure Word of God is preached and the sacraments duly administered, you may spend all your time ensuring this purity at the neglect of outward mission. Or you may feel the opposite pull, tempted to compromise the sanctity of Word and sacrament for ease of mission. You must steward both—protect the primacy of Word and sacrament while integrating it with a sustained missional focus.

In my experience, church plants that do not see fast and profound growth all experience a moment when, after they have been toiling and beating the bushes and there are not as many people in the church as they had hoped, someone says, "You know, maybe the Lord is just calling us to be a small church." This is a critical moment because there are two roads here: One leads to using this platitude as justification for simply turning inward and enjoying life together until everyone moves away or dies. The other leads to responding with, "That may be true. Maybe the Lord is calling us to be a small church. But he surely is not calling us to stop the work of mission." Isaiah was called to go to a people who would not listen—but he still went. He didn't say, "Maybe the Lord is calling me to be a minor prophet." Although we expect and work for a harvest, we keep planting faithfully whether the harvest comes or not. So steward the mission well.

Being a steward also means priests do not work for the people of their congregations. We are servants to them, we are shepherds of them, but we are not their employees. We are not service providers to the people as if we must meet the needs of consumers; we are stewards of God's church. We know we must give an account—and it will not be to the vestry, but to Jesus himself. Serving the people and serving God are in no way antithetical, for indeed God has sent us to serve the people. The people we are serving should even have input in the way we are serving them. Our leadership should be collaborative. But ultimately, as stewards, we serve the people according to the desires and will of God. We must love our people enough to risk our job to do our job, and lead them to the green pastures of God no matter the cost.

Before I left seminary to plant, I sat down with Bishop John Rogers. I asked for any advice he could give me as I stepped into a formidable work. The first thing he said to me was, "You have to teach your people how to have a priest so they will know how to care for you as you care for them." This has been some of the sagest advice I have ever received.

The people of your church plant are looking to you for an example as you model and instruct on the shape of the church. It is easy and exciting to talk about the role of the church in worship, sacraments, social justice, fellowship, music, design, art, service, etc. You must also teach them how to care for you, and that is humbling.

Your people will come to you with a preconceived notion of what the relationship between people and priest should be. Some have had adversarial relationships in the past where they see their role as lay leaders to be keeping the priest in check. Others only see themselves as receiving from you, and never consider any responsibility they have in caring for you as a person. Others truly love you, but do not know the appropriate way to show their care and concern.

You will not be the only priest who leads the church you are planting; there will be others after you. The clearer you can define the role, and the more you can teach your people to appreciate the office of the priest and care for the person in it, the healthier you and your successors and the church itself will be. The writer of Hebrews wrote to the church saying, "Obey your leaders and submit to them, for they are keeping watch over your souls, as those who will have to give an account. Let them do this with joy and not with groaning, for that would be of no advantage to you" (Hebrews 13:17). It is to the advantage of the church not to use up their leaders like so much firewood and shovel the ashes away when those leaders have finally burned out, but to cultivate their priest, encourage and share fellowship with him, care for him financially, look out for his health and that of his family—and to pray daily and vigorously for him.

You need to have direct and open conversations with your lay leadership to set a proper foundation of clergy care—that is being a good steward of your office and those who will follow you in it. Do not let your pride masquerade as humility and keep you from sharing your needs with the appropriate people in your church. Avoid a clericalism where you lead as a separated professional, but rather strike a good balance of leading in strength while walking in mutual affection and submission to one another. The relationship of the priest and the people of the church should be a beautiful thing. Many of those I have had the honor of leading as their priest are some of my dearest friends and have loved me deeply as I have loved them. We have walked through great victories and deep pain. Every ministry I have left, I have departed with significant tears. Discussions of order and systems seem a cold language to use in regard to relationships, but the ordering of the church creates proper expectations on which to build beautiful partnerships and deep friendships.

Another part of the stewardship role of the priest, even when you are a planter, is to pastor those within the church. We must love people deeply and be present in their times of joy and sorrow. In my first year as a priest and planter, someone within our fledgling group died unexpectedly. I called my mentor, King Cole, who was the priest of the church where I grew up. I told him I did not know what to do. He said, "The first thing you do is nothing. You just be with them. A great deal of pastoral ministry is ministry of your presence. Hug them, pray with them, sit with them, stay away when they need time to themselves. You can work through all the details of funerals and things later. For now, just be a physical sign of the presence of Christ." When we are striving so hard to plant and grow a church, we sometimes fall into the trap of looking at people first to see how they can aid the new church, not what the new church should provide for them. We must not neglect being pastors when we are planters.

At the same time, be wary of planting a church only by gathering people to yourself. It will stroke your ego, but what at first will make you feel needed will soon be overwhelming and cause you to despise what you once loved. You must be an equipper. As Paul says, God gave us "the apostles, the prophets, the evangelists, the shepherds and teachers, to equip the saints for the work of ministry, for building up the body of Christ" (Ephesians 4:11–12). Being a steward is equipping the saints to build up the saints.

Stewarding is also modeling. Paul says, "Be imitators of me, as I am of Christ" (1 Corinthians 11:1). The priest, with copious amounts of grace required, is the primary public model of the disciple of Christ. If you as priest and planter want to see your people engage missionally, you must do so as well. If you desire for your church to hunger and thirst for righteousness, they must see it in you. If you want to lead a church of generous people, they need to experience generosity from you. If your home is a place of hospitality, more people in your church will open their homes as well. Steward your flock through modeling life in Christ.

I purposefully list leadership last as an aspect of stewardship. It may be what we think of first when it comes to the role of the church planter, but leadership is not godly or ultimately successful if it is not built upon the rest of stewardship as laid out in the ordinal: teaching, warning, feeding, providing for the flock, seeking lost sheep. The quality of your leadership is not gauged by whether the church has fulfilled your vision, but whether your people have become more like Christ. Your value as a leader is not recognized through the bestowing of ecclesiastical titles or the awe others have for the size of your church. It is your people who are your letter of recommendation to be known and read by all.

I encourage you as a priest and planter to daily pray this prayer that comes from the service of the institution of a new rector:

> O Lord my God, I am not worthy to have you come under my roof; yet you have called your servant to stand in your house, and to serve at your altar. To you and to your service I devote myself, body, soul, and spirit. Fill my memory with the record of your mighty works; enlighten my understanding with the light of your Holy Spirit; and may all the desires of

> my heart and will center in what you would have me do. Make me an instrument of your salvation for the people entrusted to my care, and grant that I may faithfully preach the Gospel and administer your holy Sacraments, and by my life and teaching set forth your true and living Word. Be always with me in carrying out the duties of my ministry. In prayer, quicken my devotion; in praises, heighten my love and gratitude; in preaching, give me readiness of thought and expression; in worship, increase my zeal for godly preparation; and grant that, by the clearness and brightness of your holy Word, all the world may be drawn into your blessed kingdom. All this I ask for the sake of your Son our Savior Jesus Christ. Amen.[8]

Bishop

The office of bishop finds its roots in the biblical use of the Greek *episkopoi,* meaning "overseer." He is the chief pastor of the diocese, holding spiritual oversight over all the churches. His role is to see to the flourishing of the churches, clergy, and laity under his care.

The ubiquitous symbol of the episcopacy (bishops) is the crosier, or pastoral staff—the big shepherd's crook bishops carry. This symbol is given to a bishop at his consecration with the instruction to "watch over the flock of Christ," and is symbolic of his primary duties. Shepherds use a staff in many ways: to lift a newborn lamb and return her to her mother, to hook wandering sheep and return them to the fold, as an offensive weapon to fend off predators, and by gently pressing it on the sheep's sides to guide them along perilous paths on the way to green pastures.[9] It is a symbol of loving authority and should be a consolation to church planters, for the office of the bishop is meant to protect, guide, feed, and comfort you. If you get off track, he can pull you back with his hook. If you bite other sheep, he can give you a thump on the head. Church planters need this kind of fatherly oversight.

In his role in sending and supporting church planters, the bishop should first of all provide apostolic example. Something has gone wrong when our bishops become chief administrators rather than chief missionaries. Their diaconal and priestly ordination vows to be a missionary still hold after their consecration. When the archbishop prays for the new bishop, he asks God to, "Grant to this your servant such grace that he may ever be ready to spread abroad your gospel, the glad tidings of reconciliation with you, and to use the authority given to him, not for destruction, but for salvation."[10] Bishops should always be involved in the work of mission and must resist the pressures that would confine them to an office or restrict them only to service inside the walls of their churches. In the same way that a planter is the primary missional example for his people, if a bishop desires a missional diocese, he must continue to be engaged in the work himself: preaching the gospel, confirming with an emphasis on sending, connecting with the lost, doing the work of an evangelist. A missional church requires missional bishops.

The bishop is the chief direction-setter for the diocese. I pray that every bishop will see that church planting must be a primary enterprise of their diocese and accentuate it as such. Aggressive emphasis on church planting will lead to more people coming to know Christ, will provide a lasting leadership pipeline for the entire diocese, and will inspire and equip existing churches to engage in mission as well. Bishop, I know you are under immense pressure from the churches, donors, rectors, and people who already belong to your diocese to meet their needs and resource their existing ministries, but I will pray for your courage to break free from this centripetal pull and lead your diocese to reach those who are not yet a part of Christ's church.

Many clergy and laity who have a significant desire to be involved in high-level leadership in a diocese are not naturally church planters. Entrepreneurial church planters do not usually take time off from the front lines to volunteer for the standing committee, the budget task force, or the commission on ministry. This means policies are often shaped with established churches in mind, not the needs of church planting. Part of the solution is for planters to see part of their ministry as engaging in these areas. When missionaries do not take time to give leadership within their organization, they soon find themselves without the structural and budgetary support they need, and they go elsewhere leaving the institution to languish. Both the missionaries and the institutions suffer. So as a planter, serve on the committees that set direction so you can ensure planting remains a priority in the diocese. But the bishop must be engaged in these conversations as well, and ensure that church planting remains central.

Bishops also cannot do it alone. They must leverage the weight of their office to raise up others to give leadership to areas such as church planting. Many dioceses have a designated leader for planting who carries the title of Canon for Church Planting, or something similar. A canon, in modern Anglican usage, is a person set apart by a bishop or archbishop to assist in giving leadership in a particular area. In my experience, dioceses that desire to see churches planted desperately need this leader. It is essential that someone is giving passionate attention and advocacy to church planting, for the diocese will always lean toward bureaucracy and insulation. Also, the demands of effective, sustained, and healthy church planting are quite high, so the ministry needs particular attention. With all of his other duties, the bishop needs help to give close watch over this work. I encourage all bishops to delegate authority to a canon for church planting.

Delegating, however, does not mean "set it and forget it." The canon for church planting cannot advocate, create a culture, and build support structures for planting without authority, platform, and resources. The title alone is not enough.

Delegating authority means allowing the canon to set up systems and requirements to ensure healthy planters. It also means not circumventing those systems. Nothing is more frustrating than for a canon for church planting to be given the responsibility of creating church planting structures like assessment, training, and coaching only to have the bishop give exceptions to potential planters who speak directly to him. Truly delegating authority means working with the canon to create appropriate structures and then the bishop should limit his own power to approve candidates, making sure they go through the proper process under the direction of the canon without any promises of special treatment.

The bishop must give church planting a platform: he should talk about his emphasis on church planting and provide space at every diocesan event for church planting leaders to educate, inspire, and equip the diocese. I promise that the bishop will face backlash from those who get tired of hearing about church planting and want to promote other ministries. There is an important place for all godly ministries, but we should operate those ministries on the foundation of planting. More churches means more youth ministry, and more youth ministry means more church planters. Women's ministry is vitally important, so how do we leverage our women's ministries to better support church planting? The participation in church planting of those with a heart for any particular ministry serves to spread the ministry about which they are so passionate. Church planting is spreading the service of the church, so an emphasis on planting will result in more service to the poor, women's ministry, men's ministry, youth ministry, children's ministry, multi-ethnic ministry, and every other good thing the church pursues. Church planting is not in competition with these pursuits; it is the way these pursuits expand and are made stronger. So, our dioceses should give a special platform to the work of church planting because it strengthens all the rest. Keeping church planting central takes attention because church planting is easily ignored, since its focus is on people not yet in the room.

Church planting needs resources to flourish. Standing committees and budget subcommittees hold significant sway over the direction of the diocese. The bishop cannot delegate this process to the point of inattention. It is one thing to stand in front of the diocesan synod and passionately call the diocese to be a church planting diocese, perhaps even throwing out a numerical goal like "fifty churches by 2050." That is all well and good, and much needed to help shape the culture, but the bishop now must also engage in the more difficult work of fighting the good fight of the budget. The bishop should look at the calendar and budget of the diocese to see where its resources of time and money are being given. This will reveal the true priorities of his diocese.

If I may, I will speak directly to you bishops who are wondering how to best support the church planters under your care. First of all, recognize how important you are to your church planter. I cannot imagine planting without a bishop. I love my bishop and I love that the authority for the health of any church I plant does not end with me. Planters need your office, but they also need you. Your words carry great weight and your encouragement matters. They are risking more than many of your clergy and, doing so as a part of your flock, they need your particular care. So engage with your planters from time to time to build them up. Even unexpected texts or handwritten notes go a long way to making sure they know they are not forgotten. You should not micromanage them, and please don't give them planting advice if you have never planted before. They just need you.

Second, give them influence in the diocese. Your planters can feel less important than the large established churches, or suppose that their voice does not matter, but you can challenge that presupposition by doing things like seeking their counsel, publicly celebrating the work they are doing, and asking them to address diocesan gatherings. Don't unintentionally insinuate to them or to the diocese that they must prove themselves through people and money before they are worthy of attention. Yes, they are going to make mistakes. They will come on too strong sometimes, and they can be young and impulsive, but this does not make them a liability. If we are going to err, let it be toward overzealousness for mission rather than soft capitulation to insular inactivity. Your planters are some of the most creative and passionate leaders in your diocese. You will gain a great deal from their perspective, and the culture of the diocese will be moved away from being a risk-averse organization marked by its fear of failure—and shaped into a place of boldness.

Third, give your church planters a canon for church planting. Your time constraints will not allow you to be as active in their work as you may desire. Fund, find, and deploy a canon as a gift to your planters.

Finally, pray for them by name every day. Keep them in the center of your thoughts, for they are what you want all the leaders and churches in your diocese to be: engaged in mission, preaching the Word, celebrating the sacraments, pursuing holiness. Pray for their success and perseverance, and pray that more people would follow the example of these missionaries in your midst.

One reason the majority of your planters decided to plant in the Anglican tradition is that they are excited to not be planting an autonomous local congregation, but one that is connected to the greater church through their bishop. You are a gift to your church planters.

Let me close by giving a few words of wisdom to those who are learning how to relate to a bishop for the first time. I have had a bishop for my entire life, and I have worked very closely with dozens of bishops over the years, so I can speak with some experience here. Treat your bishop as you would your father, or if your relationship with your father was particularly unpleasant, relate to him as you wish you could have related to your biological father. It is okay to desire his love and encouragement. You can find comfort in his oversight. You can celebrate when he comes to visit. We respect his office—you made a vow to submit to him if you were confirmed or ordained. We also, hopefully, respect him as a godly man. He can discipline us if needed, but that should be comforting rather than scary because we all need to be corrected at times.

Remember that respect and submission do not mean that you cannot disagree or have difficult discussions, nor does it mean that a bishop is beyond correction or reproach. At the same time, like our fathers, bishops have gained wisdom we should not dismiss quickly. Many church planters come into a diocese with strong opinions about how things can be done differently to create farther-reaching mission and faithfulness. Keep that fire—the diocese needs it. But also remember that fiery young church planters come with some naivete. Bring your thoughts and your wonderful idealism to your bishop and talk it through with him. His relationship to Christ and excellent service to his church have been discerned and proven worthy by the community of the diocese, so you should approach him with an expectation of credible counsel. Equally, keep in mind that he is a normal man, so treating him with too much awe will lead you to cynicism and disillusionment because he can never live up to inflated expectations. Finally, remember that he also needs you. Encourage him, pray for him, join him under his leadership to create a diocese that plants many vibrant churches. My hope is that the longer you walk with your bishop, the more you will value him not only as an overseer, but also as a treasured friend.

Laity

I do not list the laity last as a sign of lesser importance in the work of church planting. Quite the contrary, I list them in an honored position. All the ordained orders exist within God's church to serve, build up, and send the laity into the work of ministry. The laity is an esteemed order within the church.

As Anglicans we believe in the priesthood of all believers. Using the term *priest* to describe both the ordained and lay ministries can obscure the differences between the two, and that is good. There are functions of the priestly ministry that are common to all Christians: the consecration of the world by bringing what is holy to what needs redemption, the introduction of the people to God, the proclamation of the gospel in Word and deed, engagement in the worship of God. Clergy are called out from among the people for particular authority and responsibility, but that in no way diminishes the authority unordained Christians find in Christ—nor the responsibility they share in mission. We must fight against clericalism that frames the clergy as the chief ministers or professional Christians who must do all the work of the church that requires knowledge or skill. The clergy are here to equip the saints of the laity, so there is not one minister in the church, but dozens.

Every successful church planter can tell you quickly the names of a handful of lay persons, clearly sent by God into the work, without whose labor the church plant would never have gotten off the ground. In thinking of the laity who were highly influential in the churches I have planted, I could list names for pages: Steve and Meg Morris, the young military family who loved my family well and are now the godparents to our oldest son; Todd Miller, the chemical engineer and salesman who brought calm order and invited many people to the plant; John Szoka, the retired lieutenant colonel and current state representative whose appropriate resistance made us think deeply before making any decisions; Novice and Charlotte Taylor, a retired couple ready to serve in any way asked; Tracey Laureles, the physical therapist, and her best friend and business partner Shannon Easingwood, who invited dozens of people to our new church; David and Dawn Sturkey, whose generosity in serving and giving kept the church alive during a difficult time. The list goes on: the Biglers, the Warens, the Austins, the Fishers, the Tyrons, the

Walks, and so many more people I love deeply and for whom that I am forever indebted that I have not listed here. These are the church planters. These are the unnamed heroes of the work. You are reading a book with my name on the spine, but I am simply representing their work. No church plant succeeds without names like these, and it is for the raising up and sending out of these people that the church is being planted.

Often there is one person, one couple, or one family that serves as the primary catalyst for the church plant in its very first days. It is these people whom I believe Jesus is referencing in Luke 10 when he sends out the seventy-two with instructions to look for the person of peace in every community where they would proclaim the gospel. This household welcomes the missionary sent by Christ, assists with his provision, and accepts him into their family. They serve as the entry point into the community, the first finger grip on the cliff face to start the climb. The person of peace who already has trust within their community brings credibility to the church planter who may be new to town. They leverage their network of relationships to introduce the planter and make initial connections. Paul had Lydia in Acts 16, I had Vance Tyson in North Carolina, and every other church planter has their person of peace. If you are reading this book as a lay person, I challenge you to see your calling as the person of peace who plays a significant role in initiating, gathering, funding, and providing for the church plant and welcoming the person sent to be the lead planter in your town.

As the laity, it is you who will fill the empty seats, not the preaching prowess of your pastor. It is you who will participate under the leadership of your clergy to make disciples. It is you who will both engage in the worship of God and bring others to join you. Your work will lead to the new birth and baptism of souls who are currently far from Christ. Your generosity in sacrificial giving will fund church planting work. Your calling to be a part of this church plant is not simply to be a warm body who helps create a critical mass so that the church plant can move more quickly to public worship. You are not a part of this church plant to serve your convenience or your preference. Do not sell yourself short. You have been given a much more joyous calling by Christ himself to love him, serve him, and bring others to him. You are not simply a part of a church plant; you are a church planter.

One of the most important ways the laity is called is to invite others to explore the work of the church plant. Have coffee with them, then invite them to meet the planter or become a part of the group that is praying about starting the church. The church plant needs your generosity with your resources: give generously of your money, your time, and your giftedness. See yourself as a midwife, birthing and caring for new Christians in your midst. Older laity especially can bring a credibility and consistency to a younger planter's leadership, for as others see you willing to participate and follow, they will as well.

Another call upon the laity is to pursue your vocation well. You are not working in your secular job as a placeholder, so that you are only serving God when you are directly serving in the church plant. Your vocation, no matter how unimportant in the eyes of the world, is a viable and important calling from God. It has value and meaning, and you must pursue it well as a witness to the gospel. Most of the people who will be influenced by the new church plant will live a significant portion of their lives pursuing their vocations. The church plant must seek to make disciples who do not differentiate the life of the gospel and the life of the workplace, but bring the two together in ways that transform the daily reality of serving Christ. As George Herbert penned:

> Teach me, my God and King,
> In all things thee to see,
> And what I do in anything
> To do it as for thee.
>
> A servant with this clause
> Makes drudgerie divine:
> Who sweeps a room as for thy laws,
> Makes that and th' action fine.[11]

The laity also help govern the church. In Anglican polity, the local church, under the authority of the bishop, is led by a priest in close relationship with a body of elected or appointed lay people often called the vestry. The vestry handles things like the budget, rental agreements, policy and procedures, etc. It is their duty to ensure the priest is cared for. They serve also as counselors for the priest, giving feedback and helping with decisions. That said, your church plant should not have a constituted vestry until you officially become a congregation. Until the church is a congregation as defined by your diocese, it is a mission, and a mission has different governance requirements. For example, technically the bishop is the rector of a mission, and the planter is the vicar as the bishop leads vicariously through him. Do not attempt to mimic the structure of existing churches; their ministry needs differ from that of a church plant.

There is a delicate balance in creating governance structure while planting a church. Under-structuring leads to the exhaustion of the planter due to too much responsibility being placed on his shoulders. Under-structuring also leads to a lack of accountability in key areas like finance and important legal and safety matters. On the other hand, structuring too quickly and too much makes the church plant cumbersome when it needs to be nimble. Often in an attempt to see something tangible take shape, church plants start by too quickly forming an authoritative leadership team of some sort. This rarely turns out well. The planter needs room to develop identity, discern the community, and get to know the people. In the early days of a plant, you should not be as concerned with structure as you are with organic relational ministry. In addition, it is important to have time to build relationships, to see who is truly on board with the mission of the church plant and exhibits appropriate giftedness before anyone is given a position.

I once worked with a church plant that had been given a great deal of bad advice when they first started. There were fifteen or so people involved. They were already meeting weekly in a public rented space for worship, and they had a twelve-person vestry. I'm not sure what the other three people thought about that arrangement. Do not try to import leadership structures from larger, more established churches, or recreate your experience in the previous Anglican church you attended. The time for that kind of organization will come, but to formalize leadership systems too early will quickly bog down your church plant.

Approach church structure like you would scaffolding and only put up as much as you need for your church's current size and expected growth. Don't fall behind and don't get too far ahead. In the world of IT, they call it "the hug of death" when a link goes viral and too many people click it at one time causing the website to crash because the infrastructure cannot handle the traffic. It is a hug because it is a good thing that everyone likes what you are doing, but it is death because it puts too much pressure on underdeveloped systems. At the same time, too much structure creates bureaucracy, and the people of the church plant will spend too much time in meetings and internal discussions when they should be out in the community reaching the lost.

Another problem with structuring too quickly is that most of the people do not have experience in church planting and will attempt to run the church plant as an existing church, inadvertently squashing the creativity that is needed for the new plant to be successful. This is important: a church plant is not simply a small established church; there are differences between leading a newly-starting congregation with a missional trajectory and maintaining a small church. Small-church leadership tends to make decisions that mitigate risk and ensure survival rather than aggressively pursuing mission. This kind of leadership means sure death to a church plant.

People who want a say in governing the church should first model the kind of missional and generous leadership the church plant needs. If you over-structure by writing bylaws too quickly, creating vestries too soon, or putting people in leadership before they have shown proper character and competencies, the work will become slow, ineffective, dysfunctional, contentious, and unenjoyable.

Structure should serve the ministry, not vice versa. It should be dictated by the needs of the ministry. In the early stages of the plant, the planter should ask an appropriate number of people (in the very beginning, no more than three) to serve on a temporary organizational team that provides financial controls and assists in the administrative needs of the church. Call it whatever you'd like—Advisory Team, Finance Team, Shepherd Team, etc. This team does not dictate what is spent where, but serves to keep the planter and the church above reproach in its financial systems by serving as check signers, overseeing donations, and auditing monthly bank statements. This group can then help with the legal processes like incorporation and purchasing liability insurance. That is all the infrastructure needed in the very beginning.

The planter also needs counselors who can give insight and feedback. These people should be informal at first and then more formal as time progresses. You are not establishing an authoritative body; you are building a council of advice. Do not be hasty in laying on hands in giving away authority, because it is very hard to take back without causing damage. The church planter should take time and move deliberately in formalizing leadership structures. Laity, seek first to build relationship with your planter and with those outside of the church. You can best help your church plant succeed not by seeking positions of authority, but by executing the highest office in the church—the servant.

These warnings do not sideline the laity. Rather, one of the joys of church planting is being able to help reform what it means to serve the church and the world. The laity are not limited to filling slots in a system, but are built up and released into the world. If you are reading this book as a lay person, you are the heart and soul of the church, and the success of any church plant depends on the Lord working through your service and participation.

The Role of Other Churches

The Anglican Way emphasizes that we are not autonomous congregations, so the nature of who we are should cause us to collaborate with other churches in church planting. What is often called mother-daughter church planting, when an existing church is the primary catalyst and support for a new church plant, is one of the most effective ways of starting a new church. The mother church is given vitality by the new daughter church, and the daughter church is given stability through the provision of the mother church. My dream is for every local church to one day see giving birth as a normal part of life and mission.

Here's some quick advice: First, do not do this alone. I know it is exciting and certain leaders in your church will want to take this ball and run. There are also many pitfalls and mistakes. Work closely with your canon for church planting if you have one, and get a coach to walk you through this process. A mother-daughter relationship can be a beautiful thing, or it can go quite badly.

Second, do not get locked into any one concept of this model; it can take many different shapes. Not every mother-daughter plant requires that the mother church gives away a large percentage of her people and an enormous amount of money, sending the new church out but being left weakened and grieving in the process. There are many ways to approach this work that can result in both strong mothers and children.

Third, be clear about the trajectory of the church plant. What will the relationship between mother and daughter look like in the coming months and years? Is the goal to remain forever connected, or immediately separate, or is there some timeline of growing autonomy? Canon Billy Waters serves as pastor of Wellspring Church in Denver, Colorado, canon for church planting for the Diocese of the Rocky Mountains, and leader of the Wellspring network of churches. When the churches he leads look toward planting another church, he works with them to articulate answers to three questions:

> What are we always going to share?
> What are we never going to share?
> What will we share for a little while?

These questions help outline the roles and expectations of the two churches. What is the role of the vestry of the mother church? Will it have authority over the daughter plant and for how long? What markers will indicate when this relationship needs to change? What about the rector of the mother church? Does he have a say in how things function in the daughter church, and to what limit and for how long? What about finances? Does the plant have its own budget or are the two intermingled, and who makes spending decisions? Mother-daughter plants can range in level of autonomy from being immediately their own entity to forever remaining a campus of the mother church.

Any human mother of a daughter knows that there is disagreement about the appropriate level of autonomy as her daughter grows from child to teen to adult. How much oversight in decision-making does the mother have? How does she know when to step back and let her daughter have more independence? In a family, these issues are usually worked out with tears and slamming bedroom doors. Failure to clarify these expectations lead to significant conflict in a mother-daughter church planting relationship as well, and the slamming doors cause quite a lot of damage.

Finally, and this is vitally important, put all of your decisions and agreements in writing. When things get difficult and conflict arises, people will remember conversations differently. Clarify your partnership and put it in writing signed by the rector, a representative of the mother church's vestry, and the planter of the new church.

If you are the rector of an established church who would like to see your church plant more churches, I encourage you to find training, coaching, and friendships to walk through the process with you. Planting is an expensive and risky endeavor, and your stewardship requires you to do your due diligence before entering into the process. I will give you one other warning: do not plant a church with adulterous intentions. Do not plant because you are bored or frustrated with the church you currently lead and you want to have a new focus for your affection and attention while keeping the consistency of your stable role as pastor. You will end up being involved just enough with the church plant (usually the fun parts) that you are in the way, and you will be distracted enough from your primary responsibility that aspects of the mother church will suffer as well. You must either begin the process ready to bless and give away, or you need to leave your position to go and plant the church. You cannot have the excitement of one and the stability of the other—that's cheating. To wobble in between will weaken both churches as you take payment from one but give your best to the other. You must decide if you are called to be the pastor of a church-planting church or whether you are called to go and plant.

Having babies is life-giving to the mother and to the child. It is scary and we never feel like we are ready. If you wait until you have enough people, enough money, or enough stability, you will never have kids, whether we are talking about people or churches. We must risk, but the reward is worth it. To see our children and church plants grow and bring new life to those around them is to see the work of God.

The Role of the Diocese

As previously referenced, we have two ways we might view our diocese: either it is a bureaucratic obstacle for mission that forces us to find ways to plant churches outside its confining structures, or it is an engine for church planting that ensures sustained and healthy churches. I believe the former is often true, but the latter is possible if we are intentional about it.

To be effective in the work of church planting, a diocese has four primary functions that I call the Four C's: (1) articulate its church-planting convictions, (2) shape a church-planting culture, (3) create church-planting constructs (systems), and (4) facilitate the collaboration of its churches in the work of planting.[12]

Diocese Function: Articulating Convictions

Articulating church planting convictions means seeing church planting as a command for the church. Church planting is not simply an option; it is part and parcel of the making of disciples, which is the purpose of the church. Biblically, theologically, and historically, the church has planted churches and the diocese should see itself playing an important role in this process. If this is truly a conviction, the diocese must see a lack of church planting not simply as a disappointment, but as an area of unfaithfulness that needs immediate remedy.

Diocese Function: Shaping Culture

Culture consists of the unwritten norms and expectations of an organization, so creating a church-planting culture means crafting a new normal in which church planting is the natural outcome of diocesan life. Culture is simultaneously the most neglected and, outside of the Holy Spirit, the most powerful force for the planting of new churches—far more influential than any strategy. The great business consultant Peter Drucker is purported to have said, "Culture eats strategy for lunch." What he is saying is that it is not enough to build systems or appoint leaders or make grand statements challenging the diocese to engage in the work of church planting. We must shape the culture of the diocese.

The current reality is that church planting is often seen as being done by the select few. What if a diocese so embodied its missional identity that it felt strange *not* to plant a church rather than strange when someone does? What if churches that did not birth new churches were looked upon as needing assistance to fully live into their calling, no matter their size? What if the cardinal and most influential churches of a diocese were not the largest or the wealthiest, but the churches who were most engaged in the work of mission? This is the shift we need in our dioceses.

This way of being comes down to identity and purpose. Our understanding of who we are and what we should be about shapes what we celebrate as success, what future leaders model themselves after, who is given influence, what is funded, and what is expected. The diocese should publicly celebrate missional risk and fruit, concentrate on raising up leaders for this task, ensure that people involved in church planting shape policy, craft budgets around this endeavor, and articulate not merely a hope but an expectation for church planting. Then it will see many churches planted for an enduring season.

I recognize that actually pursuing this cultural shift will cause a firestorm. Some people will lose political influence, and some churches will lose their place of prominence—and they will not go gentle into that good night. You will lose some donors when their needs are no longer catered to. Meetings will need to be run differently. Staffing will need to be reworked. This will not be easy.

A primary example of how culture has practical influence on ministry is in the area of budgeting. Often, diocesan budgets prioritize existing ministries first and then kick the can of planting down the road by promising to explore alternative ways for its funding. Most often these promises are left unfulfilled. The governing body's conscience is mollified because they gave church planting a nod, but they breathe a sigh of relief because in their minds they clearly cannot currently afford church planting. And that is true if the norm and expectation for the diocesan budget is first to fund everything needed and then if there is any leftover toss it over for optional ministries like planting churches. The problem here is that church planting should not be seen as optional, and there is never any leftover. Funding church planting is not always about finding more money that does not yet exist. It means prioritizing church planting as an essential work of the diocese. If not, then even as the diocese grows in its income, new dollars will be allocated elsewhere before they make it down the list to church planting.

Most people who volunteer for the unpleasant task of serving on budget committees have experience in budgeting for small businesses or in small local churches that have operated under an attitude of scarcity. As a result, they budget extremely conservatively. Other people join these committees in a self-serving way, wanting to ensure that the diocese funds their desired projects. Others serve good-heartedly, but do not have the experience to shape a diocesan budget. There are few people who have experience in aggressively funding mission work. Dioceses should not allow just anyone who can fog a mirror to serve on this committee. I am not disparaging the brave souls who would serve the church in this thankless way; I am exhorting the bishop to work with his standing committee to equip the budgeting team with the right people, the proper training, and a framework that values mission. This way, the budget committee is made up of people well-suited for the role who are also well-prepared to make a budget with mission and church planting at the top of their list of priorities rather than at the bottom. The bishop must not be absent from budget discussions, either. After doing the public work of exhorting the diocese to pursue church planting, he must then engage in the hard work of seeing to its proper funding. If we do not do the work of budgeting for church planting, we are placing more risk and more burden squarely on the backs of the local church planter making it even harder for them to succeed. Then if our success rate goes down, we are less likely to fund church planting. It is a death spiral. Properly resourcing mission begins with a culture that prioritizes church planting and sees the role of diocesan systems as supporting that priority.

Budgets are not the only outward and visible sign of our invisible culture. Look down the list of those who serve on important committees and leadership teams in any diocese, and you will often see many names who are doctors, lawyers, politicians, etc. Again, we need these people and their profound gifts, and in no way do I mean to insult those servants who wish to use the skills they have sharpened in their professions for the good of the church. But I am advocating for an equal number of people who bring a complementary set of skills in starting new things. How different would our dioceses be if our policy-making committees were made up of equal parts people who bring needed stability and people who are innovative risk-takers! A church-planting diocese needs a culture that asks, "How do all aspects of our shared diocesan life from our committees, to our Synods, to our ordination processes, to our selection of a bishop serve to advance the mission of the church and the starting of new church plants?"

Diocese Function: Creating Constructs

One of my favorite movie moments comes from the fantastic film *Apollo 13*. After major malfunctions on the flight's command module, the three-man crew was forced to evacuate into the lunar module. The problem was that the module was built for only two astronauts. They realized quickly that they were running out of oxygen. The air scrubbers that removed carbon dioxide and made the air breathable were being overloaded. They had filters from the command module, but those were a different shape. So back on earth, a group of NASA engineers gathered around a table covered with pieces and parts that mirrored what the astronauts had at their disposal in order to literally make a square peg fit into a round hole, "We've got to find a way to make this [the engineer holds up the square filter] fit into the hole for this [he holds up the round filter] using nothing but that [he points at the table covered with parts]."[13] In one of the most famous examples of workaround ingenuity, they did it and saved the astronauts.

Diocesan structures that were built for maintenance simply cannot produce missional church planters without a team of ecclesiastical engineers trying to find a workaround that allows a square peg fit in a round hole. Our diocesan experience for many years has been grounded in risk aversion, not mission, and our systems have been built accordingly. We will not get church planters out of systems designed to create something else. We need more than a workaround; we need to rebuild the machine.

A diocese needs seven systems in order to pursue church planting:

1. **Leadership pipeline.** Recruiting and shaping of new church planters
2. **Assessment.** Walking through discernment with potential church planters
3. **Training.** Equipping planters with the needed skills
4. **Coaching.** Providing a guide to walk beside church planters
5. **Funding.** Giving church planters needed resources
6. **Ongoing support.** Caring for the souls of church planters
7. **Strategic oversight.** Giving proper leadership to maintain these support systems

Every diocese needs these seven systems for church planting to be healthy and effective. Various church-planting networks have differed in the number of systems, but the same basic components are found in most healthy networks. There are local options for how to approach these systems, but every diocese needs an expression of each of them. My hope is that if you are in diocesan leadership, you will see the need for devoted leadership and proper funding to make these systems a reality.

Let's see how these systems might affect a diocese's church-planting budget. In my opinion, the budget should go toward effective oversight for church planting first before giving out church-planting grants. This is where a diocese often gets things backward as it takes whatever funds it has for church planting and, with a heart for equity, gives micro-grants to as many church planters as possible. So if the diocese has $50,000, ten church planters get $5,000 apiece. That is not enough to make much of a difference in a local plant. Instead, the diocese needs to focus on how its money can be used to support the largest number of planters.

First, hire a canon for church planting—it is too much work to ask someone simply to volunteer. Let your canon develop the systems that will ensure healthy and sustained church planting. Empower your canon to put together a leadership team that will develop a strategy. Part of this strategy will include training planters in fundraising. The diocesan budget carries the burden for providing the leadership systems that will result in numerous quality church planters who know how to plant a church and are all equipped to raise funds to do so. By structuring the budget this way, diocesan resources have then been multiplied and have farther-reaching effects than giving a few plants a small amount of financial support.

I hope the diocese will take the next step and also do annual campaigns, with the bishop as the chief spokesperson, to raise further funds that can be given as substantial grants to church plants. But do not give grants simply to someone who shows interest in planting in a particular area, no matter how strategic the location or attractive the planter. Grants should only be given to planters who participate with your canon to prepare properly, go about the work in a healthy way, reach certain benchmarks, and then can show they need capital to increase the momentum they have already created. This way you are ensuring the quality of your planters, creating awareness of the process of planting, and building credibility that will inspire trust from potential future donors.

Many times, I have spoken with a diocese or a donor about funding church planting and received a response of frustration or suspicion. Eventually, they tell me a horror story of giving a planter tens of thousands of dollars with nothing to show for their investment. Nearly every time, I ask more detailed follow-up questions. I find that the planter was never assessed, trained, coached, given accountability, or provided with relational support. I am all for funding church planting generously, but also for funding church planting wisely.

Diocese Function: Facilitating Collaboration

Collaboration is often an afterthought for planters and dioceses. Perhaps it comes from a familiarity with church that leads to a mistaken idea: since we know church, we should be able to plant one. This is no truer than thinking we can build a refrigerator because we use one every day. Sometimes ego and pride make their way into church planting as well, showing up as a false belief that no one else understands the situation. Whatever its cause, too many planters, churches, and dioceses pursue church planting without seeking help from those who have done this work recently, without working with other local churches, and with a disregard for the work of other dioceses.

Having started and led an organization that comes alongside church-planting efforts, I am shocked by how late in the process many people reach out for help. So many mistakes can be avoided with proper training and early collaboration.

Our Anglican interconnectedness should allow us to see those who can help us not as threats or glory thieves, but as invaluable assets. Provinces should work together to assist each other in planting. The interaction of dioceses with a geographic focus and non-geographic dioceses should be filled with communication and shared decision-making, to honor the work done by each. Local churches should support one another with wisdom, relationship, and finances. Church planters can care for and encourage the work of other planters. If raising children takes a village, planting churches takes the whole church.

Collaboration literally means "co-laboring." Seek help from others and seek it early. Intentionally support the work of others. Plant churches with the kingdom in mind. I agree that it makes things more difficult sometimes, but doing the hard work of family will result in more and stronger churches in the long run. Church planting should transcend church politics and clergy egos, to gather us around an immediate and important cause. Our unity makes us stronger. Our collective effort makes a movement for multiplication.

The Role of the Province

The province is the sphere of our polity that allows for the dioceses to relate to one another. The role of the province is to be a servant to her dioceses and people. As canon for church planting for the Anglican Church in North America, my role is to focus the province's church-planting efforts.

To pursue this end, we started the Always Forward church-planting initiative. Always Forward is a collaborative effort of the province, dioceses, local churches, and people of the Anglican Church in North America working together for the planting of new, gospel-centered, sacramental, missional churches throughout North America. We define our work as equipping a movement, strengthening our dioceses, and supporting local planters. Provinces do not plant churches, local planters do. And local planters are better supported and prepared for their work through a diocese with the proper convictions, culture, constructs, and collaboration. The province seeks to assist the dioceses in their work, and leverage the synergy that is created when more than thirty dioceses are working together in a collective effort for the planting of new churches. A diocese that desires to plant churches should not start with a blank page, but rather with a book full of the wisdom and best practices of others who are engaged in this work, and with a supportive community to encourage them, equip them, challenge them, assist them, celebrate with them, and pray for them. This is the invaluable work of the province—to see dozens of dioceses effectively engaged in the work of planting hundreds of churches together.

The Role of the Communion

The Anglican Communion is composed of around forty self-governing provinces throughout the world, bound together through a common lineage in the Church of the England. There are currently more than eighty-five million Anglicans worldwide, making the Anglican Communion the third largest Christian communion. This global family creates a network of relationships for partnership in the gospel work of church planting. I have had the opportunity to travel to many of our provinces, and have worked closely with many provincial church-planting leaders, even helping found the GAFCON Church Planting Network. I am constantly amazed by the diversity, passion for Jesus, and love for the church exhibited by these leaders.

Being a part of a global gospel movement should be important to us. The fact that our local work is connected to thousands of other local church plants throughout the world should stretch us and encourage us. Every family has its complicated relationships and its share of dysfunction, and the Communion is no different, but we should treasure our participation. Walking alongside cultures and people different from our own allows us to gain diverse perspectives on church planting that should challenge and strengthen us all. If you are a local planter, be sure to teach your people about their genealogy and show them that their difficult work is being shared in communities throughout the world. As Anglicans, they are part of an enormous family. Let that truth encourage them and provide additional credibility to your leadership as the new ideas and way of being you are teaching them find their source not in your innovation, but in the greater global community.

. . . .

When properly implemented, Anglican polity provides a biblical and effectual system of order and mission and should be an engine for church planting. We have oversight and accountability, encouragement and discipline, authority and servanthood, prayer and practical application. We have been given bishops, priests, and deacons to equip the saints for the work of ministry. We have 85 million laity to mobilize for the work of mission. Anglicanism provides the proper mix of structure and flexibility to allow for faithful and contextualized church planting that will bring many people to the knowledge and love of Christ through word and sacrament. I am so utterly convinced of this truth that I am dedicating my life to its pursuit, and I am inviting you to join me.

A Note to Non-Anglican Readers:

Okay, clearly this chapter is going to need a lot of adaptation to fit your tradition. You know your polity, theology of ordination, local governance structure, etc. much better than I do. I hope, however, as you hear me challenge my Anglican family to regain the missional heart of its organizational structures, that many of these truths apply to yours as well. How should the larger serve the smaller? How should the offices of District Superintendent, or President of the Convention, or Ruling Elder, or whatever else you have support the work of church planting? The Four Cs and the seven systems described in this chapter are equally applicable to your organization as well. Overall, how can you help reform, recreate, and rejuvenate the systems of your denomination or tradition to be an engine for church planting and not a bureaucratic barrier?

CHAPTER 13

....

Common Mistakes of Church Planters

I am not afraid of failure; I am afraid of succeeding at things that don't matter.

— *William Carey*

SUMMARY: We will make mistakes in church planting, this chapter outlines some of the most common in the hopes that we can avoid them.

"Here there be dragons." It was common practice in early cartography to illustrate dragons or sea monsters in the uncharted areas of the map to suggest unknown dangers in these unexplored lands. There are dangers in church planting as well, places where we can make errors that hinder or derail our church planting work.

As trite as it sounds, the inspirational posters and branded coffee mugs are correct: some of our best learning comes from our mistakes. Mistakes teach us what not to do, which can be as valuable as learning what we must do. Thankfully, Anglicans do not go about the work of planting in isolation but as a part of the family of the greater church, so our learning can come not only from our own errors, but also from those of the community. When someone falls through a rotten plank on the bridge, we learn not to step there.

Some of our dragons have been defined. We can hear the wisdom from those who have made this passing before us, those who have scraped their keel on the shoals and rocky shores and marked on the map the reefs on which we can easily run aground. One planter's shipwreck makes for another's safe voyage.

It is perhaps the abundance of mistakes I have made that makes me somewhat qualified to write on the work of church planting. There was the time I first started planting as a twenty-two-year-old kid that I thought I could better equip the people of my church plant for evangelism by purchasing hats and T-shirts. Some of them had logos mimicking popular brands and said things like, "The original OLD NAVY: one Savior and twelve disciples in a fishing boat." Another said, "Check Thyself Before You Wreck Thyself" with a small Scripture verse about repentance. I am cringing while writing these words. I should have been disqualified from ministry. What was I thinking? Who has ever given their life to Jesus based on bad graphic design and Christian subculture T-shirts flippantly referencing the day of judgment for sinners? I am embarrassed.

Or there was the time we thought we would reach out to the neighborhood next to the church building by holding an open house for our newly-rented space. We put out open house signs and placed door hangers on doorknobs in the neighborhood, advertising something to the effect of "New church, come visit us and see our new building. There will be cookies." No one came. What an awkward invitation. Who gets home from work, finds a door hanger waiting with an invitation from people they do not know to walk through a rented building for no particular reason and says, “Honey, get the kids ready, we are going to tour a small temporary space of some new religious group. No, Honey, they are clearly not a cult; they are serving cookies.” My eyes are now closed tightly and I am rubbing my temples.

Less ridiculous, but equally egregious, I have made decisions to meet in the wrong place at the wrong time. Before I understood the sanctity of the liturgy, I chopped it up and rewrote sections to what I thought better fit our needs. I went through a phase of trying to be more contemporary, adding cool lighting to the front of the church. I tried to be more edgy and preached for an hour on sex. I put people in leadership too early. I ignored the counsel of others because I assumed they were just not as entrepreneurial as me. I could go on, but I am now laying prostrate on the floor in shame, and I can’t reach the keyboard. I’m kidding. Sort of.

I am ever grateful that our church planting is built on the gospel of grace. It is equally important to remember that the mission belongs to God, and he can use donkeys and clueless church planters to accomplish what he wills. You will make mistakes too. You are striving to find effective ways of reaching the present while remaining faithful as the church, so you are trying new things. Some will work, others will not.

Planters are the research and development arm of the church. Do not be afraid to properly experiment, or risk, or fall short. Planting is not a safe endeavor, and you are not Jesus, so you will fail at certain things from time to time. The thing about mistakes is that we have only truly learned from them if we do not repeat them, or as Proverbs tells us in one of the more poetic passages of the Scripture, “Like a dog that returns to his vomit is a fool who repeats his folly" (Proverbs 26:11). If the skies were made of parchment, the seas filled with ink, every stalk on earth a quill, and everyone a scribe by trade, we could not endeavor to list all of the mistakes church planters make, but we can work through some of the most prevalent mistakes I have seen in my time working with Anglican church planters so we can learn from them, and hopefully not repeat them. Here there be dragons.

Mistake: Planting Unprepared

The complexity and difficulty of church planting is constantly underappreciated. One potential planter who attended a training I was leading was quite straight with me on the first day: "My bishop told me I had to come this training. I don't need it. I have been a leader in both ministry and business. I have been to church my whole life. I think I've got this. How hard can it be?" I have found that many people share this same arrogance, even if usually unarticulated.

Even more prevalent is the instance where dioceses send out church planters, even give them tens of thousands of dollars, without any assessment, training, or coaching support. Many church planters mistakenly feel they don't need any of these things. Honestly, it takes some chutzpa to be willing to engage in the risk required for church planting, and sometimes this self-confidence splashes over into arrogance. Potential planters will even pull out anecdotal evidence of their friend, cousin, or bishop who planted without preparation and did just fine. Many of these people have reached out to me after a year or two or three to admit they were wrong, that there were so many mistakes they made that could have been avoided if they had participated in more robust preparation at the beginning and coaching along the way. Don't make this mistake. As eager as you are to get off the ground, you still need a longer runway to get safely airborne.

Mistake: Planting a Worship Service Rather Than a Church

It is true that Anglican churches are worship-centric. There is a great deal of discussion on this fact in this very book. Planting a church, however, is not the same thing as planting a worship service. Our Sunday worship is a major part of our life as the church, but it is only one part. Many planters dream of starting a new church and their thoughts focus on what weekly worship will look like. Yes, that should be in the forefront of our minds, but it should not be your starting point. You are doing more than simply attempting to fill a sanctuary.

If you do begin with a full sanctuary as your principal goal, all of your methodology will be aimed at simply gathering. This is perhaps the most prevalent philosophical mistake I see planters make. There is so much more to the church outside of Sunday. How will you disciple the people? How will you govern the people? What's the plan for reaching new people after you have a significant group gathered? How will you care for the people? Mark my words: your methodology cannot be to gather people first, then figure out how to engage them in discipleship and mission. You will be creating a heavy object, then trying to push it up a hill. You need momentum in mission and discipleship that coincides with your public worship.

It is much easier to start with discipleship and mission that moves to corporate worship than to start with a weekly worship service and move to discipleship and mission. Think about all the pastors you know who have a small church and are pulling their hair out trying to get their people to engage in mission and discipleship. If your philosophy as a planter is to gather first and then teach the people to be missionaries and disciples, you are simply creating the same situation that is frustrating and burning out so many of your peers! It is like gathering a group of people in front of a hurdle and telling them to jump without a running start.

If you are planting a worship service, not a church, here is what often happens: You will gather a small group of people who will love you and the quaint Sunday service. Adding more people would then make the service lose some of its charm. Plus, all their needs are being met already, so they have no real missional motivation. So you will spend all your time planning and implementing the worship service, your church plant will grow insular, and you will plateau. Then you will linger, and then you will get frustrated, and then you will have to decide whether you are called to be the chaplain of a handful of people or you are called to go elsewhere.

Heartbreakingly, in many situations this choice simply comes down to whether the church is financially self-sustaining. If the planter is able to gather enough people to get an adequate and secure paycheck, he will perform Sunday services for the same small group of people until he dies or enough of the people die that the church wants to start talk about revitalization. In many cases, the church was not vital to begin with—it was halfway planted. Yes, there is a church service and vestry, but there is more to church than that. To think that planting is simply starting a worship service is leaving the conquest incomplete. Joshua only partially finished the mission God gave him, and because of that Israel suffered for many years.

"If I don't begin with a worship service, then what do I do?" Proper training is going to teach you how to begin planting through invitation and evangelism and then properly lead into a worship service. As important as it is, I do not have the space here to dig deep into this process. It must suffice for me to say that you will begin by building relationships and inviting others into this vision for a new church. Begin by building trust. These relationships begin to turn into others who want to share in this work. Gathering will take different forms in different places.

For many it starts like this: Begin to hold launch team meetings at your home where you share fellowship, eat together, give a short teaching, and close with compline or evening prayer. Plan elbow events where the purpose is simply to be together, invite friends, build community, and grow your launch team. As you gather you are discipling, forming, shaping, and caring. Eventually when you see sufficient growth, you can begin to hold monthly preview services to see how your missional momentum is moving. These preview services and ongoing informal gatherings in between then lead to a healthy critical mass for a weekly service.

Again, this is a very shallow description of the process of planting. Robust training will help give you a framework for all that needs to be done and teach you how to set benchmarks to help you know when to take next steps. Coaching will help you create, implement, and adapt your plan. You will need time. These things do not happen quickly.

Plant with a love for Jesus, a passion for his church, and a hunger for the lost. Plant with your goal being an active worshipping community built upon a strong foundation and driven by a common desire to be disciples and make disciples. Plant with the benefit of your local community in mind. Plant for the sake of those who do not know Jesus. Plant with the realization that you are a part of the great redemptive work of God. Don't plant simply to be a weekly event planner.

Mistake: Premature Birth

You will be tempted and pressured to move to public worship as soon as possible.[1] I cannot tell you how many times I have been ignored when I tell new planters not to move too quickly to public worship. I have even ignored my own advice and made this mistake myself.

Why am I so adamant about this? Why can our worship services put a damper on our outward focus? Weekly worship requires a lot of logistics. You need a place to meet, which often requires setup and teardown. It is fun and romantic to set up chairs for your church services—for about a month. After that it becomes a burden with no end in sight, because once you commit to public worship you will do it every Sunday of every week of every month of every year until Jesus returns. If you do not have enough bodies to share the load, you will burn out your people.

Not only do you need people to set up chairs, sound systems, Communion Tables, nursery furniture, etc., but you also need a place to store all of the stuff of the church, a trailer to haul it in, and insurance to cover it all. Your expenses have just gone up exponentially both financially and in manpower.

You will also need greeters, readers, musicians, nursery workers, and many other servants for roles during the service—every single Sunday from now on. If you do not have a critical mass, you will find your volunteers serving every Sunday and the same people who pressured you to move to Sunday worship will leave your church plant because they are worn out. Or you will have so many people out of the worship service serving in various roles that the number of people actually in the service is so few it is awkward. Also, some people will work harder than others and there will frustration and conflict. In their frustration, they will talk about how you are not growing fast enough, or some will even start to say small churches are more virtuous and suggest moving back to your living room in perpetuity.

You also have to prepare a sermon every week now, so you are giving multiple hours to that important process. Don't forget bulletins or song sheets or PowerPoint presentations someone needs to create. Every week. And there's the website to keep up. In the midst of all of this, you are still trying to develop leaders and care for the people of your church.

Your people only have a certain amount of time and energy to devote to planting this church, and now all of that energy is focused on pulling off the Sunday service. There is very little time for outward mission, deeper discipleship, and serving your community. You have just focused a significant amount of your energy inward.

No matter how hard you try, or how much you exhort your people, there is also a change in ethos and urgency when you start meeting publicly. Many will think that you have achieved your goal and will change from missionaries to consumers, settling quickly into a weekly rhythm of attendance.

As the church looks more institutional, the people will act more institutionalized. They will assume someone else is doing the work, when in actuality there is no one else. Just you and your family. And you will burn out too.

You may be thinking, *Well, we are only going to meet in a situation that requires setting up and tearing down temporarily, so we can handle it.* But what is your end game? How does this season end? Is it the building of a facility that will rescue you? That opens another can of worms. Your focus will undoubtedly shift from mission when you start talking about building, and what may have begun as a church plant focused on the lost will become a church plant focused on a capital campaign, then on construction, then on upkeep of the building. There may be a time when building a facility is the right thing to do, but many churches build too early, too small, and in the wrong location where they found the cheapest land. What began with a premature launch into public worship derails their missional focus.

Before you move to full weekly public worship, you need two things: missional momentum and critical mass. By missional momentum I mean that you already have a stream of new people coming to your launch team meetings, social gatherings, and monthly simple times of liturgy and prayer.

Your people need to be fully vested in being gatherers. They will tell you that once you start public worship, their friends will come. No, they won't. That's not how it works. What your people don't realize is that when their friends and coworkers decline an invitation to your home gathering or event by saying, "When you guys start having church services on Sundays, let me know and I'll come," they have in actuality just been politely blown off. Our people must be our method of growth, not programmatic attraction. We must have momentum as gatherers before we divert our energy toward a weekly worship event.

Critical mass is having enough people to meet the volunteer demands of a weekly worship service while also allowing for enough people to be in the seats for a corporate experience. Have you ever shown up to a party that you expected to be large and realized there were only a handful of people there? It is socially awkward. The same is true for those who would come to your worship service. There needs to be enough people that visitors do not feel like the center of attention. With regard to your volunteers, you need enough people for there to be a rotation. You have to do more than make it through one Sunday, you have to make it through 52 Sundays, 104 Sundays, 156 Sundays. Yes, growth will bring in new volunteers, but most people do not show up at your worship service and then immediately sign up to serve numerous weeks on multiple teams. There is a lag before a visitor becomes an active participant. Plus, there are many roles you do not want to put people in until you get to know them. This is why a critical mass of people is so important before you commit to a regular weekly worship service. You have to think about sustainability.

So how many people are a critical mass? I cannot fully answer this question because much depends on your context for planting. A suburban church outside of Atlanta, which can expect many families with multiple children who want well-run programs, may need more people than an urban church in the heart of Washington, DC, made up of single, career-oriented young people. But that same DC church will have to deal with a high turnover rate and will need to take that into account. A church in a community like parts of

Hawaii, where the culture is more informal and welcoming to noisy kids staying in the service, may need a different critical mass than one in a more formal university setting.

In order to give some concrete guidance here, I will hesitantly give my opinion that most churches need at minimum fifty committed adults before they begin weekly public worship services. Some Anglican leaders reading this may scoff and say, "It is a good thing I didn't wait that long to hold public worship. I've been holding worship services for five years and we still don't have fifty committed adults." May I be so bold as to say that it is very possible the reason you still do not have fifty committed adults after five years is precisely because you held public worship services too soon. There is a common phrase in church planting: start small and you'll stay small.

Don't misunderstand me. I am not saying don't gather; I am saying that for all the reasons above, you should first gather around a different purpose and with different execution than a lead-from-the-front, send-out-public-mass-invitations, rented space worship service. From the outline of the process we discussed earlier in this chapter, you can see that your launch team gatherings invite personal relationship and individual involvement. The people are not coming as watchers, they are coming as participants. You are teaching with intentionality about what the church is, what it means to be a disciple, and how we are planting this church. You are fellowshipping at elbow events simply for the value of creating community. These are not high-resource, high-commitment, high-preparation gatherings. Build the community of the church first. Clarify the function and identity of the church first. Gain momentum as people invest in the church plant by contributing financially and by bringing their friends and neighbors to investigate what you are doing. Then, when it is good and right, according to your training and coaching, move to a public expression of what has already been built in your launch team.

Your people who are clamoring for weekly worship do not understand the implications of their request. Like Ulysses, tie yourself to the mast and put wax in your ears in defense against their siren song. Wait. Hold the line. You will better position your church for mission in the community, and build a healthier congregation, if you wait until the proper time for weekly public worship.

Mistake: Failing to Act Your Age

I once visited a church plant that met in a school cafeteria. After the service, I was talking to the planter and a little girl came running by. She was perhaps two years old with a snotty nose, her hair tussled, and juice stains on the front of her pink dress. Like all two-year-olds, she clearly lacked coordination and, just as she passed us, she tripped and fell flat on her face. The planter smiled while he set her back on her feet said, “She was born on the day we launched our church. Every time I get frustrated about our development or how ineffectively we do some things here at the church, I look at her and remember that we are only that age.”

Give your church plant time to grow up. No one looked at that two-year-old girl and shook their head in disgust when she fell as if she ought to know better. Do not look at your church plant like that either. Give it time.

In the West we are consumed with progress and growth, like an angst-ridden teenager. You and many of your people will be eager to be an established church before your time.

People will say to you, "You should stop using the phrase *church plant* because we are not a plant anymore. We are meeting each week. We have a pastor. We are just a church." But do not be ashamed of the *church plant* moniker, for it covers a multitude of sins.

Imagine a new young family visits your new weekly public worship service and your nursery consists of a few hand-me-down toys, a throw rug, and one sweet elderly woman in a rocking chair who loves to hold babies. This could go one of two ways. You might tell that family, "We are a new church plant, just getting off the ground, so right now we have a safe place for your child to be cared for, but in the future we will develop a more robust nursery that not only provides safety, but spiritual formation for your child." Then they have a clear context that this is a beginning with a healthy trajectory. Perhaps they will even get excited about jumping in to help pursue that vision. They have proper expectations and see that if they choose to become a part of this church, they are choosing to join in its mission and development. On the other hand, you might pretend you are an established church, and be apologetic about the form and function of your nursery. Then the lack of a filled-out nursery is no longer perceived as a beginning but as neglect. You exchanged the title of church plant just to be called a dysfunctional established church.

Let your church act its age. Let her fall down. Don't be ashamed of her snotty nose and the juice on her dress. Don't try to hide it or pretend your church is fully grown. When kids play dress-up and wear their mom's shoes or their dad's jacket, it is cute and funny, but no one takes them seriously. So don't try to dress up your two-year-old church in adult clothes that don't fit—you are not fooling anyone. Just as in moving to public worship, you will face pressure from your people to structure. They move to what is comfortable, and structure is comfortable. Mission, evangelism, discipleship, and formation are all intangible, so in an effort to feel useful and safe, longtime church members and businesspeople press for governance, bylaws, administration, and excellence. It is difficult to focus on future trajectory, but easy to point out present imperfections. So church planters and their people can be consumed by organization, administration, and performance. I've seen planters spend hours agonizing over every detail of the page design of a song sheet, get depressed when a social event is not well attended, or trip over themselves to apologize to visitors when things are not perfect. Simply be honest: *there is so much potential, so much we are excited to see our church grow into, but we are not there yet.* And that's okay.

Although it sounds trite, the journey is the destination. Remember, church planting is all about making disciples who worship and serve Jesus, so the markers of success for your church plant are not an implemented governance structure and an error-free bulletin. Those things are not an end in themselves; they are meant to serve the work of making disciples. So relax. Yes, you need an urgency in mission, but remember to focus on the people, have proper expectations for your church plant, and only structure when the time is appropriate. Your markers for success are your people, not your structures.

Mistake: Loving the Liturgy, but Not the Lost

When we plant, we are not reproducing a style of worship or devotional practice simply for its own sake. Our liturgical way of being stems from a love and obedience to the God to whom the liturgy is addressed. Personally loving the liturgy, and wanting to lead a church where the liturgy is valued and elegantly expressed, is not enough to plant a church. You must seek first the kingdom, hunger and thirst for righteousness, and share the heart of the Savior for those who do not yet know him. Your passion must be the fame of Jesus Christ and obedient participation in his mission to make disciples of all nations—we love the liturgy because it advances this cause.

Mistake: Loving the Lost, but Not the Liturgy

Some people who come from other traditions like the concept of Anglicanism more than the reality. The idea of having a bishop who cares for you and brings accountability to you is great until he actually has to hold you accountable. The liturgy and sacraments seem like great additions to avoid a groundless worship service until you realize that the aesthetics you admire express a greater tradition to which you are submitting—that you do not get to write the liturgy; rather the liturgy is meant to rewrite your church.

If you wish to plant an Anglican church, it should be because you find value in a historic, corporate missional endeavor, and you are willing to engage in all aspects of this life. You cannot have parts but not the whole, for all aspects of the tradition give life to one another. Proper liturgical form is symbiotic with sacramental reality and episcopal polity.

If you do not desire this way of being the church in full, then you desire to plant something other than an Anglican church. I will still love you; I will even help you. I will also challenge you, however, before you dismiss the aspects of the Anglican way that are dissimilar to you and adopt an à la carte, autonomous, semi-liturgical, pseudo-sacramental approach, to press more deeply into what initially attracted you. Perhaps you were changed by the liturgy without prior knowledge of the fullness of the tradition and what it entails. Maybe your experience in autonomous churches has led you to seek an authoritative form of church structure but you are not sure about the sacraments. Or you could be searching for something transcendent that the sacraments provide but you cannot wrap your mind around having a bishop. Whatever your starting place, I pray that you will be sufficiently intrigued to explore in greater depth the way of being which inspired the practice that first captured your imagination. Our entire identity and function is meant to work in concert for the glory of Christ and the sake of the lost. Imagine if the rest is as good as the one aspect that has garnered your initial interest. In the words of every infomercial, "But wait, there's more."

Mistake: Not Building Leaders, Teams, and Systems

The initial days of church planting are highly dependent on the individual work of the planter. But also remember that you are bringing people in so you can build them up and send them out. You are inviting people not to live in the house you keep, but to be active participants in the life of the church. If you do not build leaders to share the work, you will burn out and the church will bottleneck at your capacity. If you do not organize those leaders into teams and teach them how to raise up other leaders, they will burn out and the church will be weaker. If you do not create systems for the order and care for your church, the chaos will breed frustration and conflict. Your ministry will consist of reacting to the tyranny of immediate problems, rather than the healthy growth of the church. Jesus gathered twelve, and of the twelve he poured into three, and of the three he focused on one. Eventually through these leaders Jesus sent out seventy-two, then 120, and then entrusted the entire future of the church to the apostles who saw it grow into the thousands. Church planting takes a leader who can both gather and multiply, who has the strength to bear a heavy burden and then the wisdom, humility, and boldness to allow others to shoulder it with him.

Mistake: Financial Irresponsibility

Church planting is chaotic. There is a lot of unpredictability and adaptation. Any organization, however requires administrative order to be healthy. So church planting requires a balance of both—an ordered chaos. There are areas that need to remain loose and there are aspects of the plant that need very firm order.

A primary example of the need for strategic order is the area of finances. Many planters make unintentional mistakes here. In their zeal for the people and the mission, they forget to steward well the resources needed for the work. You need to realize that managing the supply lines is part of building the army. The potential pitfalls in financial order and stewardship are many, so I will only list a few.

First, many planters undercapitalize. There's no getting around it: planting a church requires money. I have found that many planters start with a mentality of scarcity and try to determine the least amount of resources they need to get by in order to begin planting. They act embarrassed that they need money to live on when they plant, or they do not want to seem presumptuous with too large of a budget, so they begin with next to nothing. Without proper capital, the clock starts ticking the minute their feet touch the ground.

They feel pressure to find enough people to grow their church because they need giving to increase to the point it can support the planter's family. This forces compromises like rushing to public worship too early. Stress makes the planter begin to see people as commodities needed to build an operating budget rather than the focus of discipleship. It is not usually the actual ministry of working with people that burns out church planters. It is the pressure of pursuing the ministry under a financial time crunch.

In the business world, the adage is, "Time is money." In church planting, the opposite is true: "Money is time." You need time to build relationships, get to know the culture, find ways to invest in your community, gain trust, etc. There is also a significant lag between meeting people, engaging them with the concept of church planting, and seeing them commit to being a part of the process financially. Even then, most people do not tithe.

If you are reaching the unchurched, it will be a while before they can extract 10 percent of their income to give to the work of the church when they are currently living at capacity while giving nothing. If you find churched people to join you, the unfortunate current reality is the average church attender gives 2.5 percent of their income to the church, which is below the levels given during the Great Depression. Do the math: if your plant is going to cover 100 percent of your personal needs, and each giving unit gives 2.5 percent of that amount, you require forty individual giving units (an individual or a family count as one unit). That is forty individuals or families who are giving the average amount. But assuming you are reaching the unchurched, many of your people will not be giving anything at all. That means it could take sixty, seventy, or even eighty individuals or families to find the solvency you seek. For ease, we'll assume most of the families have two adults and two kids, and your church is mostly made up of families. You could have more than a hundred people coming to events or services before you cover your own expenses. And this is only taking your salary into account, not the entirety of the expenses of the church!

Here's the lesson: You cannot depend on the people of your church plant covering the expenses of your plant, including your salary, for some time. You need to raise a significant amount of capital from other sources like outside givers and sponsoring churches, so that you have what you need to plant the church.

One time, someone came up to me after I had taught on church plant finances and she said, "We are called to trust the Holy Spirit. How do you justify all of this strategy and planning when the Scripture simply calls us to have faith?" I told her that I believe God invented math. Thinking through our financial needs strategically does not deny the need for dependence on faith in the fulfillment of those needs. Jesus himself said, "For which of you, desiring to build a tower, does not first sit down and count the cost, whether he has enough to complete it? Otherwise, when he has laid a foundation and is not able to finish, all who see it begin to mock him, saying, 'This man began to build and was not able to finish'" (Luke 14:28–30). Of course, Jesus's point is the cost of discipleship, but he is employing a parable using common financial wisdom to teach a spiritual truth. Strategic planning is in no way proclaiming that we are not reliant on God's provision; we are asking the Holy Spirit to give us wisdom in our preparation and favor in its accomplishment. We must work the numbers, then pray the numbers, then ask the people of God to help be agents of God in realizing the numbers.

Henri Nouwen taught that there is no dichotomy between funding the mission and the mission itself. He said, "Fundraising is, first and foremost, a form of ministry. It is a way of announcing our vision and inviting other people into our mission."[2] Fundraising is not an unfaithful pursuit that must be endured in order to get to actual mission work; it is inviting others to join us in participating in what we believe God is doing.

This leads to our second common financial mistake: the lack of a five-year plan. You need to understand your financial situation in both the micro and the macro. How many resources will you need to get to the five-year mark? What sort of income will be required from internal and external sources to fill those needs? How does that translate into the amount of money you will have to raise each year for five years? Whether from fear of the large number or despair over not knowing how that money will be found, many planters rush into planting without a sustainable financial plan, and their planting is made much more difficult and anxious.

The third common financial mistake is a lack of controls and accountability. I have worked with planters who received funds from donors directly into their own personal accounts. That's unwise at best and probably illegal. I have seen church plants lose significant funds to embezzlement. Many church planters have no idea how the money works, how much there is, or where it goes until it is too late. I do not have adequate space to outline the processes here, except to say that you need adequate financial controls and oversight so that your funds cannot be stolen or mismanaged by you or anyone else. You should never be a signer of checks. You should never handle ministry finances using your personal accounts. You need to find assistance to maintain proper controls and accounting.

You can find help from a sponsoring church, or your diocese may have the ability to help. Keep in mind that you are not giving away the authority to approve spending, you are finding accountability so that you can be above reproach. Those who help you in this way do not have to be local, but insight and oversight are essential.

Finally, a significant financial misstep for planters is not discussing money at all until it is too late. It is no secret that the work you are doing requires resources. You must be willing to have conversations about the needs of church and ask your people to take part in filling them. It will always feel too early, and the group will always feel too small. You must push through the initial sense of awkwardness in having this discussion and address the responsibility and joy of Christian generosity in your preaching, teaching, and individual conversations. Jesus talked a lot about money, addressing the issue in half of his parables, because he understood its role in revealing our loves and where we put our trust. To fail to do the same in your church plant is to rob your people of the joy of serving as agents of God's provision, and to neglect a significant aspect of their discipleship.

One small example that profoundly impacted me early in my first church plant occurred when I was trying to organize a sermon series and my resources for preparation were woefully inadequate. I didn't have the commentaries and reference materials I needed for proper and well-informed exegesis. I was only recently out of seminary, so I had no books and no funds, and the church plant had no budget for such things. I was nervous, but I picked up the phone and called someone who was part of our burgeoning plant and who had expressed a passion for faithful preaching. I told him my situation and asked if he could help. He told me he would be glad to, and that week he brought a check for $3,000 to allow me to build a library. Not only that, but he called a woman in the church and she was excited to give as well. She told me she would give monthly to make sure I had the supplies I needed. "Pastors need books," she said, immediately endearing me to her for all eternity, "and it would be my joy to help give you what you need to minister to us through the Word of God. All you had to do was ask." *All you have to do is ask* is a phrase to live by in church planting, and not asking is a profound mistake.

Mistake: Doing Some Thing or Nothing

The silence can be deafening. All the assessment is finished. You've completed your training. You've been commissioned, prayed for, and sent out. You've moved to a new location. All the emotional and adrenaline-pumping events of the last year, all the late nights dreaming of the future church plant, all the conversations and tears and fundraising have all led to this day: you are finally planting a church. Now what? You have a laptop and a location, what do you do now? What's first? The weight of this moment can be overwhelming. All the frantic uncertainty of what lies ahead and the frenetic urgency of what needs to be done come crashing down like a silent wave. In your imagination you never pictured day one. Everything was conceptual, but today is tangible and there is a vast void of nothingness—no people, no appointments, no routines—nothing but the sound of silence. Hello darkness, my old friend.

Don't be surprised at the fear that can creep in here. It is normal. A healthy way to react to this moment is to take a deep breath and pray. Ask God to remind you that this is his church and his mission, and he is with you until the very end of the age—this is not all on you. Then remember your training. You have a plan, so work the plan. What needs to be done first? What needs to be done second? Little steps. This is a great moment to schedule a time with your coach and map out the first five days, ten days, and month. If you have not been trained, do not have a plan, and do not have a coach—well, you now know steps one, two, and three. Get assessed, get trained, and get a coach.

There are two unhealthy responses to this moment. The first is doing some thing rather than the right thing. In our frenzied desire to see quick results we feel like we need to create something. All the warnings about structuring too early or rushing to public worship too soon fly out the window, and planters start contacting other churches to obtain a copy of their bylaws or visiting schools to find a potential place to meet. Why do you need bylaws or meeting space when you don't have people? In an effort to feel like they are accomplishing something, planters make strange decisions like holing up in their home office writing copious amounts of text for a website they do not yet have, or making evening prayer worship booklets. Don't do busy work, do the right work. If you have contacts, meet with them. If you don't, then go make friends. Meet your neighbors. When Karen and I first moved to Georgia to plant, we put notes on the doors of all the houses of our neighborhood telling them that we were new and wanted friends, "so we'll be grilling out in our driveway Friday evening for anyone who wants to come by." More than twenty people came. Get out into your community, into the lives of others, and then keep working your plan. Do the right things, not just anything.

The second unhealthy response to the unnerving early days of planting is to do nothing at all. I have seen planters be overwhelmed by possibility. Perhaps they have left a busy ministry position, or a full-time job in the business world, or have just graduated from seminary. In all those cases, much of their time was dictated for them. Now they have to be self-starting, self-motivating, and self-disciplined. The stress of figuring out how to get started gives them paralysis by analysis and they end up binge-watching reruns of *The Office*. You have to wake up. I have seen church planters do very little until whatever funding they have runs out and they move on to other things. Again, work with your coach here to set up a plan for how you will spend your days, and ask your coach to hold you accountable. Pick up the phone and set up some conversations. Go to the local chamber of commerce and ask about your community. Meet with the mayor, the police chief, and the principal of your child's school to hear their perspective on the place where you are planting and the people to whom you have been called. When you are not sure what to do, ask someone to help you figure it out. Doing nothing is never the right thing, except on your day off. Then doing nothing is the something you should be doing.

Mistake: Manipulation and Marginalization

I have served in various roles, overseeing church planting on different levels for many years. Longevity has allowed me to observe church planters from their initial discernment through the first decade of their leadership in a church plant. I have lately noticed a disturbing trend: many church planters who begin healthy and strong finish poorly.

I have seen some things that begin as profound gifts in planting the church turn into liabilities when the church grows beyond the planting season and into adulthood. Specifically, church planters who have faced conflict and experienced hurt and carried the church on their shoulders, often being let down by many who offered to share the load, can develop a cynicism about help from others. The planter's long turn on watch has made him overprotective of the church plant. The planter falls into the trap of leading through manipulation and marginalization when the church gets larger.

After years of serving a small group of people where the planter could spend time with most of the people in the church to influence and disciple them, the planter has to adapt his leadership style when the people become too numerous for his individual attention. Often, instead of giving away ministry and sacrificing individual control by trusting other leaders, the planter creates a small church within the larger church—often without realizing it. He decides who is in and who is out. Those people who are in are the loyal and trusted. Those who are deemed disloyal or of less value are set out on the margins, leading to two groups within the church and eventually conflict between the two. In many cases this leads to fracture within the church or the dismissal of the planter under charges of spiritual abuse. It is heartbreaking.

Again, these situations do not occur because the planter is evil. I believe this behavior stems from years of stress caused by a disproportionate amount of responsibility for the viability and spiritual health of the church plant. When the planter has spent years dreaming, training, preparing, executing, fighting, and being wounded—all for the sake of the church plant—it is natural that the planter develops a sense of ownership of the church. He has also taken vows to be a watchman and protect the church. He usually has godly intentions, but the stress of planting, the wounds endured in the process, and the weariness of a difficult work can turn godly intentions into flesh-centered leadership. It is understandable, but it is also sinful.

I believe there are two solutions to this issue. The first is that the diocese and the local planter must be extremely intentional about the care of the church planter's soul and accountability in his work. If he pursues the work alone, he will be his own teacher and can convince himself of many false truths. Dietrich Bonhoeffer wrote,

> Everyone who cares for the soul needs a person who will care for his or her soul. Only one who has been under spiritual care is able to exercise spiritual care. That law is part of the very essence of the church. . . . Those who live without spiritual care move easily toward magic and domination over others. One finds oneself thus unable to be faithful anymore. One preaches, administers the sacraments, carries out the obligations of the office—but is faithless. Thus, the office becomes a curse.[3]

The bishop or his canon for church planting must provide care that extends beyond the self-assessment and self-reporting of "How are you doing?" An unhealthy church planter will probably not tell the truth. Trusted laity should be involved in those regular conversations as well to ensure that the planter does not inadvertently fall into sin and error. The work of the diocese in supporting the planter does not end with his deployment. I have served both as a church planter and in positions of oversight in large congregations. I can tell you that the stress of the church planter is greater, and it is exacerbated by his isolation. The diocese must care for his soul through regular check-ins, personal visits, and conversations that include the planter, his spouse, and some of his lay leaders.

The second solution to the problem of planters slipping into unhealthy leadership habits is the recognition that the planter may not be the long-term rector of the church. I have planted two churches and eventually had to leave them both. I spent ten years in one and seven in the other. Leaving those churches and those people were two of the hardest moments of my life. I ugly-cried both times. In both instances, however, I knew it was time for me to go. There was no conflict or scandal; my work was simply done there. It was time to hand the reins to another leader. The first time I transitioned, I did not handle it well and neither did our diocese. I stayed about two years too long and I did not prepare the church well for my departure, and the church suffered. The second time I had the honor of raising up a strong leader who served as my associate first. I could then utilize the trust and relational equity I had built in planting the church to help him quickly establish credibility and affection within the congregation. When it was time for the church to transition to his leadership, he was loved and trusted. The church didn't miss a beat.

Church planting is about starting things well. It is also about leaving things well. Sometimes church planters are called to start a church and remain in that parish for decades, but I have found that to be an infrequent situation. Both the planter and his oversight must be aware that the time will most likely come when it is right for the planter to hand over the rectorship to someone else. Make that transition while both the planter and the church are healthy. Do not wait to leave in crisis.

• • • •

Dragons there may be, but they are not invincible. With prayer, training, accountability, the pursuit of holiness, and communal care for the souls of all involved, we do not need to be afraid.

A Note to Non-Anglican Readers:

Mistakes are universal. Some on my list I'm sure are more pertinent to you than others, and I am confident you will come up with new creative mistakes on your own. The unavoidable fact is you will make them. Talk over this list with planters from your tradition. Are there certain mistakes that are prevalent among your planters? Do the tendencies of your tradition make you susceptible to mistakes not listed here? Mistakes are inevitable, but so is the grace of Jesus Christ.

EPILOGUE

• • • •

Go Forth to Do the Work He Has Given You to Do

My friend, I have prayed for you. Even in writing this book, I have prayed for all who would read it. I pray the Lord gives you wisdom and discernment, power and humility, favor and peace. Church planting is participating in the grand story of God's redemptive plan, and I pray that you will be ever mindful of the cosmic significance of your work. Anglicanism is a way of being a Christian and pursuing the mission of the church as a part of a great historic tradition and a modern global family, so I pray you will be ever aware of the great cloud of witnesses that surround you.

In our worship services, after the Word has been proclaimed, and the sacraments have been administered, we pray, "And now, Father, send us out to do the work you have given us to do, to love and serve you as faithful witnesses of Christ our Lord."[1] At long last, at the end of our time together in this book, may you be sent out to do the work he is calling you to do—the work of church planting in Word and sacrament.

As we practice in our liturgy, I leave you with the blessing of the church:

May the peace of God, which passes all understanding, keep your heart and mind in the knowledge and love of God, and of his Son Jesus Christ our Lord; and the blessing of God Almighty, the Father, the Son, and the Holy Spirit, rest upon you, and remain with you always. Amen.

. . . .

Acknowledgments

I am grateful to so many people who have helped in the writing and publishing of this book. First, thank you to all the wonderful people at New Growth Press; you have made this process a joy. Archbishop Foley Beach has kept the importance of church planting in front of the people of the Anglican Church in North America and trusted me with an enormous task as his Canon—thank you, Your Grace. Bishop Alan Hawkins has been a faithful friend and partner in church planting for decades—much of what is in these pages we have learned together on this journey; I am grateful for you, dear friend. King Cole—you helped instill in me a love for the Word and for the church and gave me an early example of what an Anglican priest on mission looks like; you forever shaped my life. Thank you to the Always Forward staff team—Molly Ruch and Abbi Wensyel for your support. To Ana Howland for her keen citation editing eye. I also want to thank J. R. Briggs for coaching me and encouraging me in the writing process. There can be no proper acknowledgments without thanking my mom, Delores Alger—a giver of life in so many ways. A particular thank-you to the people of the churches I have planted—Church of the Apostles (now Resurrection Church) in Hope Mills, North Carolina, and

Church of the Redeemer, Dacula, Georgia. And to the people of all the church plants of the Anglican Church in North America; you have taught me so much and hold a particular place of affection in my heart—you are the true authors of this book. Finally, thank you to the people of the cathedral at Church of the Redeemer in Greensboro, North Carolina; it is my honor to be your Dean. Most importantly we acknowledge God—Father, Son, and Holy Spirit—as the one who deserves all honor and glory and praise. "Oh, come to the Father, through Jesus the Son, And give Him the glory; great things He has done!"[1]

APPENDIX

• • • •

Contemporary Issues in Church Planting

This book is a survey of planting churches in Word and sacrament. In its scope as a general introduction to the work of planting, I was limited in my ability to go in depth into some of the complicated contemporary issues that I am certain are on the minds of some of my readers. I will not be able to provide any sort of adequate treatment of these issues here either. I do, however, want to briefly acknowledge these significant topics with a few thoughts. Be assured, my brevity is not indicative of the importance of these issues, but rather a consequence of space and focus. These subjects could, and should, be given their due respect in unique individual volumes concerned with the specificities of each.

Women in Church Planting

Women play a pivotal, essential, and vital role in the work of church planting. With that said, there are differences of understanding within the Anglican Communion on the issue of women's ordination. I will not venture into that volatile and complex topic here. Our Anglican value of subsidiarity means that the local diocese sets the norms and standards for both ordination and church planting. This book is written to serve the church in all its regional and local expressions. Whatever I have written in this book and addressed to clergy church planters should be seen as equally applicable to either gender. I am limited by my biological makeup from having deep insight into how women clergy serving as church planters need to nuance any of the instructions or implications of this book. I must leave that to the capable female authors who know the subject of church planting from a woman's perspective, of whom I am sure there are many. I encourage you to write and share your wisdom.

Church planting is not limited to clergy, however. I hope I have made that abundantly clear in these pages. Women laity serve in many powerful ways in the work of church planting. Leadership, gathering, evangelism, organization, and the many other needs of the church plant are not gender specific. Women serve according to their giftedness and capacity just as men do, with equal importance in the work of planting.

Some women have more specific roles in serving church planting. I have worked for years alongside my colleague Canon Molly Ruch as she serves as the director of the Always Forward Institute. Together we have trained hundreds of church planters. Her experience of planting multiple churches and her wisdom in what is needed for the proper pursuit of this ministry have significantly impacted the lives of many planters and, subsequently, the lives of many people in their church plants. She has taught me a great deal, has led the charge of her local church in planting more churches, and has coached many church planters. Women like Molly have a specific calling to the advancement of church planting, and I pray there continue to be more leaders like her raised up from our churches.

Some women are called to be the spouse of a clergy church planter (as men are similarly called in dioceses that ordain women). This role is profoundly important and can be quite different from church to church. Some church planting spouses desire to be an active participant in the leadership of the church plant, while others intentionally have a more limited role. I have coached planting couples in which the wife wanted to be on coaching calls, and others where she did not see that as part of her ministry. Either and both are perfectly fine. The trick is to help the planter's spouse properly manage expectations and find her place in the work. There are resources out there for spouses of planters—some better than others. Find the support, books, teaching, and coaching you need to be healthy in this process.

Although, for a variety of reasons, most current clergy church planters are men, church planting is not restricted by gender. We need faithful men and women in this work. Church planting will be healthier for more women's voices, perspectives, and leadership.

Ethnic Diversity in Church Planting

Global Anglicanism is profoundly diverse. We have family members on every inhabited continent in the world. Gatherings of global Anglicanism are graced with many colors, languages, and cultures. This global diversity, however, is not always reflected in local churches. Many of our churches throughout the world are monochromatic, and Anglicanism in North America is predominantly Caucasian.

There are many healthy conversations currently being had about this. There are also discussions on how to reach specific ethnicities within the predominant culture. For example, the church where I serve, Church of the Redeemer in Greensboro, North Carolina, is currently assisting in planting services reaching out to East African and Sudanese immigrants. How do we leverage our global diversity to build bridges on the local level? These conversations are long overdue, and I pray that our future holds the planting of many churches who see multi-ethnicity as core to their identity.

I agree with my friend and Anglican priest Esau McCaulley, who wrote, "God sees the creation of a community of different cultures united by faith in his Son as a manifestation of the expansive nature of his grace. This expansiveness is unfulfilled unless the differences are seen and celebrated, not as ends unto themselves, but as particular manifestations of the power of the Spirit to bring forth the same holiness among different peoples and cultures for the glory of God."[1] Amen. I pray Anglican church planting can be a significant factor in making this diverse picture a reality.

Church Planting and Social Justice

Our current global culture, as reflected acutely in my native United States, is struggling with very important issues of social justice including racial equality, gender equality, poverty, abuse of authority, and more. It has always been the role of the church to be a voice for redemption and healing. Church planters have the opportunity to start new congregations where advocating for the those in need and for biblical social change is an objective aspect of their mission. Many church plants start by joining with ministries that other faithful Christian organizations have already begun. There is a great need for more learning and leadership in how church planting can be a voice for godly change in our communities. Our ecclesiology teaches that the church is God's agent in the world to bring biblical truth and radical healing through the gospel. So our planting of new worshipping communities is in itself a participation in social justice. As sacramental churches, we also see our role as bringing these spiritual truths to bear in tangible ways for the healing of our cultures.

. . . .

Glossary of Selected Terms

absolution. The proclamation by a priest or bishop of the forgiveness of sins.

alb. A white robe worn in worship services of the church, representing the glory of Christ.

Anglican Church in North America. Founded in 2009, the ACNA is a faithful Anglican province with congregations throughout North America.

Anglican Communion. The global denomination made up of self-governing but interconnected regional jurisdictions called provinces, each headed by an archbishop. Since Anglicanism spread from the British Isles, the Archbishop of Canterbury has traditionally been seen as the convener of the communion, being called First Among Equals.

baptism. One of the two sacraments given by Jesus Christ, it is the sacrament of new birth into the church through the resurrection of Christ.

benediction. A prayer of blessing.

bishop. One of the three ordained orders. Bishops having varying roles, but primarily serve as the head of a diocese.

Book of Common Prayer. An authoritative book guiding the doctrine and discipline of the Anglican Church. The first edition was compiled primarily by Thomas Cranmer in 1549, based significantly on existing ancient liturgies of the church. The 1662 version is considered the authoritative standard on which all subsequent editions of the Prayer Book are based. Today, there are variations in many languages in use throughout the world.

canon. In modern usage, someone set apart by an archbishop, bishop, or dean for a particular role, such as a canon for church planting.

chasuble. A vestment typically worn over an alb by the priest celebrating the Eucharist, often used in higher-church services.

cassock. The long robe in worship services under a surplice, with colors that vary but are usually black for clergy and purple for bishops or their canons and deans.

collect. A short prayer in the liturgy usually consisting of a request and concluding with praise.

Communion (Eucharist). One of the two sacraments given by Jesus Christ, it is the family meal of the church with its roots in the Passover and its fulfillment in the wedding supper of the Lamb.

Compline. The final service of the Daily Office, said at the end of the day.

Daily Office. The daily non-Eucharistic services of the church including Morning Prayer, Noonday Prayer, Evening Prayer, and Compline. These services can be said individually or corporately and including Scripture readings assigned by the lectionary.

deacon. One of the three ordained orders. Deacons are set apart for the work of service.

diocese. A jurisdictional grouping of congregations headed by a bishop.

Evening Prayer. The third service of the Daily Office, said in the evening.

GAFCON. The Global Anglican Future Conference is a movement of orthodox Anglican provinces to "retain and restore the Bible to the heart of the Anglican Communion."

Great Tradition. The authoritative tradition of the universal church.

institution of a rector. Installing a priest as the head of a local congregation.

laity. The non-ordained people of the church.

Morning Prayer. The third service of the Daily Office, said in the morning.

narthex. The enclosed space at the entry of the church building.

ordination. The church's setting apart of people for the specific ministry roles of bishop, priest, or deacon.

ordinal. The liturgy for ordination.

priest. One of the three ordained orders. A priest often oversees a local congregation under the authority of a bishop.

province. A jurisdictional grouping of dioceses, headed by an archbishop.

rector. The priest who leads a local congregation.

stole. A scarf-like vestment worn by clergy. Priests and bishops wear the stole around their neck, hanging straight down, while deacons wear the stole over their shoulder and diagonally across their chest.

subsidiarity. A principle of governance stating that decisions are best made by the most local level possible.

Thirty-Nine Articles of Religion. A sixteenth-century document outlining the beliefs of the Anglican Church.

vestments. Special clothing worn by laity and clergy when participating in liturgical ministry.

vestry. The group of lay people who help oversee the business affairs of the local church in conjunction with the rector.

. . . .

Notes

Chapter 1

1. R. T. Beckwith, "Thomas Cranmer and the Prayer Book," in *The Study of Liturgy*, ed. Cheslyn Jones et al. (New York: Oxford University Press, 1992), 104.

2. William Tyndale, *A Brief Declaration of the Sacraments*, ed. Henry Walter (Cambridge, UK: University Press, 1850), 29.

Chapter 2

1. Anglican Church in North America, *The Book of Common Prayer* (Huntington Beach, CA: Anglican Liturgy Press, 2019), 137.

2. Tim Keller, "Why Plant Churches?" Redeemer City to City, January 1, 2002, https://redeemercitytocity.com/articles-stories/why-plant-churches.

3. Pinetops Foundation, *The Great Opportunity: The American Church in 2050* (Seattle: Pinetops Foundation, 2018), 9. To download the report, see https://www.greatopportunity.org.

4. Pinetops, *The Great Opportunity*, 10.

5. Keller, "Why Plant Churches?"

Chapter 3

1. Michael Ramsey, *The Gospel and the Catholic Church* (Peabody, MA: Hendrickson Publishing, 2009), 188.

2. Alan Hirsch and Michael Frost, *The Shaping of Things to Come: Innovation and Mission for the 21st-Century Church* (Grand Rapids: Baker Books, 2013), 255.

3. Christopher J. H. Wright, *The Mission of God: Unlocking the Bible's Grand Narrative* (Downers Grove, IL: InterVarsity Press, 2006), 62.

4. Anglican Church in North America, *Book of Common Prayer*, 649.

5. Anglican Church in North America, *Book of Common Prayer*, 130.

6. George Herbert, "Prayer I" in *The Temple: Sacred Poems and Private Ejaculations*. (Cambridge, UK: Thomas Buck and Roger Daniel, printers to the Universitie, 1633), 43, http://name.umdl.umich.edu/A03058.0001.001.

Chapter 4

1. Lesslie Newbigin, *The Household of God: Lectures on the Nature of Church* (1953; repr., Eugene, OR: Wipf and Stock Publishers, 2008), 30.

2. John Wesley, *The Journal of John Wesley* (Grand Rapids: Christian Classics Ethereal Library), 55, https://www.ccel.org/w/wesley/journal/cache/journal.pdf.

3. Ryan Nicholas Danker, *Wesley and the Anglicans: Political Division in Early Evangelicalism* (Downers Grove, IL: InterVarsity Press, 2016), 57.

4. Thomas McKenzie, *The Anglican Way: A Guidebook* (Nashville: Colony Catherine, 2014).

5. J. I. Packer, *The Heritage of Anglican Theology* (Wheaton, IL: Crossway, 2021), 28–39.

Chapter 5

1. Anglican Church in North America, *Book of Common Prayer*, 1.

2. Anglican Church in North America, *Book of Common Prayer*, 473.

3. Rosaria Champagne Butterfield, *The Gospel Comes with a House Key* (Wheaton, IL: Crossway, 2018), 14.

Chapter 6

1. Anglican Church in North America, *Book of Common Prayer*, 163ff.

2. The Welcome/Shape/Send framework and the diagram that explains it are used with permission from The Rev. Dr. Shawn McCain

and Resurrection Anglican Church in Austin, Texas, https://www.rezaustin.com.

3. J. I. Packer and Joel Scandrett, eds. *To Be a Christian: An Anglican Catechism* (Wheaton, IL: Crossway, 2020), 57, https://anglicanchurch.net/wp-content/uploads/2020/06/To-Be-a-Christian.pdf.

4. Packer and Scandrett, eds., *To Be a Christian*, 58.

5. Anglican Church in North America, *Book of Common Prayer*, 176.

6. Shawn McCain, "Mission and Evangelism 600: Church Planting in the Anglican Tradition" (online class lecture, Trinity School for Ministry, Ambridge, PA, January 2021). I asked Shawn to speak to my students on the process of discipleship at his church, Resurrection South Austin in Austin, Texas.

7. This language is a summary of Cranmer's "A Short Declaration of the True, Lively, and Christian Faith" as articulated by the Catechesis Task Force of the Anglican Church in North America. For a more complete treatment of Anglican catechesis in general and these categories specifically, read the helpful document, "Towards an Anglican Catechumenate," written by Phil Harrod and the Catechesis Task Force, which can be accessed at https://anglicanchurch.net/wp-content/uploads/2020/06/Anglican_Catechumenate_Guiding_Principles.pdf. Another great resource by the task force, "Vision Paper for Catechesis in the Anglican Church in North America," can be accessed at https://anglicanchurch.net/wp-content/uploads/2020/06/Anglican_Catechesis_Vision.pdf.

8. Anglican Church in North America, *Book of Common Prayer*, 24.

9. J. I. Packer, *The Heritage of Anglican Theology* (Wheaton, IL: Crossway, 2021), 34.

10. John Fletcher Hurst, *John Wesley the Methodist: A Plain Account of His Life and Work* (New York: Eaton and Mains, 1903), 182.

11.John Wesley, "Sermon 131-The Late Work of God in North America," in *Sermons on Several Occasions* (Grand Rapids: Christian Classics Ethereal Library), 1168, https://ccel.org/ccel/wesley/sermons/sermons.viii.v.html#viii.v-p0.3.

12. Aidan Kavanagh, "Christian Initiation: Tactics and Strategy," in *Made, Not Born: New Perspectives on Christian Initiation and the Catechumenate* (Notre Dame, IN: University of Notre Dame Press, 1976), 5–6.

Chapter 7

1. Aidan Kavanagh, *On Liturgical Theology: The Hale Memorial Lectures of Seabury-Western Theological Seminary, 1981* (Collegeville, MN: Liturgical Press, 1992), 75.

2. Anglican Church in North America, *Book of Common Prayer*, 598.

3. Anglican Church in North America, *Book of Common Prayer*, 132–33.

4. C. S. Lewis, *The Weight of Glory* (1949; repr., New York: HarperCollins, 2001), 141. Citations refer to the HarperCollins edition.

5. James K. A. Smith, *Desiring the Kingdom* (Grand Rapids: Baker, 2009), 68.

6. Anglican Church in North America, *Book of Common Prayer*, 130.

7. James K. A. Smith, *You Are What You Love: The Spiritual Power of Habit* (Grand Rapids: Brazos Press, 2016), 80.

8. Anglican Church in North America, *Book of Common Prayer*, 11–12.

9. Tish Harrison Warren, *Liturgy of the Ordinary: Sacred Practices in Everyday Life* (Downers Grove, IL: InterVarsity, 2016), 21.

10. Augustine, "Letter 189," in *The Works of Saint Augustine: Part II: Letters 156-210*, ed. Boniface Ramsey, trans. Roland Teske (Hyde Park, NY: New City Press, 2004), 3:261.

11. Anglican Church in North America, *Book of Common Prayer*, 610.

12. Stephen Lawhead, *The Paradise War* (Nashville: Thomas Nelson, 2010). Kindle edition.

13. Anglican Church in North America, *Book of Common Prayer*, 25.

14. Anglican Church in North America, *Book of Common Prayer*, 12–13.

Chapter 8

1. Thomas Cranmer, "The Preface," in *First Book of Homilies* (London: John Bill, 1562), http://www.anglicanlibrary.org/homilies/bk1intro.htm.

2. Thomas Cranmer, "The Preface," in *First Book of Homilies*.

3. Hugh Latimer, "The Second Sermon upon the Lord's Prayer," in *Sermons* (New York: E.P. Dutton, 1906; Grand Rapids: Christian Classics Ethereal Library), https://ccel.org/ccel/latimer/sermons/sermons.ix.ii.html.

4. Donald Coggin, *Stewards of Grace* (Hachette, UK: Hodder & Stoughton, 1965), 18.

5. George Herbert, "The Parson Preaching," in *A Priest to the Temple or The Country Parson, His Character and Rule of Holy Life* (London, UK: 1652; Ann Arbor, MI: Text Creation Partnership), 23, https://quod.lib.umich.edu/e/eebo/A43381.0001.001/1:12?rgn=div1;view=fulltext.

6. Hugh Latimer, "Sermon Preached on Sexagesima Sunday," in *Sermons and Remains*, ed. George Elwes Corrie (Cambridge, UK: Parker Society, 1845), 204, https://media.sabda.org/alkitab-8/LIBRARY/LAT_SRRE.PDF.

7. John Stott, *Between Two Worlds: The Challenge of Preaching Today* (Grand Rapids: Wm. B. Eerdmans Publishing Company, 2000), 125–26.

8. Hugh Latimer, "Sermon of the Plough," in *Sermons* (New York: E.P. Dutton, 1906), http://anglicanhistory.org/reformation/latimer/sermons/plough.html.

9. Charles Spurgeon, "The Story of God's Mighty Acts," transcript of sermon delivered at the Music Hall, Royal Surrey Gardens, London, UK, July 17, 1859, https://www.spurgeongems.org/sermon/chs263.pdf.

10. Hugh Latimer, "The Third Sermon of M. Hugh Latimer, preached before King Edward, March twenty-second, 1549," in *Sermons* (New York: E.P. Dutton, 1906; Grand Rapids: Christian Classics Ethereal Library), https://ccel.org/ccel/latimer/sermons/sermons.vii.iii.html.

11. Hugh Latimer, "A Sermon Preached by M. Hugh Latimer, At Stamford, November 9, Anno 1550," in *Sermons* (New York: E.P. Dutton, 1906; Grand Rapids: Christian Classics Ethereal Library), https://ccel.org/ccel/latimer/sermons/sermons.viii.html.

Chapter 9

1. William Tyndale, "The Obedience of a Christian Man," in *The Works of the English Reformers: William Tyndale and John Frith*, ed. Thomas Russell (London, UK: 1831), 1:62, https://www.richard-2782.net/obediencechristianman.pdf.

2. My first exposure to this framework came while I was a student at Trinity School for Ministry in 2002 and Michael Green was a month-long guest lecturer at the school. During a conversation the two of us shared in the library, Michael took my notebook and wrote these three phrases down. I do not know if this descriptive framework is his original idea, but I could not find a resource that references this structure in the same way that Michael wrote it for me that day.

3. Anglican Church in North America, *Book of Common Prayer*, 170.

4. Thomas Cranmer, quoted by P. E. Hughes in *Theology of the English Reformers* (Eugene, OR: Wipf and Stock, 2009), 174.

Chapter 10

1. John Calvin, "Of the Sacraments," in *Institutes of the Christian Religion*, trans. Henry Beveridge (Grand Rapids: Christian Classics Ethereal Library), https://ccel.org/ccel/calvin/institutes/institutes.vi.xv.html.

2. Augustine, "Letter 98," in *A Select Library of the Nicene and Post-Nicene Fathers of the Christian Church, vol. 1, The Confessions and Letters of St. Augustine, with a Sketch of His Life and Work*, ed. Philip Schaff (Grand Rapids: Wm. B. Eerdmans, 1956; Grand Rapids: Christian Classics Ethereal Library), https://ccel.org/ccel/schaff/npnf101/npnf101.vii.1.XCVIII.html.

3. Alexander Schmemann, *For the Life of the World: Sacraments and Orthodoxy* (Crestwood, NY: St. Vladimir's Seminary Press, 1998), 16.

4. John Murray, "Common Grace," in *Collected Writings of John Murray* (Carlisle, PA: Banner of Truth, 2009), 2:96.

Chapter 11

1. I do not know the origin of the calling/character/competency/capacity/chemistry framework, except to say it was not conceived by me, although I have used it for years with some changes over time. I have seen other iterations with slight variations as well, such as the Diocese of the Upper Midwest's process of discernment for ordination, which includes four of these five components and adds charisms and catholicity as well.

2. Charles Ridley, *How to Select Church Planters* (Pasadena, CA: Charles E. Fuller Evangelistic Association, 1988).

3. *Braveheart*, directed by Mel Gibson (Hollywood, CA: Paramount Pictures, 1995).

4. Jim Griffith and Bill Easum, *Ten Most Common Mistakes Made by New Church Starts* (St. Louis, MO: Chalice Press, 2008), 21.

Chapter 12

1. John Finney, *Recovering the Past: Celtic and Roman Mission* (London, UK: Darton Longman & Todd, 2011), 141.

2. John Whitgift, *The Works of John Whitgift: The First Portion, Containing the Defense of the Answer to the Admonition, Against the Reply of Thomas Cartwright* (Cambridge, UK: The Parker Society, 1852), 6.

3. Ignatius of Antioch, "To the Trallians," in *Early Christian Fathers*, Library of Christian Classics Series, vol. 1, ed. Cyril C. Richardson (Grand Rapids: Christian Classics Ethereal Library), 3.1. https://ccel.org/ccel/richardson/fathers/fathers.vi.ii.iii.iii.html.

4. John Chrysostom, "Homily I on Philippians i. 1, 2," in *A Select Library of the Nicene and Post-Nicene Fathers of the Christian Church, Series 1, Vol. 13, Saint Chrysostom: Homilies on Galatians, Ephesians, Philippians, Colossians, Thessalonians, Timothy, Titus, and Philemon*, ed. Philip Schaff (Grand Rapids: Wm. B. Eerdmans, 2002; Grand Rapids: Christian Classics Ethereal Library). https://ccel.org/ccel/schaff/npnf113/npnf113.iv.iii.ii.html.

5. Anglican Church in North America, *Book of Common Prayer*, 477–78.

6. Anglican Church in North America, *Book of Common Prayer*, 488–89.

7. Charles Spurgeon, "Farm Laborers," transcript of speech delivered at Metropolitan Tabernacle, London, June 5, 1881, https://www.spurgeongems.org/sermon/chs1602.pdf.

8. Anglican Church in North America, *Book of Common Prayer*, 520.

9. See Phillip Keller's wonderful book *A Shepherd Looks at Psalm 23* (Grand Rapids: Zondervan, 2007).

10. Anglican Church in North America, *Book of Common Prayer*, 506.

11. George Herbert, "The Elixer," in *The Temple: Sacred Poems and Private Ejaculations* (Cambridge: Thomas Buck and Roger Daniel, printers to the Universitie, 1633), 178–79, https://quod.lib.umich.edu/e/eebo/A03058.0001.001/1:162?rgn=div1;view=fulltext.

12. My doctoral work was centered around organizing an Anglican diocese for the work of church planting, and my dissertation developed these four Cs in detail. My initial introduction to this framework was a time of informal instruction I received from Dr. Eric Geiger based on his research into the development of leaders in the church. He has since written the first three of these components into his book *Designed to Lead* (Nashville: B&H Books, 2016), coauthored with Kevin Peck. I recommend the book highly.

13. *Apollo 13*, directed by Ron Howard (Beverly Hills, CA: Imagine Entertainment, 1995).

Chapter 13

1. Jim Griffith and Bill Easum, *Ten Most Common Mistakes Made by New Church Starts* (St. Louis, MO: St. Chalice Press, 2008), 33. In this very helpful book, Griffith and Easum discuss some of the same mistakes contained in my list, including this one, which they call "Premature Launch." They also discuss acting your age and issues of waiting too long to discuss finances. Their book further develops some of these concepts and includes other mistakes which I did not list but are equally important to avoid.

2. Henri Nouwen, *A Spirituality of Fundraising* (Nashville: Upper Room Books, 2011), 16. You can also access the chapter in which this quotation is found in at this URL: https://www.perceptionfunding.org/uploads/1/6/8/9/16891606/spiritualityoffundraisingbyhenrinouwen_267.pdf.

3. Dietrich Bonhoeffer, *Spiritual Care*, trans. Jay. E. Rochelle (Philadelphia: Fortress Press, 1985), 68.

Epilogue

1. Anglican Church in North America, *Book of Common Prayer*, 137.

Acknowledgments

1. Fanny Crosby, "To God Be the Glory," (1875).

Appendix

1. Esau McCaulley, *Reading While Black: African American Biblical Interpretation as an Exercise in Hope* (Downers Grove, IL: IVP Academic), 2020. Kindle edition.